D1562419

FOUNTAIN OF LIFE

FOUNTAIN OF LIFE

Gerard Austin
Editor

In Memory of
Niels K. Rasmussen, O.P.

The Pastoral Press
Washington, D.C.

ISBN: 0-912405-85-6

© The Pastoral Press, 1991

The Pastoral Press
225 Sheridan Street, N.W.
Washington, D.C. 20011
(202) 723-1254

The Pastoral Press is the Publications Division of the National Associa-
tion of Pastoral Musicians, a membership organization of musicians and
clergy dedicated to fostering the art of musical liturgy.

PRINTED IN THE UNITED STATES OF AMERICA

Contents

Introduction.. vii

Sources
1. Ancient Church Orders: A Continuing Enigma
   Paul F. Bradshaw.. 3

2. The Different Forms of Liturgical "Libelli"
   Pierre-Marie Gy.. 23

3. Latin Mass Commentaries from the Ninth through
   Twelfth Centuries: Chronology and Theology
   Mary M. Schaefer.. 35

4. New Research Directions in Medieval Liturgy:
   The Liturgical Books of Sigebert of Minden (1022-1036)
   Joanne Pierce.. 51

5. Using Liturgical Texts in the Middle Ages
   Tom Elich.. 69

Theology and Practice
6. "Holy Things for the Saints": The Ancient Call
   to Communion and Its Response
   Robert Taft... 87

7. "The Unbloody Sacrifice": The Origins and Development
   of a Description of the Eucharist
   Kenneth Stevenson... 103

8. The Priestly Prayer: The Tridentine Theologians
   and the Roman Canon   131
   David N. Power..

9. Sacraments Shaping Faith: The Problem of
   Sacramental Validity Today
      John A. Gurrieri.. 165

10. A Larger Vision of Apostolicity: The End
    of an Anglo-Catholic Illusion
       Louis Weil.. 183

11. Communion Services: A Break with Tradition?
       Gerard Austin... 199

12. *Fons Vitae*: A Case Study in the Use of Liturgy
    as a Theological Source
       Mark Searle.. 217

Bibliography of Niels Krogh Rasmussen, O.P. (1935–1987).............. 243

Contributors.. 247

Introduction

ON 29 AUGUST 1987 THE WORLD OF LITURGICAL SCHOLARSHIP SUFFERED A
great loss through the sudden death of Fr. Niels Krogh Rasmussen, O.P. at the University of Notre Dame in South Bend,
Indiana. At the time of his death he was fifty-two years old.

Niels Rasmussen was born and raised in Denmark. During
his student years he became a Roman Catholic and later joined
the Dominican Order in the Paris Province. Early in his career
he became a pupil of the renowned liturgist, Pierre-Marie Gy,
O.P., who until recently was Director of the Institut Supérieur
de Liturgie at the Institut Catholique de Paris. Niels studied
paleography at the Ecole Nationale des Chartres, hagiography
and codicology at the Ecole Pratique des Hautes Etudes, and
liturgical studies at the Institut Catholique de Paris. From this
last institution he received the doctorate on 28 January 1978
with the defense of the dissertation "Les Pontificaux du haut-
moyen âge" (soon to be published posthumously by Spicilegium Sacrum Lovaniense), which treated the evolution of pontificals in the ninth and tenth centuries.

His teaching career in liturgy began in 1968 and included
the following institutions: University of Aarhus (Denmark),
Institut Catholique de Paris, La Salle University (Philadelphia), St. John's University (Collegeville), The Catholic University of America, and finally the University of Notre
Dame where he was granted tenure in 1985. From that time
until his death he was Coordinator of the Ph.D. Program in
Liturgical Studies there.

His writings were extensive and scholarly, often bridging
the fields of theology and medieval history. Some of his later

publications show his deep knowledge of Renaissance and Baroque liturgy as well. Besides his work in the pontificals, he will perhaps be most remembered for his revision and English translation of Cyrille Vogel's major work in French which serves as a brilliant introduction to medieval liturgy, *Medieval Liturgy: An Introduction to the Sources*, revised and translated by William G. Storey and Niels Krogh Rasmussen, O.P. (Washington, D.C.: The Pastoral Press, 1986).

Niels Rasmussen was known and respected as a liturgical scholar not only in the United States but throughout the world. His death came as a great shock to many. They may be comforted by the words of his mentor, Pierre-Marie Gy, preaching at a eucharist offered for Niels in Paris shortly after his death: "Perhaps we can ask Jesus that the secret of those last moments of the earthly life of Niels might be in some way assumed into the agony of Gethsemani, saved by it. Lord Jesus, let your words of mercy for those who put you to death, 'Forgive them, for they know not what they do,' be even more true for Niels."

I myself mourned his death, and wanted to do something positive in his memory. I approached Virgil Funk and Lawrence Johnson of The Pastoral Press with the idea of a *Festschrift* in his memory, and they generously agreed to publish it. When I asked the contributors for their essays, I told them I wanted to do a volume on the role of liturgy as a *locus* of tradition. I thought that would be a fitting homage to someone who had worked so diligently and so well in the area of liturgical sources all his life. I told the contributors that I wanted to use as a "thread" for this volume the following quotation of Yves Congar, O.P.: "Liturgy is the privileged *locus* of Tradition, not only from the point of view of conservation and preservation, but also from that of progress and development." (*Tradition and Traditions*. New York, Macmillan, 1966, p. 429)

The authors of the studies in this volume are a cross section of the mentors, colleagues, students, and friends of Niels Krogh Rasmussen. His bibliography was compiled by two of his former students: John K. Brooks-Leonard and Joanne M. Pierce.

The title of this volume, *Fountain of Life*, is, I feel, most fitting. The death of Niels Rasmussen is for all his friends and colleagues bearable only in the context of faith, faith in a God to whom we pray: "For with thee is the fountain of light; in thy light do we see light." (Psalm 36:9)

Gerard Austin, O.P.
The Catholic University of America
Pentecost 1991

SOURCES

1

Ancient Church Orders:
A Continuing Enigma

Paul F. Bradshaw

ANCIENT CHURCH ORDERS CONSTITUTE ONE OF THE MORE FASCINATING *genres* of early Christian literature, purporting to offer authoritative "apostolic" prescriptions on matters of moral conduct, liturgical practice, and ecclesiastical organization and discipline. What these pseudo-apostolic texts have to say about the apostolic age itself may be of little interest, but they are potentially valuable sources of evidence for the thought and practices of the periods in which they were composed. Although they were apparently originally written in Greek, in some cases all that has survived are translations into other languages.

Their Discovery

Prior to 1800 only one such document was generally known, the *Apostolic Constitutions*, first published in 1563. Although its authenticity did not go entirely unchallenged, it was accepted by many as a genuinely apostolic work in the centuries which followed its discovery. During the nineteenth century, however, discoveries of other church orders came thick and fast. In 1843 J.W. Bickwell published the Greek text of a short treatise which he called "the Apostolic Church Order."[1] In 1848 Henry Tattam produced an edition of what turned out to be a transla-

3

tion into the Bohairic dialect of Coptic, made as recently as 1804, of a composite work comprising three elements—Bickell's *Apostolic Church Order*; another previously unknown document, which for want of a better title was later designated by Hans Achelis as "the Egyptian Church Order"; and a different recension of the final Book 8 of the *Apostolic Constitutions*.[2] This collection is usually called the Clementine Heptateuch or Alexandrine Sinodos.

In 1854 Paul de Lagarde edited a Syriac version of a document generally referred to as the *Didascalia Apostolorum*;[3] and in 1856 he published a Syriac translation of the *Apostolic Church Order* and the Greek text of a work known as the *Epitome* of *Apostolic Constitutions* 8, or alternatively by the title which appears in some manuscripts, "The Constitutions of the Holy Apostles through Hippolytus."[4] In 1870 Daniel von Haneberg produced the Arabic text of what claimed to be the *Canons of Hippolytus*;[5] and in 1875 Philotheos Bryennios discovered the only known Greek text of the *Didache*, or "Teaching of the Twelve Apostles," which he published in 1883.[6] In the same year Lagarde disclosed the existence of a Sahidic dialect version of the Bohairic collection earlier published by Tattam,[7] and in 1899 Ignatius Rahmani produced a Syriac document, the *Testamentum Domini*, which capped all other apostolic claims by feigning to be the words of Jesus himself to the apostles after his resurrection.[8] In 1990 Edmund Hauler edited a fifth-century palimpsest which contained—unfortunately with many lacunae—Latin translations of the *Didascalia*, the *Apostolic Church Order*, and the "Egyptian Church Order."[9] Finally, in 1904 George Horner contributed Arabic and Ethiopic versions of the Alexandrine Sinodos to the Bohairic and Sahidic texts earlier published by Tattam and Lagarde.[10]

Their Relationship

As the various church orders began to appear, it rapidly became obvious that they were more than merely parallel examples of a particular type of literature. Parts of the different documents exhibited such a marked similarity to one another that it clearly pointed to a direct literary relationship. But what was that relationship? How did these various pieces of the jigsaw puzzle fit together?

There was no shortage of theories, and almost every possible combination was suggested. Thus in 1891 Achelis proposed that the genealogy ran from the *Canons of Hippolytus* through the so-called "Egyptian Church Order," and also another work subsequently lost, to the *Epitome* and then to *Apostolic Constitutions* 8[11] while in the same year F.X. Funk suggest-

Table 1: The Pieces of the Puzzle

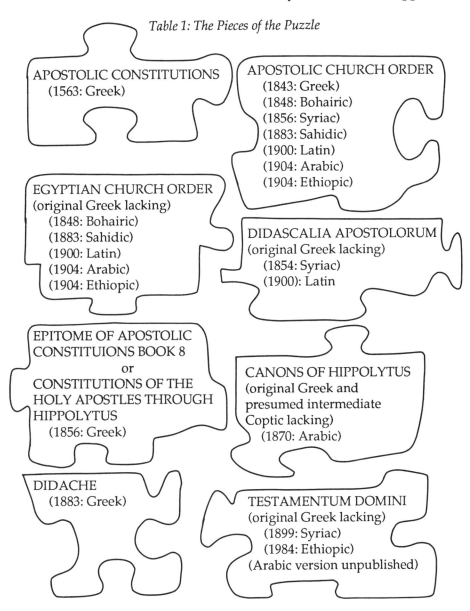

APOSTOLIC CONSTITUTIONS
(1563: Greek)

APOSTOLIC CHURCH ORDER
(1843: Greek)
(1848: Bohairic)
(1856: Syriac)
(1883: Sahidic)
(1900: Latin)
(1904: Arabic)
(1904: Ethiopic)

EGYPTIAN CHURCH ORDER
(original Greek lacking)
(1848: Bohairic)
(1883: Sahidic)
(1900: Latin)
(1904: Arabic)
(1904: Ethiopic)

DIDASCALIA APOSTOLORUM
(original Greek lacking)
(1854: Syriac)
(1900): Latin

EPITOME OF APOSTOLIC
CONSTITUIONS BOOK 8
or
CONSTITUTIONS OF THE
HOLY APOSTLES THROUGH
HIPPOLYTUS
(1856: Greek)

CANONS OF HIPPOLYTUS
(original Greek and
presumed intermediate
Coptic lacking)
(1870: Arabic)

DIDACHE
(1883: Greek)

TESTAMENTUM DOMINI
(original Greek lacking)
(1899: Syriac)
(1984: Ethiopic)
(Arabic version unpublished)

ed almost exactly the opposite order: *Apostolic Constitutions* 8 —› *Epitome* —› "Egyptian Church Order" —›*Canons of Hippolytus.*[12] When Rahmani published the *Testamentum Domini* in 1899, he claimed that it was a second-century work from which *Apostolic Constitutions* 8 and the "Egyptian Church Order" were both derived, with the *Canons of Hippolytus* in turn being dependent upon the latter. In 1901 John Wordsworth propounded the theory that there was a lost church order from which all the known ones were derived.[13]

What is ironical to later eyes is that at this stage nobody proposed a combination that would have put the "Egyptian Church Order" first in this line. Instead, it was unanimously judged to be descended from one or other of the documents to which it had close similarity. It was not until 1906 that Eduard von der Goltz suggested that this anonymous text might in reality be a genuine work by Hippolytus of Rome, the *Apostolic Tradition*, previously believed to have been lost.[14] This theory was taken up and elaborated, first by Eduard Schwartz in 1910, and then quite independently and much more fully by R.H. Connolly in 1916.[15] Although a few scholars still entertain doubts about its attribution to Hippolytus or its Roman origin,[16] it is now universally accepted that this document is the original source of the other church orders from which it was formerly presumed to be derived.

Thus, as can be seen from Table 2, a family tree can now be established for the whole collection of church orders with a high degree of certitude. Because they claim to be apostolic, most of them reveal neither the names of their true authors, nor the place and date of their real origin, and hence such questions usually have to be answered largely on the basis of the internal evidence of the documents themselves. Though there may still be some division of opinion over the precise date or provenance of certain individual texts, the conclusions reached by scholarship suggest that the majority originated in the third and fourth centuries, chiefly in Syria and Egypt.

It is agreed that the *Didache* constitutes the earliest extant example of this literature, though a debate still continues over its dating, some judging it to be contemporary with New Testament works, others placing it early in the second century, or even later.[17] The author of the *Didascalia* seems to have been aware of the *Didache* when he wrote early in the third century, and the author of the *Apostolic Church Order* incorporated part of it directly into his work. The compiler of the *Apostolic Constitutions* in turn used the *Didascalia*, the *Didache*, and the *Apostolic Tradition*. The *Apostolic Tradition* also formed the basis of both the *Canons of Hippolytus* and the *Testamentum Domini*, and even the *Epitome* of *Apostolic Constitutions* 8 appears to have had access to it, since it reproduces it at a few points in preference to the version of it in the *Apostolic Constitutions*.

That it has been possible to put these particular pieces together in what appears to be their correct order should not fool us into thinking that the whole church-order puzzle has been solved. It would be rather like thinking that once the literary relationship between Matthew, Mark, and Luke had been established, no further critical work on the Synoptic Gos-

Table 2: Relationship Between Individual Church Orders

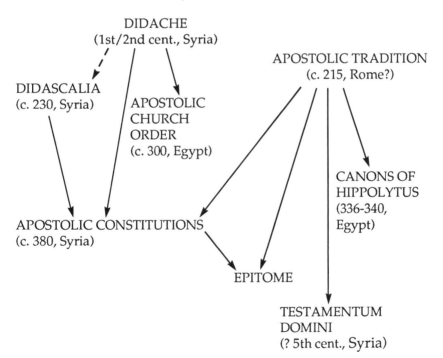

pels was necessary. Other questions still remain with regard to the church-order literature, and it is to these that we now turn.

The Text

Although no new church orders have been added to the list of discoveries since the beginning of the twentieth century, some new manuscripts of various recensions have been found, including in some cases a few small fragments of otherwise missing Greek originals. These have affected the task of establishing the text, and consequently better editions have since been produced for some of the individual documents. Thus, Willy Rordorf and André Tuilier have published a new edition

Table 3: Collections of Church Orders

APOSTOLIC CONSTITUTIONS (Greek)			
Books 1-6:	Book 7:	Book 8:	
Didascalia	Didache	Apostolic Tradition	
VERONA PALIMPSEST LV (53) (Latin)			
Didascalia	Apostolic Church Order	Apostolic Tradition	
ALEXANDRINE SINODOS (Sahidic, Bohairic, Arabic, Ethiopic)			
	Apostolic Church Order	Apostolic Tradition	Apostolic Constitutions Book 8
CLEMENTINE OCTATEUCH (Syriac)			
Testamentum Domini (in 2 books)	Apostolic Church Order		Apostolic Constitutions Book 8
CLEMENTINE OCTATEUCH (Arabic)			
Testamentum Domini	Apostolic Church	Apostolic Tradition	Apostolic Constitutions Book 8

of the *Didache*,[18] Arthur Vööbus one of the *Didascalia Apostolorum*,[19] and René-Georges Coquin one of the *Canons of Hippolytus*.[20] In the case of the *Apostolic Constitutions*, the edition by Funk in 1905 has generally been treated as definitive,[21] even though its tendency to play down the heterodoxy of the work by preferring orthodox variant readings wherever possible was criticized by C.H. Turner soon after it appeared.[22] Fortunately, however, a new edition, making use of a wider range of manuscripts and free from this tendency, has recently been published by Marcel Metzger.[23]

In the case of the *Apostolic Tradition*, it is commonly assumed that Bernard Botte's edition[24] or the English translation by Geoffrey Cuming[25] presents us—at least substantially—with what the author originally wrote. This assumption, however, is very much open to question. All that can be offered are attempts at reconstruction of the missing Greek original on the basis of the various extant translations into other languages and the adaptations made of it in other church orders. Such a task is by no means straightforward, and there remains considerable uncertainty over the true reading of many parts of the work,[26] which ought to lead to much greater circumspection in its citation than is commonly employed.

The original Greek of the *Testamentum Domini* is also lacking, and reliance has usually been placed on the Syriac version published by Rahmani, but here there are two problems. First, his edition was based on only one family of manuscripts, while a different manuscript tradition seems to underlie the text of the *Testamentum Domini* found in the West Syrian Synodicon,[27] which may offer indications of better readings at some points. Second, even if the earliest text of the Syriac can be established,[28] it is not certain that it always reproduced accurately the original Greek, especially as there are also extant Arabic and Ethiopic versions of the document with significantly different readings. These are both probably dependent upon a lost Coptic translation. Until recently any comparison with these versions was extremely problematic, as neither had ever been published, but Robert Beylot has now produced a critical edition of the Ethiopic,[29] which goes some way to meet the difficulty, though the quality of his work has been questioned.[30] Since both these versions are later than the Syriac, many differences can be dismissed as the emendations—intentional and unintentional—of translators and copyists, but at least at some points they may retain older readings. The doxologies in the Ethiopic, for example, have a much simpler—and hence seemingly more primitive—form than those in the Syriac.[31]

The Collections

Until relatively recently no attention was paid to the fact that the majority of the church orders were known to us not as individual documents at all but only as part of larger collections of such material. Even now only two scholars in the last thirty years, Bernard Botte and J.M. Hanssens, have tried to explore the nature of that inter-relationship. As can be seen from Table 3, there are four such collections:

(a) the *Apostolic Constitutions*;

(b) a Latin translation of three Greek works thought to have been made about the same time as the *Apostolic Constitutions*, but known to us only through one manuscript, a fifth-century palimpsest;[32]

(c) the collection known as the Alexandrine Sinodos, or the Clementine Heptateuch, found in several different language versions—in the two dialects of Coptic (Sahidic and Bohairic), in Arabic and in Ethiopic—of which the Sahidic is the oldest and the others are all in one way or another ultimately dependent on it;

(d) what is known as the Clementine Octateuch, which is found in two different forms in two different languages, Syriac and Arabic, neither of which has yet ever been published in full. It consists of the *Testamentum Domini*, followed by material included in the Alexandrine Sinodos, except that the Syriac version differs from the Arabic in omitting the text of the *Apostolic Tradition* of Hippolytus, and consequently dividing the *Testamentum Domini* into two books in order to retain the eightfold form.

What is particularly interesting about these collections is that the various church orders tend to appear in them in the same sequence. Thus we have the *Didascalia*, the *Didache*, and the *Apostolic Tradition* in the *Apostolic Constitutions*; and the *Didascalia*, the *Apostolic Church Order* (which we saw earlier itself incorporates part of the *Didache*), and the *Apostolic Tradition* in the Latin palimpsest. The Alexandrine Sinodos retains the latter two works in the same order as in the Latin translation, but appends to them another version of *Apostolic Constitutions* 8. The same is true of the Octateuch, though here the *Testamentum Domini* is prefixed. It appears impossible to dismiss all these similarities as merely coincidental, and it seems that there is a literary relationship between the collections as well as between the individual church orders.

One simple answer—that there is direct dependency—must be ruled out. The Latin translation is certainly not derived from the *Apostolic Constitutions*, nor is the latter a retranslation back into Greek from the Latin: its Greek is too close to that of the sources—where we can check it—for such an idea to be conceivable, and in any case one has the *Didache* and the other has the *Apostolic Church Order* as its middle document. It is equally difficult to imagine that the Sahidic version of the Sinodos obtained its material from anywhere except a Greek source, and the same is true of the Syriac version of the Octateuch; indeed the colophon attached to the *Testamentum Domini* in this collection explicitly affirms that it at least was translated from Greek into Syriac by James of Edessa in the seventh century.

Thus we need to seek some other solution to their similarities. Botte proposed the existence of an early Greek "tripartite collection," subsequently lost, which consisted of the *Didascalia*, the *Apostolic Church Order*, and the *Apostolic Tradition*—in that order.[33] This would mean that the Latin collection was a translation of that work, while the author of the *Apostolic Constitutions* would have been influenced by it with regard to his order, but for some reason preferred to replace the *Apostolic Church Order* with the *Didache*, since the two were similar to one another.

Botte's theory, however, still leaves a number of difficulties. It suffices to explain the relationship between two of the collections, but is not really adequate when it comes to the other two. If the author of the Sinodos had a triple collection in front of him, why should he discard the first of its three works but retain the other two? Botte suggested that it may have been because the *Didasacalia* did not lend itself as easily as the others to the division into separate canons which we find in this collection. But, in any case, why should both the Sinodos and the Octateuch have chosen to add to this supposed triple collection a version of *Apostolic Constitutions* 8? That cannot surely be put down to coincidence, especially as there is nothing at all to suggest that this particular extract ever circulated on its own. Moreover, at the very least we seem obliged to posit the existence of an earlier, Greek form of the Octateuch, from which both our present versions, the Syriac and the Arabic, are ultimately descended. The Arabic cannot be descended directly from the Syriac, because the Syriac lacks the *Apostolic Tradition* (presumably omitted because it was so similar to the material in the *Testamentum Domini*), and the Syriac was obviously aware of a previous eightfold form of its material, since it divided the *Testamentum Domini* into two in order to retain that structure after the omission of the *Apostolic Tradition*.

It looks, therefore, as though we are forced to take seriously something like the more complicated theory put forward by J.M. Hanssens.[34] He held that originally only the *Apostolic Church Order* and the *Apostolic Tradition* circulated together in the fourth century. From this combination developed two further collections: one comprising the *Didascalia*, the *Apostolic Church Order*, and the *Apostolic Tradition*, from which the *Apostolic Constitutions* and the Latin translation were derived; the other made up of the *Apostolic Church Order*, the *Apostolic Tradition*, and a version of *Apostolic Constitutions* 8. This latter document would thus have constituted the original Greek collection of which the Alexandrine Sinodos was a translation; and our conjectured Greek Octateuch would then have been an expanded form of this, prefixed by the *Testamentum Domini*, since the supposed words of Jesus himself would naturally be placed before, and not after, what were then taken to be injunctions of the apostles.

Although the outlines of the process of transmission and aggregation of the various documents may thus be discerned, many questions of detail still remain unanswered. To give just one example, how are we to account for the existence of an Ethiopic version of the *Testamentum Domini*? Was it derived from our conjectured Sahidic Octateuch, and if so, why were the rest of its contents not translated as well? Was it perhaps because they already existed in the Ethiopic version of the Sinodos, or does the Ethiopic *Testamentum* emerge by some other route?

"Living Literature"

Even if we can begin to see *how* the various church orders were transmitted and combined, our puzzle is still far from complete. We may have been able to account for the process at a physical level, but that does not explain *why* it ever happened at all. Why should anyone take the time and trouble repeatedly to copy out these texts, translate and revise them, and combine them with others? What lies behind this gigantic spider's web?

Strange though it may seem, this is not a question which those who have made use of the documents as historical source material have often stopped to ask. They have simply plundered what they wanted to fit the picture of the early church that they were attempting to paint, without asking themselves why it ever came to be there in the first place, and what this might have to say about its value as historical evidence. The editors, copyists, or translators expended considerable time and energy on their work not merely out of a desire to preserve antiquity for its own sake, but because they believed that the source-document they were using had some practical relevance to the life of their own churches. Thus when they encountered something that did not correspond with their own experience—for example, injunctions which advocated practices contrary to those of their own tradition, or the omission of something with which they were familiar and which they regarded as important or essential—they could only conclude that the text before them really ought to accord with what they knew, that the traditions of their own church must be those which had been prescribed in apostolic times, and hence there was no alternative but to correct the text so that it did truly harmonize with apostolic teaching and practice as they understood it.

This development can be seen not only between the individual church orders in the series, as each one revised its predecessor, but also in the process of the copying of manuscripts, the translation from one language to another, and even the aggregation into collected works. At each step along the way, the aim was not simply to reproduce exactly the last example of the material but to amend and update it. Thus, these texts are not always copies or translations in the sense in which we generally mean those words, but are instead really versions of the original, and frequently differ markedly from one another. Prayer texts may be modified, for example, or even entirely omitted, if they do not resemble the prayers with which the copyists or translators were familiar; and additional prayer-material from their own tradition may be inserted among that from the source-document.

The church orders, therefore, should not be treated in the same way as other ancient works. When we encounter variant readings between different manuscript traditions, we are not always looking at accidental dislocation and copyists' errors, as we might be, for example, in the works of Augustine. We are frequently seeing deliberate emendations designed to alter the sense of the text. This of course makes the task of restoring the original more difficult than it is in other types of literature. But we must also keep in mind that, in looking at this material, the original is not the only important historical source: we should be equally interested in the changes which were made by the first, second, and even third translators, as indicating something about the world in which each lived, about what had changed and what had remained the same in the ongoing life of the church, about the matters which were of vital importance to each translator's generation and those issues which had now ceased to be of concern.

Perhaps the best way of thinking of this material is as "living literature," constantly growing, changing, and evolving as it moves from generation to generation, or from one ecclesiastical tradition to another, with each stage, and not just the first, offering valuable source-material for historical study. Indeed, we may even be mistaken in what we regard as the beginning of the process, as the original documents in the series. If we may vary the metaphor a little, and look upon the literature as a great river which is made up of a number of smaller tributaries, what we consider the sources of the streams may perhaps not be where the water first begins at all, but only where it bursts forth into our view from beneath the ground—another stage in its long journey and not the point at which it is formed.

Sources

There are certainly signs which suggest that at least some of the documents are made up of a number of different strata of material. They may have been drawing upon older sources which are otherwise unknown to us, or may themselves have gone through a number of different editions, as it were, being amplified and revised in response to changing situations, before attaining the forms which we mistakenly treat as "the original text."

For example, it is acknowledged that the *Apostolic Constitutions* probably made use of other sources besides the works known to us, especially in Book 7, where prayer texts of a strongly Jewish character are found.[35] It has also been recognized that not only is the first half of the *Apostolic Church Order* dependent upon the first part of the *Didache*, but part of the second half appears to imply a very primitive stage of the evolution of the Christian ministry and does not seem entirely consistent with what is written elsewhere in the document. Thus, this too may well be a composite work bringing together a number of earlier written sources.[36]

Most scholars now subscribe to the view that the *Didache* also evolved by stages, but are divided over the number of redactions, and the relative antiquity of different parts of the work.[37] At the very least, the first part of the document, usually known as the "Treatise on the Two Ways," seems older than the rest. It is paralleled in Jewish material and also turns up elsewhere in early Christian literature,[38] which implies that it once had an existence of its own. It is even possible that the work known to the author of the *Apostolic Church Order* may not have been the complete *Didache* but some earlier stage in its evolution.

Some scholars have begun to suggest that a similar process of evolution may also be true in the case of the *Apostolic Tradition*.[39] It would appear from the Latin translation that at one time it circulated in at least two different forms, one with a longer and the other with a shorter ending, and there are other signs in the text which may point to more extensive revisions—statements which do not quite harmonize, practices described twice, and so on. However, it is difficult to know how many of these should be attributed to the actions of the author himself, bringing together older written sources which did not cohere with one another, and how many should be attributed to subsequent copyists and translators revising the original text.

Indeed, it would perhaps be better to think of the various church orders not as works by a single author at all, but rather as having had a succession of editors who shaped the stream of tradition which came down to them, both before and after it emerges to our sight in documentary form.

Fact or Fantasy?

Looked at in this light, therefore, can we discern any overall trends in the development of this material? Why were the different editors modifying it? As A.F. Walls has pointed out,[40] there is a change in the way in which the term "apostolic" seems to be understood as the literature evolves. In the earlier documents it appears to have a more dynamic sense, meaning "that which is in accordance with the witness and teaching of the apostles," whereas the later documents become pseudepigraphical, with the various injunctions explicitly attributed to the apostles themselves, either collectively or individually.

Not only is there this change of form in the gradual development of the literature, but there is also a change of content. Most of the earlier documents—the *Didache*, the *Didascalia*, and the *Apostolic Church Order*—are principally concerned with the Christian life as a whole, with the moral conduct of the members of the church. It is only in relation to the welfare of the whole community, therefore, that they deal with those who are its leaders, and consequently are naturally more concerned about the personal qualities which such ministers should display than with the process of their institution. Moreover, the *Apostolic Church Order* contains no strictly liturgical material at all; the *Didascalia* merely alludes obliquely to liturgical practices; while the *Didache* includes only very brief liturgical directions together with prayer texts for the eucharist or *Agape*, all of which may be later additions to its original nucleus.

With the *Apostolic Tradition*, however, we move into literature of a very different kind. Here, at least in its extant form, exhortations concerning Christian behavior and the moral qualities required of ordained ministers have almost entirely disappeared, and are replaced by directives about the correct procedure to be adopted in the appointment of ministers, the texts of the prayers to be used in the ordination rites and in the celebration of the eucharist, the ritual to be followed in the administration of baptism, and other such matters. It is the ordering of the church and its liturgy which is now the principal focus. This trend continues in the derivatives of this document, so that, for example, whereas the *Didascalia* was concerned with the proper disposition of different groups of people—ordained, lay, male, female, and so on—within the Christian assembly, the *Testamentum Domini* concerns itself instead with the proper arrangement of the church building and its furniture.

These shifts in form and content suggest that, as time passed, the purpose of the church orders changed, and their "apostolic" pedigree needed to be more firmly underscored and reinforced by more emphatic claims if it were to have any authority. This in turn raises the suspicion that not all editorial hands were necessarily modifying the received text in order to correspond with the actual historical practice of their own churches. At least to some extent, they may have been indulging in an idealizing dream—*prescribing* rather than *describing*—imagining what the organization and liturgy of their community would be like if they were allowed to have their own way and impose their idiosyncratic ideas on the rest of the congregation. Thus we may sometimes have less of a factual account than a clever piece of propaganda, which required the guise of alleged apostolic prescription to promote its cause. This has long been suspected with regard to at least some parts of the later documents, but there is no reason to think that any of the church orders are free from this tendency, still less that they constitute the official handbook of a local church, as earlier scholars tended to suppose.

On the other hand, this does not mean that they should simply be dismissed as historical sources. Beneath what may be fanciful embroidery in theology and practice there is undoubtedly some foundation based on the reality of either of the local tradition or of influences from other churches. But the evidence needs to be sifted with care, and reliance should not too readily be placed on the unsubstantiated testimony of a church order, without corroboration from other sources.

The change of emphasis in subject-matter also provides some clues as to why certain texts were retained and others dropped in the development of the collections of church orders which we considered earlier. It was not merely that the *Didascalia* did not lend itself easily to division into separate canons, as Botte suggested: the problem was not simply one of form but of content. What the *Didascalia* had to say was not the sort of apostolic material which later generations wanted to preserve. It was no longer relevant to their needs, and so ceases to appear in the later canonical collections. This may also explain why copies of the *Didache* do not exist in the wide variety of languages in which the other church orders are found: its moral teaching was no longer important enough for anyone to consider it worthwhile to translate and copy it, and its meager liturgical provisions were too archaic to be reconciled with the contemporary practice of the translators' world.

Equally, it explains why the *Apostolic Tradition* was translated, copied, amended, and expanded so many times: its subject-matter was exactly what later eyes were looking for—the beginnings of liturgical rubrics and canon law. Similarly, it explains why *Apostolic Constitutions* 8 should have been abstracted from the totality of the work and grafted on to the later collections, even though it partially duplicated the contents of the *Apostolic Tradition*: it too contained just the sort of material people wanted. Finally, it explains why ultimately there were no more church orders, why the *genre* simply died out: eventually apostolic fiction ceased to be used as a source of authority in the mainsteam churches of both East and West, and collections of liturgical texts and canon law were produced which derived their authority instead from individual living bishops and genuine synodical assemblies. It was only in the lesser Oriental Churches that the pseudo-apostolic directives continued to be respected and carefully preserved, and even came to constitute the foundation of much liturgical practice, while elsewhere the original Greek texts were allowed to disintegrate: they had served their purpose and were no longer of practical use.

The *Apostolic Church Order*, however, constitutes a fly in the ointment, upsetting the neatness of this theory of development. Although it is not a liturgical document, it continues to make an appearance alongside the *Apostolic Tradition* in every single collection of church orders. Nevertheless, perhaps even this can be explained. The *Apostolic Tradition* refers in its opening words to an earlier work (or to the first part of the same work) on the subject of spiritual gifts. No trace of this has ever been found. But it is possible that someone mistakenly thought that the *Apostolic Church Order* was this missing text and placed the two together in that order to form the nucleus of all other later collections. If they were thereafter looked upon as a single work, then it is less surprising that this short treatise managed to retain its place even when its subject-matter had ceased to be of interest to copyists and translators.

* * * * * *

The jigsaw puzzle is far from solved, and other pieces still need to be inserted. For example, published versions and recent critical editions are still lacking for several parts of this literature. Moreover, although what in scripture studies would be called "source criticism" has to some extent been done, the equivalent of serious "form-criticism" and above all "redaction criticism" still wait to be tackled: what shaped the material in its development and what we can learn about the world of the various editors and translators who transmitted and revised it?

Perhaps the whole church order literature is not so much a simple jigsaw puzzle but, as F. Loofs suggested at the end of the nineteenth century,[41] a giant kaleidoscope capable of being arranged in a variety of patterns wherein each person can see the image that he or she wishes to find. Yet, in spite of the apparent morass which first impressions present, if we are willing to take account of the total complexity of the literature and avoid the practice of simply abstracting pieces without reference to their context—what one might call the "hit and run" approach to historical sources—we can begin to discern an underlying pattern and a logical progression in its development, which may help us to understand it better.[42]

Notes

1. J.W. Bickell, *Geschichte des Kichenrechts*, vol. 1 (Giessen, 1843) 107-132.

2. Henry Tattam, *The Apostolical Constitutions or the Canons of the Apostles in Coptic with an English Translation* (London, 1848).

3. P.A. de Lagarde, *Didascalia Apostolorum Syriace* (Leipzig, 1854 = Osnabruck-Wiesbaden, 1967).

4. *Reliquiae Iuris Ecclesiastici Antiquissimae* (Leipzig, 1856) 1-23.

5. D.B. von Haneberg, *Canones S. Hippolyti Arabice* (Munich, 1870).

6. P. Bryennios, *DIDACHE TON DODEKA APOSTOLON* (Constantinople, 1883).

7. P.A. de Lagarde, *Aegyptiaca* (Göttingen, 1883 = 1972) 209-291.

8. I.E. Rahmani, *Testamentum Domini Nostri Jesu Christi* (Mainz, 1899 = Hildesheim, 1968); English translation by James Cooper and A.J. Maclean, *The Testament of Our Lord Translated into English from the Syriac* (Edinburgh, 1902).

9. Edmund Hauler, *Didascaliae Apostolorum Fragmenta Veronensia Latina. Accedunt Canonum qui Dicuntur Apostolorum et Aegyptiorum Reliquiae* (Leipzig, 1900).

10. George Holner, *The Statutes of the Apostles or Canones Ecclesiastici* (London: Williams & Norgate, 1904); later edition of the Arabic by Jean and Augustin Périer, *Les 127 canons des apôtres*, Patrologia Orientalis 8/4 (Paris, 1912).

11. Hans Achelis, *Die Canones Hippolyti*, Texte und Untersuchungen 6/4 (Berlin, 1891).

12. F.X. Funk, *Die apostolischen Konstitutionen, eine litterarhistorische Untersuchung* (Rottenburg, 1891 = Frankfurt: Minerva, 1970).

13. *The Ministry of Grace* (London: Longmans & Green, 1901) 18-21. A similar view was taken by A.J. Maclean, *The Ancient Church Orders* (Cambridge: University Press, 1910) 141-173.

14. "Unbekannte Fragmente altchristlicher Gemeindeordnungen," *Sitzungsberichte der Preussischen Akademie der Wissenschaften* (1906) 141-157.

15. Eduard Schwartz, *Uber die pseudoapostolischen Kirchenordnungen* (Strasbourg, 1910); R.H. Connolly, *The So-Called Egyptian Church Order and Derived Documents* (Cambridge: University Press, 1916 = 1967).

16. Notably J.M. Hanssens, *La Liturgie d'Hippolyte*, Orientalia Christiana Analecta 155 (Rome: Pont. Institutum Orientalium Studiorum, 1959; 2nd edition, 1965); Jean Magne, *Tradition apostolique sur*

les charismes et diataxeis des saints apôtres (Paris, 1975); and most recently Marcel Metzger, "Nouvelles perspectives pour la prétendue *Tradition Apostolique*," *Ecclesia Orans* 5 (1988) 241-259.

17. The most recent claim for an early date was made by Joan Hazelden Walker, "A Pre-Marcan Dating for the Didache: Further Thoughts of a Liturgist," *Studia Biblica 1978* III (Sheffield, 1980) 403-411; but her argument is flawed, since it cannot be assumed that Christianity developed at the same speed in every place: a more primitive theology does not necessarily mean an earlier date.

18. Willy Rordorf and André Tuilier, *La Doctrine des douze apôtres*, Sources chrétiennes 248 (Paris: Editions du Cerf, 1978). See also W. Rordorf, "Une nouvelle édition de la Didachè (problèmes exégetiques, historiques et théologiques)," *Studia Patristica* 15 (1984) 26-30; A. Tuilier, "Une nouvelle édition de la Didachè (problèmes de méthode et de critique textuelle)," *Studia Patristica* 15 (1984) 31-36.

19. Arthur Vööbus, *The Didascalia Apostolorum in Syriac*, Corpus Scriptorum Christianorum Orientalium 401, 402, 407, 408; Scriptores Syri 175, 176, 179, 180 (Louvain, 1979). See also Sebastian Brock and Michael Vasey, *The Liturgical Portions of the Didascalia*, Grove Liturgical Study 29 (Nottingham: Grove Books, 1982).

20. *Les Canons d'Hippolyte*, Patrologia Orientalis 31/2 (Paris, 1966). See also Paul F. Bradshaw, *The Canons of Hippolytus*, Alcuin/GROW Liturgical Study 2 (Nottingham: Grove Books, 1987).

21. F.X. Funk, *Didascalia et Constitutiones Apostolorum* (Paderborn, 1905 = 1979).

22. C.H. Turner, "A Primitive Edition of the Apostolic Constitutions and Canons," *Journal of Theological Studies* 15 (1913) 53-65; "Notes on the Apostolic Constitutions," *Journal of Theological Studies* 16 (1914) 54-61, 523-538; 21 (1920) 160-168.

23. *Les Constitutions apostoliques*, Sources chrétiennes 320, 329, 336 (Paris: Editions du Cerf, 1985-1987).

24. *La Tradition apostolique de saint Hippolyte* (Münster: Aschendorff, 1963, fourth edition 1972).

25. G.J. Cuming, *Hippolytus. A Text for Students*, Grove Liturgical Study 8 (Nottingham: Grove Books, 1976).

26. See, for example, the recent contributions by Anthony Gelston, "A Note on the Text of the *Apostolic Tradition* of Hippolytus," *Journal of Theological Studies* 39 (1988) 112-117, and G.J. Cuming, "The Post-Baptismal Prayer in the *Apostolic Tradition*: Further Considerations," *Journal of Theological Studies* 39 (1988) 117-119.

27. Arthur Vööbus, editor, *The Synodicon in the West Syrian Tradition*, Corpus Scriptorum Christianorum Orientalium 367, 368; Scriptores Syri 161, 162 (Louvain, 1975).

28. One of my doctoral students, Grant Sperry-White, is currently

engaged in producing a new edition and translation of the Syriac text, and I am grateful to him for the substance of this paragraph.

29. Robert Beylot, *Le Testamentum Domini éthiopien* (Louvain: Peeters, 1984).

30. See the review by the late Roger Cowley in the *Journal of Semitic Studies* 31 (1986) 292-295.

31. Compare the Syriac "to you be praise and to your only-begotten Son our Lord Jesus Christ and to the Holy Spirit honorable and worshiped and life-giving and consubstantial with you, now and before all worlds and to the generation of generations and to the ages of ages" (Rahmani, *Testamentum Domini* 99) and the Ethiopic "Glory to the Father, to the Son, and to the Holy Spirit, now and always and to the ages of ages" (Beylot, *Le Testamentum* 206).

32. Most recent edition by Erik Tidner, *Didascaliae Apostolorum Canonum Ecclesiasticorum Traditionis Apostolicae Versiones Latinae*, Texte und Untersuchungen 75 (Berlin: Akademie-Verlag, 1963).

33. Bernard Botte, "Les plus anciennes collections canoniques," *L'Orient syrien* 5 (1960) 331-349.

34. *La Liturgie d'Hippolyte* 171ff.

35. See the recent study by David A. Fiensy, *Prayers Alleged to Be Jewish: An Examination of the Constitutiones Apostolorum*, Brown Judaic Studies 65 (Chico, CA: Scholars Press, 1985).

36. See Adolf Harnack, *Die Quellen der sog. apostolischen Kirchenordnung* (Berlin, 1886); Alexandre Faivre, "Le texte grec de la Constitution ecclésiastique des Apôtres 16-20 et ses sources," *Revue des sciences religieuses* 55 (1981) 31-42.

37. For a discussion of some recent theories, see F.E. Vokes, "The Didache Still Debated," *Church Quarterly* 3 (1970) 57-62. See also S. Giet, *L'Enigme de la Didachè* (Paris: Ophrys, 1970).

38. It is, for example, found in the second-century *Epistle of Barnabas* and in the Latin *Doctrina Apostolorum*.

39. See the works cited in Paul F. Bradshaw, "The Liturgical Use and Abuse of Patristics," in Kenneth Stevenson, editor, *Liturgy Reshaped* (London: SPCK, 1982) 137-138.

40. "A Note on the Apostolic Claim in the Church Order Literature," *Studia Patristica* 2 (1957) 83-92.

41. "Die urchistliche Gemeindeverfassung mit spezieller Beziehung auf Loening und Harnack," *Theologische Studien und Kritiken* 63 (1890) 637.

42. The most important recent study is by Alexandre Faivre, "La documentation canonico-liturgique de l'église ancienne," *Revue des sciences religieuses* 54 (1980) 204-219, 237-297.

2

The Different Forms
of Liturgical "Libelli"

Pierre-Marie Gy

IN THE COURSE OF THE PAST TWENTY YEARS NIELS RASMUSSEN, MYSELF, and a few others, particularly Michel Huglo, have often discussed the topic of liturgical *libelli*. This question plays a prominent part in the doctoral dissertation of N.K. Rasmussen which, I hope, will soon be published. M. Huglo deals with them both in his study "Les libelli de tropes et les premiers tropaires-prosaires"[1] and in his *Livres de chant liturgique*.[2] I will here attempt to sum up my own research, as it has developed within a prolonged conversation with the above-mentioned colleagues as well as with those who commonly deal with the question of liturgical *libelli*, whether in the liturgical domain or in related disciplines.[3]

From the outset one must underline the basic importance of *libelli* as a category in the liturgy and elsewhere, while at the same time warning against the distinction too neatly made between *liber* and *libellus*. The *Thesaurus Linguae Latinae* had already indicated that in ancient texts such a distinction could not ordinarily be given a technical significance. A mistake may have been made in this regard, but it was one which had the advantage of stimulating historians in their research about what we call *libelli*, many of which they found.

Having said this, I will try to give both consistency to and a balanced appreciation of the practical definition of the liturgical *libelli* which I proposed to Niels Rasmussen in 1980 and which M. Huglo kindly took into account in his study "Les libelli de tropes." It includes four elements which are best considered as not too separate from each other:

1. The *libellus* consists of a booklet or a small number of booklets (no more than three or four).

2. At the beginning these booklets or booklet were independent.

3. The *libellus* is not bound.

4. From the liturgical point of view, the *libellus* does not include all the functions of a given ministry, for example, that of a bishop, or the whole of the liturgical year, but only a particular action or specific feast.

Number of Booklets

The first element of this practical definition inevitably includes a choice of method, somewhat in the same way as we must establish, by common agreement, the distinction in terms of size between portable and non-portable books.[4] If such a convention were adhered to, the name *libellus* would not be given to Paris B.N. 1143 (five booklets); however, on the basis of its contents (the Office and Mass of Corpus Christi, of which it is probably the original manuscript[5]), this manuscript ought to be considered a real *libellus*. Likewise, the name *libellus* is to be given to Mende Evêché s.c., the book of the sacristan of the cathedral of Mende around 1300.[6] This manuscript consists of only one booklet today, but probably at the beginning it consisted of two.

Originally Independent Books

Regarding this second criterion, the catalogues of manuscripts do not generally give sufficient information. We would need to know the differences in size and number of lines; likewise, a difference in script can indicate that a booklet was not written in the same region as the others. For example, the ff. 90r-116v of Paris B.N. lat. 13764 form a small ritual book of the

monastery of Saint-Amand, bound afterwards with three manuscripts, principally hagiographical, of Saint-Remi of Reims.[7]
In the Paris B.N. lat. 933, a Benedictine collectar-ritual book
from Lagrasse in the Diocese of Carcassonne, the primitive
manuscript (dating from before the introduction in 1080 of the
monastic reform of St. Victor of Marseille and which was corrected after that date according to this reform[8]) includes in ff.
155r-162v a booklet, in twelfth-century Italian script, of the
dedication of a church, which should be added to the three
witnesses used by Andrieu to establish the text of the Roman
Pontifical of the Twelfth Century.[9]

A liturgical section in the middle of a manuscript in which
the general arrangement and script are homogenous only justi-
fies the name *libellus* in a wider and improper fashion, and in
my opinion it would be better to avoid such an appellation, as
in Paris B.N. lat. 1984A, a Carolingian moral collection, for ff.
87r-104r, a funeral ritual which contains the most ancient (Ambrosian) testimony of the Office of the Dead. We could have a
copy of a *libellus* here, but, on the other hand, it could be an example of an abridged version, an *excarpsus* directly produced
from a complete book. This last explanation is surely the better
one for the liturgical section of a collection discovered by A.
Wilmart which he designated a "Benedictine booklet from Gellone."[10] This collection of 107 ff., copied approximately between 804 and 812, contains among other things a group of sev-
en Masses for the main feasts of the year, which in all
likelihood were drawn directly from the Gregorian Sacramentary, and to which were subsequently added, on a double sup-
plementary folio, two votive Masses from the Supplement of
Aniane. Niels Rasmussen, who discovered this last distinctive
feature, rightly uses the expression *cartula missalis*, and he has
shown that *cartula* first existed independently.[11]

A similar observation could be made for the liturgical por-
tion of a manuscript of Mont-Blandin, preserved at the Royal
Library of Brussels, which is precisely entitled *Liber Sacramentorum Excarpsus*.[12] Here again, it could be a case either of a copy
taken from a sacramentary *excarpsus* which would formerly
have existed in independent form, or an *excarpsus* produced by
the author of the manuscript himself. But in cases like this, it
should be remembered that the Carolingian era used abridged

sacramentaries along with major sacramentaries. We will soon come to the testimony of Alcuin on this subject.

It often happened that a complementary booklet was added to a preexisting liturgical book, without this booklet ever having been destined to be used alone. Here also, one would hesitate to use the designation *libellus*.

Finally, it goes without saying that a fragment of a liturgical manuscript is not the same thing as a *libellus*. The great contemporary liturgical repertories have at times lacked precision in this regard. However, they did so because of the conviction that the *libelli* offer us a key—not necessarily the only one—for understanding the manner in which liturgical books were put together. In this regard, M. Huglo has shown the role played by the *libelli* in the genesis of tropers; the thesis of N. Rasmussen will demonstrate that same role in the genesis of pontificals.

Absence of Binding

Not bound, the booklet or booklets of a *libellus* can be joined together or bound subsequently, depending on the situation.[13] Frequently the wear and tear of the front-facing page of a first folio shows that the booklet was used without binding. For example, this can be noticed in the first folio of the customary book for the sacristy of the Mende cathedral, which we mentioned earlier, or again for f. 1r and especially for f. 8v of Rouen A 566 (175), a booklet of votive Masses *per hebdomadam*, copied at Saint-Amand, used (and completed) subsequently at Saint-Denis.[14] In other cases the front side of the first folio had been left empty, and the text only begins on the reverse side. This is the case for a *libellus missae* of Benediktbeuren copied circa 800 and containing Masses (prayers and readings) of Ascension and Pentecost (both the vigil and the feast itself).[15] It was an analogous preoccupation which led, in a certain number of library catalogues dating from the end of the thirteenth century, to the practice of noting for each volume, not the first words of the first folio, but the first words of the second one, and similarly the last words of the penultimate folio.

The absence of binding explains why *libelli* are generally not as well preserved as books.[16] It also leads us to suppose that *li-*

belli were in fact very numerous, but that they more easily wore out, were torn, or were lost. At Muri in the twelfth century the catalogue notes: *Sunt adhuc hic opuscula libellorum satis utilia, que oportet servare et meliorare et non destruere.*[17] At Saint-Pons de Tomières in 1276 the catalogue indicates: *Item sunt viginti volumina caternorum quasi inutilia.*[18]

To avoid losing the *libelli*, collections of them were assembled from the Middle Ages onwards. Hardly any effort was made to group these around a common subject. On the basis of what we can see in the preserved manuscripts, some libraries had some sort of tradition of binding *libelli*, whereas others did not. Thus, Saint-Martial of Limoges, whose manuscripts are kept at the Bibliothèque Nationale in Paris, has numerous collections of *libelli*. Bernard Itier, *armarius* of this monastery during the entire first quarter of the thirteenth century, mentions for example that in 1205 he had bound, along with the treatise of Julian Pomerius on the contemplative life, four booklets, until then independent.[19] The first three contain, respectively, the cosmography of Bernard Silvestris, a treatise on computing time, and some sermons. The fourth is a twelfth-century liturgical *libellus* of the Office of St. John the Baptist. It is, however, very rare that medieval manuscripts yield such precise information to the historian.

Specific Purpose of "Libelli"

The fourth point brings me to the heart of this presentation. I will briefly consider three periods: the pre-Carolingian period, the period from the Carolingian liturgical reform up to the twelfth century, and finally the thirteenth century which determined the liturgical books up to the end of the Middle Ages and even—to some degree—beyond that.

From the era before Charlemagne we have various liturgical fragments, but we do not have, it seems to me, any *libelli* in the sense that I have tried to define them. However, a passage from the *Historia Francorum* by Gregory of Tours has led liturgical historians for a century to ask if *libelli* were not at the origin of the sacramentary. Concerning St. Sidonius, bishop of Clermont in the middle of the fifth century, Gregory writes: *Contigit autem quadam die ut ad festiuitatem basilicae monasterii inuitatus accederet, ablatoque sibi nequiter libello per quem sacro-sancta sollemnia agere consueuerat, ita paratus a tempore cunctum festiuitatis opus explicuit, ut ab omnibus miraretur.*[20] In spite of the difference between local liturgies, it was tempting to find an echo of this text in the structure of the manuscript of Verona, long designated as the Leonine Sacramentary, which seems in effect to be the case. According to A. Stuiber (Bonn, 1950), it may be a collection of *libelli sacramentorum romani.*

If we turn to the Carolingian era, we again have important evidence on the role of *libelli* from Alcuin, assuming that he allowed the establishment of a distinction between *libellus* and sacramentary. My intention here, however, is not to examine the meaning of the texts by Gregory of Tours and Alcuin, but to consider the *libelli* in themselves. For the ninth and following centuries there are three cases to distinguish.

1. Extracts from a sacramentary for a given feast or for the great feasts, extracts not necessarily destined for poor parishes or travelling priests. For the Office, Msgr. P. Salmon and I have noticed that in the tenth and eleventh centuries the abridged books are perhaps as numerous as the complete ones, but in my opinion it is a case of abridged books rather than *libelli* as such.

The manuscript Montserrat 72, an Andorran collection of the twelfth century and examined by the Catalan liturgist J. Bellavista,[21] is particularly interesting as a sort of abridgement of all the liturgical books for the use of a poor church, but it should be considered in the context of the Hispanic *liber misticus*. Before leaving this category, I would like to note that all known *libelli missae* from the Carolingian or post-Carolingian era are derived from sacramentaries and do not shed any light on the genesis of the sacramentaries.

2. In the case of that book which, since the second half of the thirteenth century, has been called the pontifical and the book which in the sixteenth century received the name ritual, the situation is different. It has been greatly clarified by N.K. Rasmussen. Although we cannot say that the *libelli* are, strictly speaking, at the origin of the pontifical, they did serve abundantly in the same way as the pontificals, and perhaps over all were more numerous than the pontificals. For example, the will of the bishop Riculf of Elne in 915 mentions: *ad ecclesiam*

consecrandam quaterniones duos, ad visitandum infirmum quaterniones duos, ad ordinationes ecclesiasticas quaternione uno:[22] we do not have the impression that this bishop used any other book for this type of liturgical function.

The main contribution of Niels Rasmussen is that, while analyzing the ten or twelve pontificals of the ninth and tenth centuries, he notices that three of them (Leiden 111.2, Reims 340, and Vat. lat. 7701) contain one or several *libelli*. In particular, the manuscript of Leiden, namely, the pontifical of Beauvais, is nothing other than a collection of *libelli*. To this it is necessary to add that the *libelli*, independently from the pontificals, seem to have have been particularly used for the liturgy of the sick and the dead.

3. The use of *libelli* is particularly suitable for new offices. This question has been studied under the aspect of the distinction between liturgical manuscripts and hagiographical manuscripts by E. Munding in his treatment of the manuscript Sankt-Gallen 566, which is a list of lives of saints dating fom the tenth century. Munding makes reference, according to circumstances, to different sources going from the great passionaries to the *quaterniones*.[23] In general, the first have been preserved, whereas the second have disappeared. Still in the hagiographical field, B. Bischoff studied a series of small hagiographical or festive manuscripts which still had the marks of folds;[24] these had presumably been transported from one place to another to spread the cult of a saint. It must equally have been the case, without folding, for the *libelli* of the Office and the Mass of the Feast of All Saints, an example being Munich Clm 14704, 121-144, from Freisingen: B. Bischoff definitely assured me in 1980 that, from a paleographical point of view, this *libellus* may be dated during the episcopate of Anno (854-875). The English paleographer and liturgist, Sir Francis Wormald, has also considered as a group the illuminated hagiographical *libelli* from the tenth to the end of the twelfth century: some contain euchological elements and others do not.[25]

For the thirteenth century, I will examine three cases, beginning with the one having the most general importance: the liturgical *libelli* in the library of Boniface VIII in 1295; the *libellus* of the Office of Corpus Christi circulated by Urban IV along with the Bull instituting this feast; finally, the use of *libelli* in the liturgy of the Friar Preachers such as it was established between 1254-1256.

The 1295 catalogue of Boniface VIII's library[26] contains 523 manuscripts, including 108 liturgical manuscripts (*libri ad divinum officium*), which is a considerable proportion. According to each particular case, it is indicated whether a manuscript is a *liber* or a *quaternus*, but in some cases the catalogue mentions *quaterni* in the plural, that is, one work in several *quaterni*. Adopting that hypothesis, I counted a total of twenty-four works in *quaterni*, fourteen being liturgical: here again the proportion is high. Among the liturgical *quaterni*, five or six can be linked to the pontifical (papal coronation [two copies], preparation for the papal Mass, consecration of virgins, episcopal blessings, *ordines*), and an equal number have a hagiographical or festive character (thus the Office of the Trinity by John Peckham and the Office of Corpus Christi to which I will return later). Finally, there is a *quaternus* which we would call a *Kyriale*, and a group of *quaterni* (n. 419) whose description seems rather to correspond to an incomplete antiphonary. In their variety these *quaterni* are, depending on circumstances, supplements to preexisting liturgical books or booklets, supplements which were more convenient to use separately.

For the Office of Corpus Christi, the catalogue of 1295 contains two copies of a *liber* (nn. 294, 295), one of a *quaternus* (n. 288), and one of *IIII quaterni, in quibus est officium de corpore Christi cum nota* (n. 418). The last one may correspond to Paris B.N. lat. 1143, which the papal catalogue of 1311 proves belonged to the library of Boniface VIII.[27] The *quaternus*, apparently not noted, is explained in a passage of Urban IV's Bull instituting the feast where the pope prescribes its celebration with the elements of the Office *que cum proprio misse officio vobis sub bulla nostra mittimus interclusa:*[28] the liturgical *quaternus* is in that case included under the crease of the Bull. We don't have any such *quaternus de Corpore Christi* originating directly from the Roman Curia, but two indirect copies are still extant. They include both the Bull *Transiturus* and the un-noted text of the Office *Sacerdos in Aeternum* with the corresponding Mass.[29]

The liturgical books of the Friar Preachers, as established between 1254-1256 under the rule of the master general, Humbert de Romans, probably represent the most elaborate state of liturgical organization at the time, with a complex combination of choral and individual celebration, and of memorized liturgical practice and developing written culture.[30] As a rule the new liturgical books of 1254-1256 respond to all that was needed, but for three exceptions. The first consists in the *libellus* of the Little Office of the Virgin Mary, which was given to novices just long enough for them to learn it by heart.[31] I will not consider here whether the book of the Hours was originally a *libellus*.

Among the Preachers *libelli* were provided for two other circumstances, namely, funerals and processions, and it was the responsibility of the cantor to keep and distribute these books.[32] At funerals, each priest was expected to say all the numerous orations in the rite for the deceased. As for processions, it was provided that only the cantor would use the part of the processional containing the rubrics, which were grouped at the front, whereas the noted part would be recopied in the desired number of examples.[33] In itemizing the processional manuscripts, M. Huglo has been surprised by the large proportion of Dominican processionals among those preserved. This is due, on the one hand, to the cultural level of the Dominican nuns of the Middle Ages; but, on the other hand, I think, due to the link in the last centuries of the Middle Ages between the development of reading and writing, and the dwindling of memorization in the culture of that time.

These three thirteenth-century usages of *libelli* (those in the library of Boniface VIII, those of the Office of Corpus Christi, and those of the liturgy of the Friar Preachers between 1254-1256) provide us with concrete examples of how, from the liturgical point of view, the *libellus* does not include all the functions of a given ministry, but only that of a particular liturgical action or a specific feast. Further examples and insights will be provided by the forthcoming publication of Niels Rasmussen's doctoral dissertation, *Les Pontificaux du haut moyen-âge*.

Notes

1. Study published in R. Jacobsson, ed., *Pax et Sapientia: Studies in Text and Music of Liturgical Tropes and Sequences in Memory of Gordon Anderson*, Studia Latina Stockholmiensia 29 (Stockholm: Almquist & Wiksell International, 1985) 13-22.

2. Michael Huglo, *Livres de chant liturgique*, Typologie des sources du moyen-âge occidental 52 (Turnhout: Brepols, 1988) 64-75.

3. I believe it might be worth reconsidering the categorizing of pre-Carolingian and Carolingian *libelli precum*, as some fit the criteria indicated below, and others attain more considerable proportions in respect to size. On the other hand, mention could be made, by way of comparison, of the *libelli* containing conciliar canons, for instance, those of Lateran IV; several of these are among the manuscripts used by A. García y García, *Constitutiones Concilii Quarti Lateranensis* (Vatican City: Bibloteca Apostolica Vaticana, 1981). We could also mention the synodal booklets of the parish priests of the thirteenth century; see O. Pontal, *Les Statuts de Paris et le synodal de l'Ouest* (Paris, 1971) 71, 107-108. See also in a general way Msgr. Emile Lesne, *Histoire de la propriété ecclesiastique en France*, vol. v (Lille: R. Giard, 1938) 368-375; also P.R. Robinson, "The 'Booklet'," a Self-Contained Unit in Composite Manuscripts," in *Codicologica 3: Essais typologiques*, eds., A. Gruijs and J.P. Gunbert (Leiden, 1980) 46-69.

4. S.J.P. Van Dijk and J. Hazelden Walker, *The Origins of the Modern Roman Liturgy* (Westminster, MD: Newman Press, 1960) 32. They proposed the establishment of the height of twenty centimeters as the boundary between a portable and a non-portable breviary.

5. See my book *La Liturgie dans l'histoire* (Paris: Saint-Paul/Cerf, 1990) 423-438.

6. I believe the inventory of 1380 designates it as the "libretum de divinis officiis qui est in subsacristia." See my "Livres liturgiques de l'Eglise de Mende," *Mens Concordet Voci. Mélanges Martimort* (Paris, 1983) 500-501.

7. See E. Palazzo, "Les deux rituels d'un libellus de Saint-Amand," in *Rituels: Mélanges offerts à Pierre-Marie Gy*, eds. Paul De Clerck and Eric Palazzo (Paris: Cerf, 1990) 423-438.

8. See J. Lemarié, *Le Bréviaire de Ripoll*, Scripta et Documenta 14 (Abadia de Montserrat, 1965) 107.

9. *Le Pontifical romain au moyen âge*, vol. 1, *Le Pontifical romain du XIIe siècle*, Studi e Testi 86 (Vatican City: Biblioteca Apostolica Vaticana, 1938) 176-195.

10. A. Wilmart, "Un livret bénédictin composé à Gellone au commencement du IXe siècle," *Revue Mabillon* 12 (1922) 119-132.

11. N. Rasmussen, "Une *cartula missalis* retrouvée," *Ephemerides Liturgicae* 83 (1969) 482-484.

12. Bruxelles B.R. 10127-44, 125r-135r (K. Gamber, *Codices Liturgici Latini Antiquiores*, 2d ed. [Fribourg: Universitätsverlag, 1968] n. 856).

13. The catalogue of Christ Church, Canterbury (Cambridge Univ. Libr. Ii.3.12, circa 1170, ed. Montague Rhodes James, *The Ancient Li-*

braries of Canterbury and Dover [Cambridge: University Press, 1903] 7-12) mentions a work preserved *in quaterno*, at the same time distinguishing it from those which are bound *in asseribus* (in wooden boards), *in pergameno, in corio*. The majority of medieval manuscripts which have been preserved are *in asseribus*. Those which have only supple bindings are rarities. On this see B. Van Regemoster, "La reliure souple des manuscrits carolingiens de Fulda," *Scriptorium* 11 (1957) 249-257; also the works of J. Vezin: "Communication sur des reliures souples des XIIe et XIIIe s., " *Bulletin de la Soc. Nat. des Antiquaires de France* (1976) 168-171; "Paléographie et codicologie," *Ecole Pratique des Hautes Etudes, IVe Section* (1978) 583-586; "Une reliure carolingienne de cuir souple (Oxford, Bodleian Library, Marshall 19)," *Revue française d'histoire du livre* (1982) 235-241 (was a manuscript which pertained to St. Augustine of Canterbury); "Une reliure en cuir souple estampé du XIIIe s. (Paris, B.N. lat 6637 A)," ibid. 243-249.

14. On this manuscript see Eric Palazzo,"Un *libellus missae* de Saint-Amand pour Saint-Denis: Son intérêt pour la typologie des manuscrits liturgiques," *Revue bénédictine* 99 (1989) 286-292. He gives here a very good example of monography of a liturgical *libellus*. See also his "Les deux rituels d'un *libellus* de Saint-Amand (Paris: Bibliothèque Nationale, Lat. 13764," in *Rituels: Mélanges offerts à Pierre Marie Gy* 423-436.

15. It is one of the elements of the palimpsest of Munich Clm 6333 published by E. Munding and A. Dold, *Benediktinische und Liturgische Texte aus Clm 6333*, Texte und Arbeiten 1 (Beuron, 1930) 15-18.

16. Hincmar, for example, claims to have found the life of St. Sanctinus in "quaternunculos valde contritos" at the monastery of St. Sanctinus of Meaux (AASS Oct. V, 586-588, n. 7-13).

17. Gustav Heinrich Becker, *Catalogi Bibliothecarum Antiqui* (Bonn: Apud M. Cohen et Filium, 1885) 252.

18. L. Delisle, *Le Cabinet des manuscrits de la Bibliothèque Nationale*, vol. 2 (Paris, 1874) 548, n. 256 bis.

19. Paris B.N. lat. 2770, 179r: "Anno 1205 fecit me ligare Bernardus Iterii armarius, et quatuor quaterniones ultimos qui antea non erant mecum adiunxit."

20. *Historia Francorum* II, 22.

21. See J. Bellavista, *L'antifoner de missa de Sant Romà de les Bons* (Andorra, 1979).

22. PL 132:468D.

23. Emmanuel Munding, *Das Verzeichnis der St. Galler Heiligenleben und ihrer Handschriften in Codex Sangall no. 566*, Texte und Arbeiten 1 (Leipzig: O. Harrassowitz, 1918) 3-4.

24. B. Bischoff, "Uber gefaltete Handschriften, vornehmlich hagio-

graphischen Inhalts," *Mittelalterliche Studien* 1 (Stuttgart: A. Hiersemann, 1966) 93-100.

25. Francis Wormald, "Some Illustrated Manuscripts of the Lives of the Saints," *Bulletin, The John Rylands Library* 35 (1952) 148-166.

26. A. Pelzer, *Addenda et Emendanda ad Francisci Ehre Historiae Bibliothecae Romanorum Pontificum tum Bonifatianae tum Avenionensis*, vol. 1 (Vatican City, 1947) 4-24.

27. F. Ehrle, *Historia Bibliothecae Romanorum Pontificum*, vol. 1 (Vatican City: Typis Vaticanis, 1890) 28, n. 27.

28. Gy, *La Liturgie dans l'histoire* 228.

29. Ibid. 235-236.

30. See the doctoral dissertation of Thomas W. Elich, *Le Contexte oral de la liturgie médiévale et le rôle du texte écrit* (Paris: Institut Catholique et Université Paris-IV, 1988).

31. See at the Couvent Saint-Jacques in Paris at the end of the thirteenth century, John of Montlhéry, *Libellus de Instructione Novitiorum*, ch. 3 and 4, in Humbert of Romans, *Opera Vita Regulari*, ed., J.J. Berthier, vol. 2 (Rome, 1889) 129: "Facta autem confessione generali, et traditis sibi horis beatae Virginis ad repetendum vel addiscendum . . . Item, postquam sciverint horas beatae Virginis cordetenus, tradant eas magistro novitiorum, qui custodiat eas."

32. Humbert of Romans, *De Officio Ordinis*, ch. 8, "De Officio Cantoris," in *Opera de Vita Regulari*, ed., J.J. Berthier, vol. 2 (Rome, 1889) 239: "Item debet procurare quod aliquid armarium habeatur in choro vel in sacristia vel alibi, prout videbitur locus magis deputatus ad hoc, in quo libri omnes de choro reponantur, praeter libros processionales; et inde, per ipsum, vel per alium si praelato visum fuerit, deportentur ad chorum tempore officii, prout necessarii fuerint, et postea reportentur. Ipsius autem est distribuere ipsos libellos per chorum, prout videbitur expedire, sive pro funeribus, sive pro processionibus."

33. See Gy, *La Liturgie dans l'histoire* 125.

3

Latin Mass Commentaries from the Ninth through Twelfth Centuries: Chronology and Theology

Mary M. Schaefer

IN THE PREFACE TO THE REVISED ENGLISH EDITION OF *MEDIEVAL LITURGY: An Introduction to the Sources* the editors and translators note the reason Cyrille Vogel gave for compiling such a source book: "the difficulty so many medievalists seem to have in undertaking the study of the medieval liturgy."[1] As recently as 1981 Vogel had observed that "the sources themselves are still imperfectly catalogued and . . . agreement among specialists is still far from complete."[2] The purpose of this article, in a collection dedicated to the memory of Niels Rasmussen, is to bring up to date the information on those commentaries of the ninth through twelfth centuries which offer a theological reflection on the liturgy of the Mass.[3] Commentaries which confine themselves to historical or rubrical data are not included. The documents are ordered according to the date where that is known, or arranged in relative chronological order. Brief biographical and bibliographical data together with the authors' major sources are noted.[4]

The ambitious yet restricted cultural program of the Carolingian renaissance is well known. Maintenance of these cultural gains was a struggle for the tenth and early eleventh centuries.[5] The twelfth-century renaissance was broad and complex; its contributions must be investigated on a number of fronts.[6] In the visual arts, whether architecture, sculpture, painting, or illumination, schools of artists and artisans from the British Isles to Italy developed characteristic regional expressions. This mobile society and its artists took to the pilgrimage roads; hence the migration or transmission of influences from one region to another. Truly foreign influence—the Byzantine—also appeared in some centers of religious culture. In the early twelfth century these were generally monastic; increasingly, cathedral churches and their bishops provided the fertile cultural matrix needed. This makes the period both a delight to the connoisseur and a challenge to the specialist. The thirteenth century would refine and harmonize the artistic energies of Europe, and in its course present a synthesis in keeping with the high scholasticism of the universities.[7]

The situation in the arts and the study of the Bible is echoed on a smaller scale by the liturgical genre of the Mass commentary, developed in the medieval West by Carolingian interpreters.

Carolingian and Post-Carolingian Period: Ninth to Eleventh Centuries

The Carolingian author noted for the use of all types of allegory,[8] Amalarius of Metz, briefly bishop of Trier (d. ca. 850) provided in the third book of his *Liber Officialis*[9] the fertile if fanciful soil that would be tilled and re-tilled by subsequent generations of Mass commentators.

Less well-known is Amalar's contemporary and theological antagonist, Florus, deacon of Lyons (d. ca. 860). The latter's *De Actione Missarum* ("Concerning the Canon of the Mass") is a tissue of quotations from the Fathers[10] interlarded with his own modified patristic commentary. The position of Florus can be summarized in part. The church is a community which spans the whole world. The whole church is a holy priesthood (1 Peter 2:9). The eucharist is the mutual offering of priest and church (i.e., assembly of the people); the priest prays on behalf of the people, and the people the priest. Through Christ their head, the one true mediator and priest, their every prayer and "action of thanksgiving" is offered. The ministerial priesthood "exhibits" the ministry of offering and supplicating which is the action of all the faithful.

Florus' position on the participants and offering of the Mass finds a follower in chapter 40, attributed to Remigius of Auxerre (ca. 840-908), of the Pseudo-Alcuinian *Liber de Divinis Officiis*.[11] Although Remigius is Florus' best-known copier, he does not hand on the "whole Florus." Half of chapter 39 of this work is a radical synopsis of Amalar.[12] In the treatise *De Corpore et Sanguine Domini*[13] abbot John of Fécamp (ca. 990-1078) incorporates substantial verbatim segments of the *De Actione Missarum* which relate to the eucharist and its institution.

The imposition of the reform of the Roman Mass inaugurated by Pope Gregory VII (1073-1085) and its consolidation were assisted by Bernold of Constance (ca. 1050-1100), priest and monk of St. Blasien in the Schwarzwald. Chapters 1 to 23 of his *Micrologus de Ecclesiasticis Observationibus*[14] seem to have been responsible, more than any other single factor, for establishing Roman usage in the shape and text of the Mass ordinary in German-speaking lands. About the year 1100 the bishops of Hungary decreed that the order of Mass set out in the *Micrologus* was normative in their territory.

Liturgical historian and canonist, Bernold is partially dependent on Amalar, although he expresses uneasiness with the more arbitrary applications of number symbolism. In Bernold's presentation the priest's gestures constitute a kind of objective sign of Christ's saving acts. Read as a tableau, they invite subjective participation in the events of the passion or in Christ's ethical attitudes. Bernold's commentary contributes to a progressive restriction of liturgical roles to the priest.

Early Twelfth Century:
1100-1115

The genre of the Mass commentary flourished in the twelfth century. The first three listed here, from the region of the Meuse and lower Rhine rivers, represent monastic theology still under the spell of the great Carolingian monastery of Corbie and its abbot, Paschasius Radbertus.

The *Liber de Sacramentis* of Petrus Pictor (fl. Flanders 1100)[15] is a eucharistic tract of twenty-six chapters with prologue and epilogue, the whole written in rhyming hexameters. Each chapter is introduced by a theological proposition, in prose, inspired by the *De Corpore et Sanguine Domini* of Paschasius Radbertus (written 831-833), the first systematic treatise on eucharistic doctrine written in the West[16] and an important medium for transmitting patristic teaching to the Middle Ages, albeit with a Carolingian twist and a diminution in the understanding of symbol. Petrus separates the doctrinal material from those inventive allegorical sections which deal with the priest's actions. He addresses priests directly in chapters 21 through 26.

Important patristic motifs include the activity of the Word; the notion of the eucharist as celestial banquet and medicinal food; the analogy of sacramental incarnation to explain the "transferal" of the bread into the body and blood of Christ; and the divinization of those who receive it. If we follow the patristic categories of presence set out by Johannes Betz,[17] it can be seen that Petrus understands Christ to be actively present in the Mass as host of the meal; the sacrifice of the cross is present in memorial; finally, Christ is substantially present in the saving food.

Another proponent of the Gregorian reform is Blessed Odo, abbot of St. Martin's, Tournai, and then bishop of Cambrai (d. 1113). His *Expositio in Canonem Missae*[18] faithfully copies the text of the Roman Canon and provides a literal exposition of it which, while bearing the individual stamp of the author, is informed by the notion of the *circumastantes* as co-offerers of the Mass found in Florus of Lyons. Odo's exposition of the narrative of institution is based on that of Ambrose in *De Sacramentis*. Other patristic ideas include the centrality of the Word, the analogies of creation and sacramental incarnation for eucharistic change, and the divinization of those who participate in the Mass. Odo notes the role of the Holy Spirit in the consecration of the bread and wine. He transmits Florus' thought to later commentators, who receive it only partially.

Rupert of Deutz (ca. 1075-1129) completed the *De Divinis Of-*

ficiis[19] in 1111 or at the latest 1112; it was his first major work. A prolific writer, exegete, and theologian, his old-fashioned monastic theology earned for him charges of heresy as regards its eucharistic teaching. Surprisingly, the complex imagery which Rupert uses with great symbolic impact seems to have aroused no such ire. In much of the Mass commentary, he is inspired by Amalarian rememorative allegory although maintaining the patristic perspectives transmitted by Paschasius: the Wisdom-Christology motif of the tree of life in paradise and Christ as high priest of the eucharistic banquet; and the Word taking up bread and wine from the altar and "transferring" them into his body and blood. Rupert understands that the sacrifice of the cross is present in the Mass; that Christ divinizes the members of the church by forming one *persona* with them; and that the whole assembly is co-offerer of the Mass.

Honorius Augustodunensis (active ca. 1098-1150s) is an enigmatic reforming historian and theological popularizer whose works rehearse many of the themes which animated the early years of the twelfth century.[20] Perhaps born in Ireland, he seems to have been monk and finally hermit; his latest activity is localized in Regensburg, southern Germany. The *Gemma Animae*,[21] an example of liturgical catechesis counted among works written in England before 1110, was more likely edited in Germany ca. 1140. Honorius borrows from Amalar and, in Book I which treats of the Mass, utilizes Isidore of Seville's etymological comments and method. He retains a residue of patristic thought particularly with respect to Christ's activity.[22]

But in chapters 45 and 83 the liturgical ministers are tragedians who play out their roles in the ritual drama of the Mass. The presider's action is explained as impersonation of Christ in his passion; the people are mainly passive. Another stratum in Honorius' work, that of doctrinal exposition, awards to the people a more integral participation which does not generally extend to communion. The Mass is celebrated daily, Honorius says, to refresh priests; to provide for the first communion of neophytes; and to inculcate in the minds of the faithful for their imitation the memory of Christ's passion.[23] In Honorius, as in Petrus Pictor, two different modes of explaining the Mass are found side by side. One expounds the *veritas* or truth of Christ's real activity as high priest of the church's sacrifice.

The other explains the liturgical rites as figure of the reality: the self-offering of Christ on the cross. Since the literal meaning of the readings and prayers is no longer accessible to the majority of worshipers, allegory affords them an opportunity for subjective appropriation of the ministerial action.

Another approach is taken by that group of authors I have termed "history of salvation theologians." In the undated *Sermo V*[24] the influential canonist Ivo (bishop of Chartres 1090-1115) works out a typological concordance of Augustinian inspiration between the "sacraments" of the old covenant which prefigure, and those of the new covenant which commemorate, the salvific acts of Christ's life. The first part of the Mass, which takes place openly before the people, corresponds to the levitical sacrifices offered at the altar of holocausts outside the temple at Jerusalem. Ivo relates the liturgy of the eucharist to priestly activity at the altar of incense and in the Holy of Holies. Although the unique priesthood of Christ as set forth in the Letter to the Hebrews is Ivo's middle term, Christian and Old Testament priesthood are the poles of his argument which reduce attention paid to the activity of Christ and the faithful in the Mass. Therefore the priest is awarded a certain mediatorial role vis-à-vis a passive people.

The brief *De Sacrificio Missae*,[25] attributed to Alger of Liège (entered Cluny in 1121) lies within Ivo's horizon of influence and reflects on themes which appear in correspondence written ca. 1109-1115 between the bishop of Chartres and abbot Pons de Melgueil. Of much greater moment is the lengthy poem *Versus de Mysterio Missae*[26] by the humanist Hildebert of Le Mans (ca. 1056-1133), from 1125 archbishop of Tours. Inspired by Amalar in his treatment of the first part of the Mass, Hildebert draws on Ivo's *Sermo V* for expounding the liturgy of the eucharist. Indeed, parallels with Petrus Pictor's *Liber de Sacramentis* have led to the theory that the latter poem was dependent on the *Versus*. Although it retains residues of the narrative monastic theology which still flourished in the Mosan-Rhenish region, Hildebert's poem is less doctrinal and Paschasian in content. Most of Hildebert's poetry was written in the period 1100-1115; this lengthy one in unrhymed distychs may date from around 1112. If so, it concludes a flourishing period for the Mass commentary which lasts little longer than a decade.

Mid-Twelfth Century

The energies expended on the narrative genre of the Mass commentary were directed elsewhere after ca. 1115. The birth of the scientific theological disciplines may go far toward explaining the accusations of heresy hurled against writers like Rupert of Deutz and Honorius. Early scholasticism represented a new, disciplined approach to reflection on liturgy when it subjected sacramental praxis to systematic analysis. Canonists too had something to contribute to the self-understanding of the church. Despite sometimes high-flown titles, commentators on the Mass recycled ideas and images from the beginning of the century or extracted technical terminology from recently developed theological treatises without presenting the whole construct. The first two works listed in this section were written in the heady academic atmosphere of Paris in mid-century. The latter two are late blooming examples of monastic theology from the Cistercian context.

The gains achieved when the schools introduced an analytic approach to explain doctrines such as eucharistic presence would be offset by losses. Once the Berengarian issue established the agenda, patristic concepts of Christ's active presence as liturgist and priest, the presence in memorial of the cross, and the consequent relationality of substantial or somatic presence would cease to figure in Mass commentary. The notion that Christ is the chief actor in liturgy would find a place in the treatise on sacramental theology forming a separate stream from the theological exposition of liturgy, where the ministers enjoyed a new prominence.

The sea-change marking the birth of early scholasticism is reflected in the *Speculum de Mysteriis Ecclesiae*, ascribed to Hugh of St. Victor (d. 1141) in the Migne Patrology.[27] Shown to be based on Hugh's lectures and the *Summa Sententiarum*, it can be dated ca. 1160. Its stated aim is "to explore what each thing in the church represents mystically." Chapter 7 treats at length of the celebration of Mass; it is indebted to Ivo's typological analysis of the priesthood and sacrifice in Old Testament terms. Pseudo-Hugh is particularly interested in the priest's representative role (cf. Hildebert) and in eucharistic conversion, although he does not yet utilize the language of transubstantiation. Christ is presented as victim in the Mass; nothing is said about his priesthood. The priest "acts in place of Christ" who is located corporeally in heaven; he has the "power of offering" Christ's body and blood.

John Beleth's popular *Summa de Ecclesiasticis Officiis*[28] was mined for material by Mass commentators of later periods. Its title is misleading; unaffected by scholastic method, it is a grab bag of historical tidbits indebted to the Latin Fathers, Bede, Amalar, Rupert, and Honorius, as well as to Gratian and the decretalists. Beleth omits a discussion of the central part of the Canon; the popular audience to whom this *Summa* was directed was evidently not privy to the "secret" prayers. His is the first Mass commentary to use the term *transsubstantiare*, from the early 1160s applied to eucharistic conversion by the scholastics. The third of its four recensions appears to have been written at Paris between 1160 and 1164.

A brief letter of the English-born Cistercian abbot Isaac of Stella to John bishop of Poitiers, the *Epistola ad Joannem Episcopum Pictaviensum de Officio Missae*, was written between 1165 and 1167.[29] This exposition of the Canon, inspired by Ivo of Chartres' *Sermo*, focuses on the priest's piety. The "actions" of the Canon are related to the stages of the soul's ascent to God in the ascetical and mystical life: the theme of divinization dear to monastic theologians.

The *Libellus de Canone Mystici Libaminis*[30] has been given various attributions, dates, and provenances. It may well record a sermon preached at Clairvaux by Richard the Premonstratensian in the middle to late twelfth century. Its chief source is Honorius' *Gemma Animae*, chapters 49 to 56, wedded to number symbolism. The traditional content of monastic theology is combined with scholastic focus on the sacrament of the altar and its sanctifying effects for the individual.

Close of the Twelfth Century:
1180s to 1200

Lengthy works and increasing clericalization are characteristic of this period.

Since D. Van den Eynde, the *Tractatus de Sacramento Altaris*, a condensation of many sources with a diversity of theological perspectives, has been given to Stephan II, bishop of Autun (d. 1189).[31] The corrected dating eradicates claims about its precocious utilization of scholastic concepts. The Mass commentary (chapters 12-20) includes both literal and allegorical explanations. The author's analysis of the priestly office as representation of Christ is detailed and nuanced. Although he paraphrases Odo of Cambrai with respect to the people's participation in the liturgy, he does not understand the liturgy as their offering nor the priest as their representative.

A shadowy figure who promises to say nothing of his own devising, Robert Paululus (probably a priest of Amiens, d. after 1184) wrote *De Caeremoniis, Sacramentis, Officiis et Observationibus Ecclesiasticis* utilizing wide-ranging sources but especially the commentaries of Rupert of Deutz, Isaac of Stella, and the *Gemma Animae*.[32] But his choice and arrangement of authorities result in a theological construct in which the priest is the chief actor, bearing "the person of the true and high priest" Christ, and acting as the latter's intermediary with the people. Old Testament levitical priesthood is the sole model for Christian sacrificing priesthood; the eucharistic sacrifice is that of the priest, who prays that it be carried to the heavenly altar by "his" guardian angel. The offering of the church becomes the priest's offering; its goal is his divinization. Finally, the people's Amen at the doxology is attestation of the priest's continence. The Mass is understood as an exercise of the priest's private devotion; the people participate vicariously in his sacrifice.

For Robert, Christ is present in the earthly liturgy by virtue of his "representation" in the transubstantiated offerings of bread and wine, which are converted by the power of the whole Trinity working *ad extra* rather than by the activity of the Word, as was characteristic in the early part of the century.

The two commentators on the Mass in the final years of the century are Italian: Sicard of Cremona and Lothar of Segni (Innocent III, elected to the papacy in 1198). A century later Durand of Mende (d. 1296) would copy extensively from both commentaries for his very popular *Rationale Divinorum Officiorum* (ca. 1291).

Sicard, bishop of Cremona from 1185 until his death in 1215, wrote the *Mitrale seu de Officiis Ecclesiasticis Summa*[33] probably before 1198, since it shows no indication of acquaintance with Lothar's suddenly popular treatise. Book II gives an extensive exposition of ordination rites and distinguishes, for each of the clerical grades, the "substance of the sacrament" from the integral rites which add to its solemnity. Book III is entitled "Concerning the Duties of the Ministers of the Church." Its subject, the Mass, is approached from the perspective of the ministers. It is not very original, making intensive use of Honorius' *Gemma Animae*, John Beleth's *Summa*, the *Liber Pontificalis*, Amalar, and Rupert.

Sicard explains why the bishop is titled vicar of Jesus Christ. He uses Rupert's explanation of eucharistic conversion but substitutes the language of transubstantiation, attributing instrumental power to the priest. Of the priesthood he exclaims, "Great dignity, wonderful power, most high and terrifying office!" To a greater degree than most commentators, Sicard makes a place for the activity of the Holy Spirit. As Christ filled bread and wine with the Holy Spirit, so the Holy Spirit effects this sacrament. Elsewhere, Sicard states that the dominical words are the essential consecratory form, whereas the remainder of the liturgy adds to the solemnity.

He, and Lothar as well, distinguish the manner of offering of ministers and people: priests offer by their acts, the people by their devotion. During the Canon the people should not be disturbed at their prayers. Sicard is, however, egalitarian on the matter of communicating: if priests celebrate Mass several times a day, then "religious laity" should also be allowed multiple communions. Indeed, it seems that the customs of the church of Cremona allowed for frequent communion by properly disposed laity, an anomaly judging from the general evidence.

Lothar of Segni comments on the pontifical Mass of the Apostolic See, "mother and teacher of the other churches," ca. 1195-1197 in *De Missarum Mysteriis*, when still a deacon.[34] Besides the Latin Fathers and councils, his sources include Florus of Lyons, Remigius of Auxerre, in a major way Rupert, and Honorius; Hugh of St. Victor, Gratian, and Peter Lombard; Peter Comestor, Robert Paululus, and Peter of Poitiers. William Durand (d. 1296) would incorporate large tracts of this work into his *Rationale*.

Lothar stresses the "help" which the Mass, preeminent sacrament, offers for following the commandments and obtaining salvation. Like Sicard, he is interested in ordination rites and those grades of clergy who exercise liturgical ministries. In addition, he sets out the degrees of power which the ordained enjoy. He terms priests "mediators between God and humanity" when they preach to and intercede for their flock; indeed, at the entry rite Christ appears before the assembly "in the person of" the bishop. The bishop or priest makes the ritual offering to the whole Trinity, and so is active subject; the faithful offer the "sacrifice of praise" by joining their devotion to the priest's action.

Lothar restricts the use of the phrase *in persona Christi* to the bishop of Rome's allegorical representation of Christ in the first part of the Mass. In the Canon the presider's role is described as instrumental representation of Christ. However, the presider offers not only in his own name but "in the person of the whole church." His own acts must be carried out in communion with the church.

* * * * * *

These soundings of three centuries of liturgical-theological commentary on the Mass show a startling change of paradigm. What happens within the Carolingian period sets the parameters for the genre in the West. From the whole church as active subject of the liturgical action (Florus) and Christ as the high priest active in the liturgy (Paschasius), notions based on literal exposition of the text and the patristic witness, favor shifts to Amalar's subjective approach: "I say what I think." Eventually commentators collect what everybody else said without digesting it, forcing the material to fit their own theological positions.

Amalar's success in seeking out symbolic explanations which are not anchored in the actual prayers and texts of the liturgy—what the liturgy says about itself—gradually leads to the loss of understanding of the liturgy's true content. The way is then opened for that clericalization and privatization of the eucharist which is writ large and clear in the commentaries of the closing years of the twelfth century. From now on, the split between the public worship of the church and the private devotion of ministers and people, between liturgy as narrative expression of the church's faith and sacramental theology as scientific investigation of disputed questions, is established.

Are there, many centuries later, lessons to be learned from this? It is ironic but telling that a partial systematic synthesis which accounts for only some of the aspects of the mystery celebrated can take for granted the virtual exclusion of the people from the table of the Lord. When, for whatever reason, the liturgical action is no longer accessible to the people who celebrate it; when liturgy ceases to embody the authentic theological content of ecclesial prayer as witnessed to by the integral tradition, it must reclaim its roots and its essence. Investigation of Vogel's "liturgical antiquities" provides gains beyond those of pure scholarship. Light is thrown on the dynamics operative in the Roman liturgical renewal of our own day.

Notes

1. Revised and translated by William G. Storey and Niels Krogh Rasmussen (Washington, D.C.: The Pastoral Press, 1986) xv. Originally published 1962-1966.

2. Ibid. xvii.

3. Ibid. 12-15. See my *Twelfth Century Latin Commentaries on the Mass: Christological and Ecclesiological Dimensions*, Doctoral Dissertation, University of Notre Dame, 1983 (Ann Arbor: University Microfilms), with the additional evidence supporting the summary presentations here. The theme of this article was discussed, shortly before his death, with Professor Rasmussen, who had assisted me with this aspect of the dissertation.

4. This revises the comprehensive but dated survey of *expositio missae* literature done by Adolf Franz, *Die Messe im deutschen Mittelalter* (Freiburg im Breisgau, n.p., 1902; reprinted Darmstadt: Wissenschaftliche Buchgesellschaft, 1963). I am grateful to Professor Roger Reynolds, generous as always in sharing bibliographical information.

5. Beryl Smalley, noting the "dramatic pause in the history of Bible studies" during this period, attributes it to the emphasis placed by religious reformers on the liturgy "at the expense of study." See *The Study of the Bible in the Middle Ages* (Notre Dame: University of Notre Dame Press, 1964) 44-45. Whether or not occasioned by too much prayer, there is a similar hiatus in doctrinal writing and liturgical commentary.

6. *Renaissance and Renewal in the Twelfth Century*, eds., R.L. Benson and G. Constable (Oxford: Clarendon, 1982). The literature is enormous. This was the era of the giant Bibles; see Walter Cahn, *Romanesque Bible Illumination* (Ithaca: Cornell University Press, 1982).

7. Erwin Panofsky, *Gothic Architecture and Scholasticism* (New York: Meridian, 1957).

8. Parallels can be drawn between the different "senses" of Scripture and the types of allegory: rememorative (events in salvation history); typological (fulfillments of the Old Testament); moral (ethical admonitions); eschatological or anagogical (references to the consummation at the end of time). Sicard of Cremona quotes Amalar (n. 9 below, I.19.2-16, pp. 114-120), who had quoted Bede (*De tabernaculo et vasis eius*, I.6, PL 91:410B): "It is history when the thing is referred to with simple speech . . . It is allegory when with words, or mystical things, the sacraments of the church are signified . . . Tropology is a moral word concerning the institution or correction of morals, and is made with frank words . . . Analogy is speech leading to higher things, as concerning future rewards, or the future life" (PL 213:47A-C).

Although allegory's excesses are well known, its use made the ceremonies of the Mass intelligible to simple priests and laity so that they could participate devoutly. In twelfth-century usage, allegory serves a variety of theological and ecclesiological positions.

9. I.M. Hanssens, ed., *Amalarii Episcopi Opera Liturgica Omnia*, vol. 2, Studi e Testi 139 (Vatican City: Biblioteca Apostolica Vaticana, 1948). The *Liber Quare*, a liturgical catechism based on Amalar, omits comment on the Mass (G.P. Götz, ed., Corpus Christianorum, Continuatio Mediaevalis 60 [Turnholt: Brepols, 1983]).

10. PL 119:15-72. P. Duc, *Etude sur l'"Expositio Missae" de Florus de Lyon suivie d'une édition critique du texte* (Belley: Chaduc, 1937) is rare. Florus names Cyprian, Ambrose, Augustine, Jerome, Gregory, Fulgentius, Severianus, Vigilius, Isidore, Bede, and Avitus at the beginning of his work.

11. For the text attributed to Remigius, see PL 101:1246C-1271B.

12. PL 101:1244C-1246B.

13. PL 101:1085-1098.

14. *Micrologus de Ecclesiasticis Observationibus*, ed., Jacobus Pamelius (Antwerp, 1565); Melchior Hittorp, *De Divinis Catholicae Ecclesiae Officiis et Mysteriis* (Cologne: Canlenium and Quentel, 1568); PL 151:977-1022. See V.L. Kennedy, "For a New Edition of the *Micrologus* of Bernold of Constance," *Mélanges en l'honneur de Monseigneur Michel Andrieu*, Revue des sciences religieuses, volume hors série (Strasbourg: Palais Universitaire, 1956) 229-241. The manuscript ma-

terials he was collating at his death are on deposit at the Pontifical Institute of Mediaeval Studies, Toronto. A date of 1089 is accepted as plausible by S. Bäumer, "Der Micrologus ein Werk Bernolds von Konstanz," *Neues Archiv* 18 (1893) 440-441. This would place its writing one year after his *De Veritate Corporis et Sanguinis Domini*, a collection of patristic texts and synodal decrees together with an addition by Bernold, gathered to counter Berengar's eucharistic heresy.

15. *Petri Pictoris Carmina*, ed., L. Van Acker, CCCM 25 (Turnholt: Brepols, 1972) 9-46. The poem has been variously attributed to Peter of Blois, Hildebert of LeMans, Anselm of Canterbury, and Bernard of Clairvaux, and the poet's activity to ca. 1170.

16. *Paschasius Radbertus De Corpore et Sanguine Domini*, ed., B, Paulus, CCCM 16 (Turnholt: Brepols, 1969).

17. M. Schmaus et al., eds., *Handbuch der Dogmengeschichte* IV/4a: *Eucharistie in der Schrift und Patristik*, ed., Johannes Betz (Freiburg: Herder, 1979) 52ff.

18. PL 160:1053-1070. See my "Twelfth Century Latin Commentaries on the Mass: The Relationship of the Priest to Christ and to the People," *Studia Liturgica* 15:2 (1982/1983) 82-84. Odo's commentary may have been written between 1109 and his death in 1113.

19. PL 170:11-332; *Ruperti Tuitiensis Liber de Divinis Officiis*, ed., H. Haacke, CCCM 7 (Turnholt: Brepols, 1967). He treats the Mass in Book I, chs. 28-37 (through the gospel) and Book II, chs. 1-20 (beginning with the creed), with addenda on the history of its ceremonies, the use of leavened or unleavened bread, and the decoration of altars and churches.

20. V.I.J. Flint, *Ideas in the Medieval West: Texts and Their Contexts* (London: Variorum Reprints, 1988) for her collected articles; M.-O. Garrigues, "L'Oeuvre d'Honorius Augustodunensis: Inventaire critique," in *Abhandlungen der Braunschweigischen Wissenschaftlichen Gesellschaft* 38 (1986) 7ff., esp. 83-91; 39 (1987) 123ff.; 40 (1988) 129ff. I am indebted to Prof. Robert D. Crouse for recent publications on Honorius.

21. PL 172:543-738.

22. See especially his *Sacramentarium* (PL 172:737-806), a work of theological reflection, and *Eucharistion* (PL 172:1249-1258), the latter in a forthcoming CCCM edition edited by M.-O. Garrigues.

23. *Gemma Animae*, I.36 (555B-c).

24. PL 162:535-562.

25. PL 180:853-856.

26. Hittorp, pp [523]-528; PL 171:1177-1196.

27. PL 177:335-380. See H. Weisweiler, "Zur Einflussphäre der 'Vorlesungen' Hugos von St. Viktor," in *Mélanges Joseph de Ghellinck, S.J.* (Gembloux: Duculot, 1951), II, 526-581.

28. PL 202:13-166; *Iohannis Beleth Summa de Ecclesiasticis Officiis,* ed., H. Douteil, CCCM 41, 41A (Turnholt: Brepols, 1976).

29. PL 194:1889-1896; English translation by Michele Daviau, "A Letter on the Mass," *The Way* 6 (1966) 321-327. For the date see G. Raciti in *Dictionnaire de spiritualité* 7 (1970) 2020.

30. PL 177:455-470. See G. Macy, "A Bibliographical Note on Richardus Praemonstratensis," *Analecta Praemonstratensia* 52 (1976) 64-69.

31. PL 172:1273-1308. See D. Van den Eynde, "On the Attribution of the 'Tractatus de Sacramento Altaris' to Stephan of Baugé," *Franciscan Studies* n.s. 10 (1950) 33-45; idem, "Le 'Tractatus de Sacramento Altaris' faussement attribué à Etienne de Baugé," *Recherches de théologie ancienne et médiévale* 19 (1952) 225-243. His sources include Amalar, Odo, Rupert, Ivo, Hildebert, Hugh of St. Victor, Otto of Lucca's *Summa Sententiarum,* Pseudo-Hugh's *Speculum,* and Peter Comestor's *Historia Scholastica.*

32. PL 177:381-456.

33. PL 213:13-434.

34. PL 217:773-916; also see entry in Vogel, *Medieval Liturgy* (1986) 15. The commentary on the Mass begins with Book II. Book IV provides a lengthy excursus on contemporary questions pertaining to eucharistic theology.

4

New Research Directions in Medieval Liturgy: The Liturgical Books of Sigebert of Minden (1022-1036)

Joanne Pierce

ONE OF THE MOST IMPORTANT QUESTIONS IN THE AREA OF MEDIEVAL LITurgy today concerns the evolution of the structure of the Mass, the *ordo missae,* in the West. The medieval celebration of the Mass developed, in part, in response to the particular spiritual needs of northern European culture; the influence these needs had on the actual structure of the eucharistic service determined the form of the Tridentine Mass in the sixteenth century, as well as the *ordo missae* produced as a result of the reforms of Vatican II. Thus, if the eucharist is to be celebrated most fruitfully in response to the cultural needs of the twenty-first century, one must first understand clearly the reasons and stages which determined its medieval shape.

In this article contemporary theories about the evolutionary stages of the *ordo missae* will be summarized, and one specific medieval text will be discussed as a primary example. Some of the new directions for further research which arise from the study of this one important manuscript will conclude the dis-

51

cussion, directions which concern both the eucharist and other liturgical celebrations as well.

In order to study the medieval eucharistic celebration (and indeed the complexity of the medieval liturgy as a whole), it is important to select key texts (often still in unedited, manuscript form) from specific medieval cities and dioceses. The liturgical life of the medieval church was quite rich, and included a great deal of local variation. One of the most important of these medieval cathedrals was that of the German city of Minden, on the river Weser; and one of the most important medieval eucharistic texts for the study of the evolution of the Mass was part of the liturgical life of that city.

Just after the turn of the eleventh century (1022), a new bishop was installed in the then-important see of Minden. His name was Sigebert (d. 1036), and, in addition to his political role as advisor to the Holy Roman Emperor, he was also concerned with the liturgy of his cathedral. Sigebert ordered a set (a *corpus*) of nine liturgical books for use in his church; this *corpus* survives almost complete to this day, one of the oldest and largest of these sets still extant.

It is one of these books, the *libellus precum*, or prayerbook,[1] which is today considered such an important key in understanding the evolution of the medieval Mass. As will be seen, this manuscript contains (among other texts) the unique *ordo missae* known as the *Missa Illyrica*; this elaborate order of Mass is a perennial footnote in many modern histories of the eucharist.[2] As will be seen, this text can no longer be relegated to footnotes; it is an important example of how the Christian liturgy (here, the eucharist) is adapted to respond to the needs of a particular culture, and how that culture, in turn, influenced the development of the Mass as a whole.

Observations on the Sigebert Corpus

Before turning to a more complete exposition of the text and study of the *libellus precum*, however, more should be said about the Sigebert *corpus* as a whole. Eight of the original nine manuscripts still survive—a rare event in itself. Unfortunately, none are today at Minden; after various travels, the texts are presently held in four groups, at four different libraries.

After the city of Minden had been ceded to Brandenburg-Prussia at the Peace of Westphalia (1648), several of these manuscripts were removed from the Minden cathedral and became part of the Royal Library in Berlin (opened to public use in 1661). Due to the turmoil caused by World War II, this group of manuscripts has been further subdivided. Three of them are held in Berlin's Preussischer Kulturbesitz: a gospel book, a graduale book, and a book of hymns. One is held at the Deutsche Staatsbibliotek, also in Berlin: the sacramentary. Two are presently at the Jagiellonian University Library in Cracow, Poland: a book of tropes and an epistle lectionary.[3]

However, two of the Minden manuscripts had been removed from the cathedral before 1648. Sometime before 1557,[4] the famous Lutheran theologian Matthias Flacius Illyricus visited Minden and either borrowed or bought[5] two of the Sigebert manuscripts. They were part of his personal library at the time of his death in 1575, and when his widow sold that library to Duke Heinrich Julius of Braunschweig (Brunswick)-Lüneberg in 1597, both passed into his possession. Today, these two are in the manuscript collection of the Herzog August Bibliothek in Wolfenbüttel, Germany (a public research library based on this ducal collection): an antiphonary, and the above-mentioned book of prayers, the *libellus precum*.[6]

Since it is unusual for such a large set of liturgical books to have survived for so long a time, it is important to re-establish the fact that all these manuscripts are indeed part of the eleventh-century Minden group. This has been done[7] by comparing the external format of the manuscripts, as well as by finding common points of contact in their content.

All of the manuscripts, both the "noted" books (those with St. Gall neumes), e.g. the antiphonary, as well as the "text" books (those which contain only prose/script), e.g. the *libellus precum*, are physically alike. All of the "noted" books have the same size and style of script, right down to the fine strokes and intense black color of the ink; the layout of the pages is also very similar. The same is true of the "text" books; the script (late Carolingian minuscule) is so similar that the manuscripts could almost have all been produced by the same scribe.[8]

In addition, several other external characteristics are shared by all the manuscripts: these include page format, spacing, and decoration. For example, larger illuminated initials are done in a characteristic "Minden" style in all eight books: interlace, knobbed ends of tendrils, red lines and dots banding the legs of the letters, and a palette of a pastel green/gold/ vivid blue, and brick red.[9]

Due to the limited and incomplete nature of the contents of one of the books, the *libellus precum*, this study of internal connections among the manuscripts was limited to two categories: first, hagiography (i.e., the study of which saints are singled out for special mention in the manuscripts); and, second, the service of the veneration of the cross found in most of the manuscripts. The hagiographical question is a simple one: which saints appear to be particularly important in the calendars of each manuscript, and are these the same ones in all the manuscripts? Several common names do appear to hold a particular significance, lined with gold in litanies, and with especially decorated feast days: Sts. Peter and Lawrence (universally venerated, as well as being patrons of the cathedral at Minden) and St. Gorgonius (a saint venerated locally in this part of Germany, and also one of the saints to whom the cathedral was dedicated); St. Afra (another regional German saint); and Sts. Gall, Magnus, Otmar, and Ulrich (specially venerated at the Benedictine abbey of St. Gall, whose scribes possibly produced the manuscripts).

Since the *libellus precum* contains a number of prayers within an *ordo* for the veneration of the cross, the liturgy of Good Friday was taken as a second point of comparison among the books. When the texts describing the veneration of the cross in the various manuscripts were compared, a clear pattern for the celebration of that service at Minden emerged. The rubrics given in the sacramentary, the music prescribed in the gradual and antiphonary, and the rubrics and private prayer texts for the bishop's use found in the *libellus precum* all interconnect to form a consistent order of service.

> 1) Two acolytes bring the veiled cross from the sacristy; a procession of the ministers is formed, and they follow.

> 2) Two priests *in choro* sing: *Popule meus*, with verses *Quia eduxi/Quia [ego] eduxi/Quid ultra*.

3) Two other priests following behind the cross in the procession, sing, after each verse, the Greek verses of the Trisagion:
Agios O Theos, Agio Iskiros, Agios athanatos, Eleison Imas.

4) The choir, after each verse, then sings the Latin verses of the Trisagion:
Sanctus Deus, Sanctus Fortis, Sanctus Immortalis, Miserere nobis.

5) During this, this cross is set up at the altar (*ipsum altare*) for the veneration rite.

6) The bishop prostrates himself on the carpet provided (between the cross and the altar), along with the other ministers; the cross is held by two acolytes, and a kneeler (*oratorio*) is placed before it.

7) The singing continues as above, until the cross reaches the altar (the place where it is to be venerated); then the bishop removes the veil, intoning the antiphon "Ecce lignus" and the psalm "Beati immaculati."

8) First the bishop (*pontifex*) adores and kisses the cross, then other bishops (*episcopi*), priests, and deacons, and other (clerics) according to their rank, and then the people.

9) The music that accompanies this rite (*Ad detergendam crucem*) is:
Ant: *Ecce lignum crucis* (verse: *Beati immaculati in uia*)
Ant: *Crucem tuam adoramus* (verse: *Deus misereatur nostri*)
Ant: *Crucem tuam adoramus* (verse: *Miserere mei Deus*)
Prosa (*Item unde supra*): *Cum fabricator mundi mortis*
Ant: *Crux fidelis*
Hymn: *Pange lingua* (*Versus Fortunati*)

10) Then the cross is put back in its "proper place."

The *libellus precum* provides private prayers for the bishop to recite while he himself is venerating the cross (step 8 of the above outline). The first group is a series of penitential prayers to be said at the first of the three genuflections the bishop would make as he approached it to venerate it with a kiss. Next come three more prayers for forgiveness, to be said at the second genuflection; and then yet another group of private prayers for the third genuflection.

When the bishop reaches the foot of the cross, he is to kiss the ground and say another prayer, *humiliter ac uenerabiliter*.

He next kisses one foot of the crucifix with the versicle "Crux mihi certa salus," and the other with "Crux Domini mecum." Each hand of the *corpus* is then kissed, with the versicles "Crux mihi refugium" and "Crux mihi sit uera defensio quam semper adoro." After he rises, he recites another "general prayer" *ad sanctam crucem*; and then a formula for a trinitarian blessing is given.[10]

Clearly, a comparison of the texts provided in the various Minden manuscripts has yielded important information about this one particular service for the veneration of the cross. It is important to point out that, apart from this, very little work has been done in comparing the liturgical texts of these manuscripts, a task which could tell much about the liturgical life of an important medieval *ecclesia particularis*.

The Libellus Precum and the Missa Illyrica

Historically, the scholarly spotlight has fallen on one of these manuscripts, the prayer book itself. It is one of the two held at Wolfenbüttel, under the signature of *Codex Helmstadiensis* 1151. The manuscript is actually a combination of a prayer book and an *ordo missae*, complete with rubrics and other invariable prayers and versicles.[11] At this time, the *ordo missae* was often contained in a booklet separate from the larger sacramentary, which itself contained Mass formularies for the temporal and sanctoral cycles, as well as the text of the Roman Canon itself.

As mentioned above, a large section of the manuscript was edited in the sixteenth century by the Lutheran theologian Matthias Flacius Illyricus: the eucharistic section[12] was published in 1557 under the title *Missa latina*. In reference to its famous editor, the text has more commonly been known since its publication as the *Missa Illyrica*.[13]

Some time before Flacius Illyricus took possession of the manuscript, it had become separated from its two identifying features: a small dedication miniature of Bishop Sigebert, and the small ivory carving of Sigebert which had been on the original cover of the book.[14] Flacius Illyricus did not mention which manuscript was the source of his *Missa Illyrica*; therefore, the original manuscript and its place of origin remained a mystery for some three hundred years. The manuscript source of the edition, *Helmstadiensis* 1151, was not positively identified until 1894 by Adalbert Ebner.[15]

The manuscript's city of origin was not determined for another ten years. In 1905, this was conclusively shown to have been the Westphalian city of Minden by Joseph Braun, S.J.[16] from hints within two prayers of the manuscript itself. The first was a prayer within the series of pre-Mass vesting prayers to accompany the donning of a rather uncommon episcopal vestment called the *rationale*;[17] and the second, one of a series of *Suscipe sancta Trinitas* prayers at the offertory, which refers to "this" [the] congregation of St. Peter"[18] (one of the patrons of the Minden cathedral). Braun correctly identified the German city of Minden as containing the only cathedral which was both dedicated to St. Peter and whose bishop had the right to wear the *rationale*.[19]

Since its original publication in the sixteenth century, the *Missa Illyrica* has been the subject of much controversy, most of it undeserved. Much of the discussion centered around the problem of the date of the *Missa* (how ancient the text really was) and the extent to which the text seemed to support "Lutheran" or "Catholic" eucharistic theology and practice (for example, if the texts appeared to support communion under both species by the laity;[20] or whether the underlying theology of the prayers stressed shared communion or priestly sacrifice). Possibly because of its original publication by the vocal Lutheran Flacius Illyricus, and the rather anti-Roman tone of the accompanying commentary (the essay *Quaedam Observationes*), the text was even placed on the Index by Pope Sixtus V (1585-1590).

Contemporary Liturgical Significance of the Missa

Obscured for centuries by these polemical arguments, the true historical significance of the text has gone unrecognized until relatively recently in the area of liturgical studies. The real importance of the *Missa* in liturgical history is its crucial role as a "benchmark" *ordo* in the study of the evolution and history of the *ordo missae* in the West. In this regard, special attention must be paid to the large number of sacerdotal *apolo-*

giae (private prayers of the priest during the Mass which express his sinfulness and unworthiness) found at many points in the text. In 1954 the liturgical historian Boniface Luykx proposed a new theory of the evolution of the *ordo missae* in the West, based on a study of Carolingian and Ottonian liturgical manuscripts.[21] He concluded that distinct stages in this evolutionary process were marked by the type and number of sacerdotal *apologiae* added at various "soft spots"[22] in the *ordo*. These "soft spots" can be thought of as "lulls" in the verbal "action" of the eucharist (or other service). For example, a liturgical movement or gesture which is originally unaccompanied by any "covering" prayer tends to attract these private prayers at later stages of development. Processions are one type of this kind of liturgical "soft spot"; another category would be actions performed by the presider alone during the *ordo*, such as kissing the altar or washing his hands. As will be seen, this process of adding on prayers to "fill up" the structure of the liturgy becomes more and more pronounced as time goes on.

According to Luykx's hypothesis, there are overall three categories or stages of development, each successively more elaborate. The process begins in the ninth century with the apology type of *ordo missae*. Here the number of communion prayers is multiplied, as are certain kinds of offertory prayers (e.g., the *Suscipe sancta Trinitas* texts), and variable forms of the *Memento etiam* prayer within the Roman Canon.[23] The custom of attributing authorship of some of these penitential prayers to noted Fathers of the church (e.g., Augustine, Ambrose) is already common by this time.

The next stage is marked by a Frankish type of *ordo missae*. Here the quantity and style of text found at the original "soft spots" is elaborated, and indeed, more prayer texts and versicles are added to other available "moments" in the *ordo* (e.g., the preparation and vesting of the presider in the sacristy, the censing of the altar, preceding and following the reading of the gospel,[24] and at the commixtion of the bread and wine at the fraction). Here too, apology-type prayers are introduced and tied together by rubrical directions.

The third type is named after the area in which Luykx hypothesizes that it first develops: the Rhenish *ordo missae*, from the Rhineland area of Germany.[25] The *Missa Illyrica* is a clear example of this type, at root, a longer, more elaborate and elastic *ordo* to be used by a bishop at a large, formal celebration of Mass. Apologies and other interpolated prayer texts are held together by long blocks of rubrics; prayers of recent composition begin to displace older, shorter prayers at some points (for example, at the washing of the presider's hands[26]). The pre-Mass preparation and vesting of the presider and assistants is made even longer and more elaborate,[27] as is the entry rite itself. An organized and specific thanksgiving rite after Mass is also added. Assisting ministers and other clerics are now given private prayers and particular responses during the Mass liturgy. The multiplication of several elements, including kissing/veneration gestures, priestly confession prayers, handwashings at the offertory, and private texts/versicles during communal, sung moments (e.g., the *Sanctus*), contributes to the increasing privatization and clericalization of this type of *ordo missae*.

New Edition of the Manuscript

The eighteenth-century edition[28] of the *Missa* is not adequate for modern scholars, who now need the best possible access to the text in the light of these new research directions.[29] In addition, the manuscript in which the *Missa* is found has never been edited in its entirety, and contains other material vital to the study of medieval spirituality, for example, prayers to accompany the veneration of the cross, and an incomplete section of other, more general prayers.[30] Therefore, the decision was made, in consultation with Niels Rasmussen, O.P., then associate professor of theology at the University of Notre Dame, to prepare a fresh edition of the entire manuscript. As has been noted above,[31] this fresh edition of *Helmstadiensis* 1151, the *libellus precum* ("prayerbook") of Sigebert of Minden, was prepared as a Ph.D. dissertation in the Department of Theology, University of Notre Dame.

A new codicological description of the manuscript introduces the actual edition. To facilitate analysis and comparison with other published editions of earlier sources and contemporary *ordines*, the text has been broken down into a series of 231 liturgical "units." The 121 folia of the manuscript contain a number of relatively independent subsections, including individual prayers with titles, series of *preces* or versicles and responses, and blocks of free-standing rubrics. Each has been assigned a separate number; for longer series of pairs (for example, versicles and responses) further subdivisions are made using letters of the alphabet. Each line of an individual unit is also assigned a number. The critical apparatus is presented at the bottom of each page (usually two or three units), using Jean Deshusses' edition of the Gregorian Sacramentary as a model.[32] Since there is only one copy of the manuscript, the apparatus consists of only one tier, which includes information on discrepancies between the manuscript and the reprinted edition in Martène, as well as scriptural references and other *loca parallela* for each unit. Such references include contemporary and related *ordines*, as well as earlier sacramentaries, *libelli precum*, or collections of prayers.

New Directions for Future Research

Several important findings may be found in the new edition's accompanying commentary on each individual prayer text or other liturgical "unit." Perhaps the most striking are the following.

First, much more study needs to be done on the origin and classification of these penitential prayers called apologies. Fernand Cabrol's study of the *apologiae* in the DACL,[33] done at the beginning of the century, attempts to classify and trace the evolution of individual texts and groups these prayers. However, it is of questionable value and is sorely in need of updating. There needs to be a complete modern study of these prayers as a *genre*, in order to trace their origins and eventual use in medieval eucharistic *ordines* and *libelli precum*. Not only should the texts be listed and classified (according to place of origin and various forms and uses), and an *incipit* index provided, but ideally a verbal concordance for these texts should also be compiled, as Deshusses and Darragon have done for the prayer texts of the major sacramentaries.[34] One learns quickly when working with *apologiae* that they are very plastic prayer forms; compilers seem to have had few qualms about "mixing and matching" *incipits* with different sections or bodies of text. Perhaps many researchers drop the topic of the evolution of the *ordo missae* in the West as a fruitful line of work precisely because the history of the apologies is so ill-defined.[35]

A related problem for both the study of the *apologiae* as well as of the *ordo missae* in general is accessibility of the sources. Many of the manuscript sources are transcribed only in Migne, Martène, or Wilmart, and need to be re-presented in modern editions. Only then, for example, can Luykx's theory really be tested, although it has been at least partially supported in the distinction made among the various stages of *ordo missae* evolution.[36] Unfortunately, the area can appear, at both first and second glances, to be almost unmanageable.

Second, many of the prayer texts interpolated into the structure of the eucharist in the Sigebert prayerbook prove to stand in striking contrast to the form and spirit of classic Roman liturgical prayer. Roman collects, for example, are always plural, communally oriented, spare and almost terse in their address to God and expression of petitions.[37] The apologies (and other related prayers) found here are in contrast, highly individualistic, almost solely presider-oriented, fulsome of expression, and imbued with a spirituality of "rejection of the world and worldly things." In many ways the Sigebert prayerbook is one of the fullest (if not finest) collections of prayers which express this flavor of medieval spirituality.[38]

Third, it is clear that slowly, from the ninth century on, a kind of private devotional service is introduced into the public celebration of the Mass. Some of the prayers are taken from collections of devotional prayers compiled in the ninth century for lay persons.[39] Here, in the eleventh century, we see many of these prayers, as well as others of new composition, inserted at virtually every possible point for the presider (and in some instances, his assistants) to recite, often as other, communal chants and prayers are being recited, for example, the *Gloria*.[40] They are strongly penitential in nature, and focus on the bishop/priest presider as unworthy representative, offerer of the holy sacrifice on behalf of himself and any number of intentions (and the people as a whole).[41] This devotional pattern survives (in a less florid form) in the Tridentine Missal, which in turn influences the *Ordo Missae* of Paul VI. There, some of these private prayers become optional (e.g., vesting prayers); while some become communal (e.g., the *Confiteor*); others remain for the presider alone (e.g., the versicle "Lord, wash away my iniquity, cleanse me from my sin," at the *lavabo*). The very structure of the Mass is still affected: three options for a brief penitential rite during the introductory rites remain even to this day.

Fourth, there is a need for a comprehensive study, in the style of Jungmann, of the *ordo* for the veneration of the cross; both of the evolution of the ritual actions, as well as of the varied and various accompanying prayers. Some work on individual prayers has already been done,[42] but a systematic analysis is still lacking.

Fifth, each of the other volumes of the Sigebert *corpus* must be studied. In order of decreasing significance,[43] these would be: the antiphonary, the gradual, the troper, the sacramentary, the hymn book, and the two lectionaries. Such a study would not only serve to flesh out further the local liturgical life of an important medieval see, but would also contribute to a wider task: the refinement of the classification system and nomenclature used for early medieval liturgical books in general (which have often been grouped in anachronistic categories).[44]

Doubtless, further research could take many more directions besides those specifically delineated here.[45] It is my intention only to point out the tip of the iceberg in terms of the potential impact that editions and analyses of the Sigebert books could have on the area of medieval liturgical studies. Perhaps others who are interested in the area of medieval liturgy will contribute to this on-going discussion.

Notes

1. It is also the subject of the author's recent dissertation: "Sacerdotal Spirituality at Mass: Text and Study of the Prayerbook of Sigebert of Minden [1022-1036]," Unpublished Ph.D. Dissertation, University of Notre Dame, April 1988. The dissertation is currently under consideration for publication through the Medieval Institute at the University of Notre Dame. Niels Rasmussen inspired and directed this dissertation for four years; after his untimely death, Dr. William Storey graciously undertook the task of overseeing the project till its completion.

2. For example, Louis Bouyer, *Eucharist*, trans., Charles Underhill Quinn (Notre Dame, IN: University of Notre Dame Press, 1968) 379, 384; and N.M. Denis-Boulet, *La Messe et le culte de l'eucharistie*, part 2 of *L'Eglise en prière*, ed., A.-G. Martimort (Tournai: Desclée & Co., 1961) 297, n. 3; 377, n. 4. See also Cyrille Vogel, *Medieval Liturgy: An Introduction to the Sources*, trans. and rev., William G. Storey and Niels K. Rasmussen (Washington, D.C.: The Pastoral Press, 1986) 162-163.

3. The signatures of these manuscripts are as follows:

Wolfenbüttel:	*codex Guelferbytanus* 1151 *Helmstadiensis* (the book of prayers) *codex Guelferbytanus* 1008 *Helmstadiensis* (the antiphonary)
Berlin: Preussischer Kulturbesitz	*theol. lat. oct.* 1 (the book of hymns) *theol. lat. qu.* 15 (the gradual) *theol. lat. qu.* 3 (the gospel lectionary)
Berlin: Deutsche Staatsbibliothek	*theol. lat. fol.* 2 (the sacramentary)
Cracow:	*theol. lat. qu.* 11 (the troper) *theol. lat. qu.* 1 (the epistle lectionary)

4. Publication date of the section of the *libellus precum* known as the *Missa Illyrica*, see above. Illyricus' edition was reprinted five times over the following two hundred years. The two most accessible for the modern scholar are those found in Edmond Martène, *De Antiquis Ecclesiae Ritibus* (1737), hereafter referred to as DAER, *Lib.* I, *Cap.* IV, *Ordo* IV, cols. 489-528 (reprinted Hildesheim: G. Olms, 1967), and PL 138:1301-1336.

5. For further discussion of how Flacius Illyricus actually came into possession of the manuscript, see Oliver K. Olson, "Der Bücherdieb Flacius," *Wolftenbütteler Beiträge* 4 (1981) 111-145.

6. This manuscript is the main subject of the author's dissertation. See above, note 1.

7. The author was able to travel in Europe during the academic year 1985-1986, and personally compare all of the manuscripts, with the exception of those in Poland. Grateful acknowledgement must be made of the financial assistance provided by the following: the Fulbright Commission; the Grawemeyer Committee of the University of Louisville (KY); the Zahm Grant program of the Office of Advanced Studies at the University of Notre Dame; the Department of Theology at the University of Notre Dame; and the Liturgisches Institut in Trier, Germany.

8. My own confirmation of a 1905 observation by Dr. Milchsach, head librarian of the Herzog August Bibliothek, as cited in Joseph Braun, "Alter und Herkunft der sog. *Missa Illyrica*," in *Stimmen aus Maria Laach* 69 (1905) 143-155.

9. See Wilhelm Vöge, "Die Mindener Bilderhandschriftengruppe," in *Repertorium für Kunstwissenschaft* 16 (1893) 198-213, especially 203, 212-213. He describes a characteristic Minden "Palette."

10. See numbers 206-222 in my fresh edition of the manuscript, "Sacerdotal Spirituality," Chapter III. See also the general discussion of the veneration of the cross, 128-130 and 431-439.

11. Such an arrangement was not uncommon at this period. Note, for example, the case of the pontifical of Hugh of Salins (eleventh century), edition by Jean Lemarié, "Le Pontifical d'Hugues de Salines, son 'ordo missae' et son 'libellus precum'," *Studi Medievali*, ser. 3, 19 (1978) 363-425.

12. For ease of reference, texts in the *Missa* will be cited both according to the corresponding columns in the Martène DAER reprint, as well as the numbers assigned in my edition of the complete manuscript. The *Missa* itself can be found there as numbers 1-205.

13. For a good discussion of the *Missa* in the light of the life and works of Flacius Illyricus himself, see Oliver K. Olson, "The 'Missa Illyrica' and the Liturgical Thought of Flacius Illyricus," unpublished Ph.D. dissertation, Universität Hamburg, 1966.

14. Both are now held in Berlin, the Preussischer Kultursbesitz, under separate signatures: *theol. lat. qu. 3 frag.* (the dedication miniature); and *Elbenbeintafel theol. germ. qu. 42* (the ivory carving).

15. See his revised edition of Valentin Thalhofer, *Handbuch der katholischen Liturgik* I (Friburg im Breisgau: Herder, 1894) 103, n. 2.

16. Joseph Braun, "*Missa Illyrica*," see note 6, above.

17. Martène, col. 493; my edition, number 30.

18. Martène, col. 510; my edition, number 136.

19. The findings of both Ebner and Braun appear to have been overlooked (or disregarded) by some later scholars. Emmanuel Bourque, for example, in his *Etude sur les sacramentaires romains, 2e partie: Les Textes remaniés* (Vatican City: Pontificio Istituto di Archeologia Cristiana, 1958) still refers to the source as a "lost" Heidelberg manuscript. See Tome 2, pp. 333-335, number 418.

20. The disputed text is actually a distribution formula to be used in giving communion to the people (Martène, col. 516; my edition, number 189). Flacius transcribed the text as "Corpus et sanguis Domini nostri Jesu Christi prosit tibi . . .", and so the wording has remained in the succeeding reprints of the *Missa*. However, a reexamination of the manuscript itself reveals that the words "et san-

guis" have actually been written on the page in pencil above the first line of the text (which itself is written in black ink). The script of the penciled-in words is not Carolingian, and appears in fact to date from some centuries later. Comparison of the letters with examples of script known to have been done by Flacius Illyricus himself yielded indefinite results: the group of letters to be compared (eight) was simply too small a sample to use in making a clear determination.

21. Boniface Luykx, *De oorsprong van het gewone der Mis* (Utrecht-Antwerpen, 1954), later translated into German by Johannes Madley and reprinted as "Der Ursprung der gleichbleibenden Teile der heiligen Messe (*Ordinarium Missae*)" in *Liturgie und Mönchtum* 29 (1961) 72-119. This issue was published under the separate title *Priestertum und Mönchtum*.

22. For more complete discussion on the role of "soft spots" in liturgical evolution, see Robert Taft, *Beyond East and West: Problems in Liturgical Understanding* (Washington, D.C.: The Pastoral Press, 1984), chapters 10 and 11. See also Anton Baumstark, *Comparative Liturgy* (Westminster, MD: Newman, 1958).

23. The *Missa* has six of these variable texts.

24. The *Missa* has twenty-three during the readings/gospel.

25. The abbey of St. Gall is credited with being the source of this new kind of *ordo*, which then spreads to the rest of the area through the abbey of Reichenau and the influential see of Mainz. Since St. Gall and Reichenau were important centers of manuscript production, the new *ordo* traveled quickly through the Ottonian and Salic empire; Sigebert probably had his Minden manuscripts made for him at one of these two abbeys, or a daughter abbey under their influence.

26. The older *Lavabo inter innocentes* versicle is augmented by the newer *Largire sensibus nostris* prayer, or dropped altogether (Martène, cols. 492 and 505; my edition, numbers 12 and 98).

27. The *Missa* has thirty-five separate gestures and texts at this point.

28. Comparison of the subsequent printed editions of the *Missa Illyrica* show them to be essentially Flacius Illyricus' edition, with occasional minor changes.

29. Luykx's theories were used by Jungmann in the fifth edition of *Missarum Sollemnia* (1962, never translated into English). Other contemporary scholars working in the area of ninth- to eleventh-century liturgy also refer to Luykx, but all of these studies are limited by the lack of modern editions of relevant *ordines*, most importantly, the *Missa Illyrica*. See, for example, Bonifacio Baroffio and Ferdinand Dell'Oro, "L'*Ordo Missae* del vescovo Warmundo d'Ivrea," *Studi Me-*

dievali, ser. 3, 16 (1975) 795-824; Joaquim O. Bragança, "O 'Ordo Missae de Reichenau," *Didaskalia* 1 (1971) 137-161; Jean Lemarie, "Le Pontifical d'Hugues de Salines, son 'ordo missae' et son 'libellus precum'," *Studi Medievali*, ser. 3, 19 (1978) 363-425; and Niels Krogh Rasmussen, "An Early 'Ordo Missae' with a 'Litania Abecedaria' Addressed to Christ (Rome, Bibl. Vallicelliana, *Cod.* B 141, XI. Cent.)," *Ephemerides Liturgicae* 98 (1984) 198-211.

30. The *Missae*, or *ordo missae* section, runs from nos. 1-205 in the new edition; the prayers for the veneration of the cross (nos. 206-222) and the incomplete list of general prayers (nos. 223-231) follow this eucharistic section, and are not included in the Martène edition.

31. See note 1 above.

32. Jean Deshusses, *Le Sacramentaire Grégorien*, tome 1: *Le Sacramentaire, le Supplément d'Aniane;* tome 2: *Textes complémentaires pour la messe;* tome 3: *Textes complémentaires divers.* Spicilegium Friburgense 16, 24, 28 (Fribourg: Editions Universitaires, 1971, 1979, 1982).

33. Fernand Cabrol, "Apologies," DACL 1.2 (1907) cols. 2591-2601.

34. Jean Deshusses and Benoit Darragon, *Concordances et tableaux pour l'étude des grandes sacramentaires*, SSF Subsidia 9-11 (Fribourg: Editions Universitaires Fribourg Suisse, 1982).

35. The necessity for this further study has been expressed strongly by Niels Rasmussen in "An Early 'Ordo Missae'": "That much still remains to be done is shown by the fact that scholars have not yet been able to establish more than a very simple typology for the mass orders . . . before pursuing this task of establishing a more exact typology it is important to make the texts available" (p. 200).

36. Another important aspect of Luykx's theory also must be evaluated: the real influence of St. Gall, Mainz, and Reichenau as liturgical/artistic centers in the Carolingian and Ottonian periods.

37. The essential "soberness and sense" which is the hallmark of ancient Roman prayer; see Edmund Bishop, "The Genius of the Roman Rite," in *Liturgica Historica* (Oxford: The Clarendon Press, 1918) 19.

38. A related problem, of course, is the question of why these apologies disappear so suddenly from the *ordo missae* by the turn of the eleventh century. Are they legislated out (as some liturgical scholars believe) through the liturgical reforms of Gregory VII, or (as others hold) does the spread of the practice of auricular confession satisfy the penitential impulse, to which the apologies were composed as a response?

39. For example, the ninth-century Prayerbook of Charles the Bald, of which there exists only a sixteenth-century edition by Ninguada, under the title *Liber Precationem Quas Carolus Calvus* (etc.) (Ingolstadii: Davidis Sartorii, 1583).

40. For example, Martène, col. 499; my edition, numbers 68-70.

41. This shift in the theological "view" of the presider is complemented by a more subtle shift in the Christology of many of the prayers: a focus on the divine Christ as triumphant victor. Many prayers, especially those in the Good Friday *ordo*, are specifically addressed to Christ. For further discussion, see Joseph Jungmann, *The Place of Christ in Liturgical Prayer* (Staten Island, NY: Alba House, 1965).

42. See, for example, Lilli Gjerlow, *Adoratio Crucis* (Oslo/London/ Boston: Norwegian Universities Press, 1961), and André Wilmart, "Prières médiévales pour l'adoration de la croix," *Ephemerides Liturgicae* 46 (1932) 22-65.

43. In terms of the inclusion of interesting "local" material.

44. My thanks to Père Pierre-Marie Gy, O.P. for helpful discussion on this last point.

45. The strong Irish/Celtic influence on a number of the manuscript's prayer texts (seen in the analysis of these individual units) suggests another line of research, as does the wider topic of the interconnections among politics, art, and liturgy in the Ottonian period, interconnections strongly made in the liturgical texts of some of the other Sigebert books.

5

Using Liturgical Texts
in the Middle Ages

Tom Elich

THOSE WHO STUDY LITURGICAL SOURCES HAVE LONG RECOGNIZED THAT
the origins of liturgical texts lie in an oral process of improvisation.[1] The remark of Hippolytus is well-known: "When giving thanks to God, it is not at all necessary for the bishop to ut-
ter the same words as have been written, as though reciting
them from memory; but let each pray according to his ability."[2] A good deal of work has been done on how improvisation operates in traditional oral cultures. The oral-formulaic
theory of Milman Parry and Albert Lord, for example, shows
how the poet or singer draws on a stock of familiar phrases
and sentences to construct a narrative which is never exactly
the same a second time but which is nevertheless profoundly
traditional.[3] Understanding the processes of improvising liturgical prayer may help us to analyze early liturgical texts, their
meaning, style, and structure.

Already with Hippolytus, however, there is a role for written prayer texts. They serve as an example of the kind of
prayer considered orthodox and suitable. The written text
seems to play a greater role in the fifth century with Sidonius
Apolinarius. Gregory of Tours admires his outstanding ability
to improvise.[4] Yet, Sidonius, though apparently he can do as
well without a written text, is accustomed to take to the altar a

libellus with which he celebrates solemnities. He did not necessarily read what was in his fascicule; it may simply have been used as a fixed point for his improvisation. Gregory mentions that he had compiled a collection of Masses composed by Sidonius, but this work is unfortunately lost.

We do, however, have a number of these *libelli* of which the most famous collection is the Verona Sacramentary.[5] These small, unbound booklets used for a particular feast or liturgy have a complex relationship to the more elaborate and comprehensive liturgical books, as Niels Rasmussen has shown for the pontifical[6] and Michel Huglo for the troper.[7] In this volume Pierre-Marie Gy develops further the different forms taken by the liturgical *libellus*.

The story of Sidonius also illustrates the complex relationships which can exist between the written text and the oral performance of the text. While liturgical historians have, for the most part, concentrated on the hard data of written texts, it is also important to give some attention to the oral side of liturgical history. At the level of liturgical performance there is a certain continuity throughout the Middle Ages with the oral improvisation of the early church's liturgy. We do not so much pass from improvisation to written text, but from improvised text to memorized text to read text.[8] In this evolution writing plays a greater and greater role in regulating and determining the liturgical event.

The importance of memorized texts in the history of liturgy was also recognized by Niels Rasmussen in his classification of episcopal liturgical documents: he begins with what he calls the non-document, the memorized text.[9] The medieval references he quotes, however, do not illustrate "non-documents" as would be the case with purely oral improvisation. Rather, they illustrate the case where written texts have been memorized and then recited (more or less accurately) from memory. This is not a different type of document, but refers to how the written liturgical text was used in the performance of the liturgy.

Medieval Europe provides a largely oral context for the use of liturgical texts until the gradual development in the twelfth and thirteenth centuries of a more literate mentality. This latter period corresponds to the rise of universities: the monastic rumination of *lectio-meditatio-oratio* gives way to the *lectio-*

quaestio-disputatio of the new scholastic theology. The twelfth-century theological debates on the eucharist bring into conflict oral, popular performance on the one hand, and literate, intellectual hermeneutics on the other.[10] In the same period, civil administration begins to rely more on written documents and archives.[11] The new literate mentality of the late Middle Ages has its repercussions in the area of liturgy. A fixed, transportable, written text is used to create uniformity at different times and places at the expense of the diversity characteristic of local, "oral" cultures. The written text assumes control: the liturgy is organized and regulated in writing, and what was once recited from memory is now principally read from the book.

This shift in attitude to the liturgical text is sometimes difficult to see clearly because reading (the Scriptures, for example) has never been entirely absent from the liturgy, because some liturgical texts are fixed in writing quite early, and because the clergy who use liturgical texts are more literate than most other people. Nevertheless, it seems possible to say that it was normal for much of the Middle Ages to experience the liturgy without relying on the book at every moment. It was used only when necessary. Having the book and knowing how to read it is one thing; feeling constrained to read from it is another.

To illustrate this evolving use of the liturgical text in the Middle Ages, we will look in turn at music, memorization, and the form of books.

Liturgical Music

Until the ninth century, liturgical music was performed and handed on orally. It is the best example of "pure" orality in medieval liturgy. Isidore of Seville described the situation well: "Unless sounds are held in one's memory, they perish because they cannot be written down."[12] The introduction of the Roman liturgy into Frankish territory under the Carolingians included not only texts and rubrics but also chant. However, these liturgical reforms of Charlemagne did not produce the unity he desired.

Towards the middle of the ninth century, Amalarius of Metz was upset by the discordant antiphonaries in his province. When Pope Gregory IV was unable to lend him an authorized copy, Amalarius went to the monastery of Corbie where he was able to compare his tradition with authentic Roman books. He found differences not only in order, but also in the texts, and he discovered many responses and antiphons which they did not sing in Metz. He was astonished to discover how much mother and daughter differed from each other. His response was to compile yet another antiphonary, drawing the best from both.[13] In the eleventh century, Guido of Arezzo still complains of disaccord between master and pupil, saying that there is not one antiphonary, nor even a small number of them; they are as numerous as the masters of each church.[14] Such diversity of texts, common to all liturgical books of the period, can be explained by processes of written transmission, though it shows that the full potential of written texts for achieving uniformity is not yet being exploited.

The transmission of the music, however, is more complex. Nothing in the prologue of Amalarius indicates that he was able to compare the music as well as the text of the antiphonaries. The earliest musical notation in the form of neumes appears in short isolated pieces in the ninth century; fully notated books and those for which notation was planned when copied date from the tenth century. In any case, it is not possible to read the music from such a text; these neumes give an indication of the direction of the melody and of how it is to be sung, but they are only useful to those who already know the melody by heart. Aurelian of Réomé is the first to describe neumes but he insists that the art of music, if not inserted into the memory, is not retained.[15] At the end of the ninth century, Hucbald proposes a method of singing a piece without a master. He combines the alphabetic letters of the monochord with neumatic notation.[16] The system is perfected by Guido of Arezzo with the development of the staff which he describes in detail.[17] Pope John XIX is astounded that boys know chants they have never heard.[18] Square notation on the staff becomes common in the twelfth century and leads to proportional notation in the thirteenth. Up to this point, the musical text could only serve as a support to chant that was basically known and executed from memory; now a melody could be accurately read.

With more complex part-music in the liturgy and with a

new orientation towards the book, reading music is what cantors began to do. A manuscript illumination graphically illustrates the new practice of reading a musical text while singing in the liturgy: two or three tonsured clerics, dressed in copes, sing before an open book resting on a lectern. It appears quite suddenly in the second quarter of the thirteenth century as an illustration for Psalm 97, "Sing to the Lord a new song." By the end of the century this illumination of singers before an open book has become general in Paris, in the north of France, in England, and even in the low countries.[19] It seems this liturgical scene was introduced into the Parisian schema of psalter illustration which centered on the figure of King David. Early thirteenth-century illuminations of Psalm 97 suggest that it may originally have been part of this cycle showing David directing singers or playing the organ.[20] These examples have more in common, however, with earlier portrayals of cantors which always show them singing from memory.[21]

The mechanisms of learning, teaching, comparing, correcting, and performing chant from memory are quite different from using a notated antiphonary. A melody can be learned only by hearing it. So singers need to travel to learn or to teach new music. A melody can only be checked by comparing it with what another cantor sings. So cantors often travel in pairs. Regional differences are only noticed by those who move from place to place.

A good example of how this process worked comes from a digression on Gregorian chant in the Life of Saint Gregory. John the Deacon, writing about 873, argues that the Gauls regularly had the opportunity to learn the Gregorian chant but were unable to keep it pure.[22] They mixed in their own melodic elements, and they lost the delicate inflection of the chant through their naturally barbaric voices. While visiting Rome, Charlemagne notices the difference and asks: "Where is water the most limpid, in the stream or at the source? We, then, who till now have been drinking the polluted water from the stream must go back to the unfailing source." He leaves two clerics with the pope in Rome and, after receiving good instruction, they return to restore the chant in Metz; from here the restoration spreads through all of Gaul. A good while later, after the death of these two clerics, Charlemagne notices a difference between Metz and the other churches in Gaul. "We will go back to the source," he says. At his request the pope sends him two cantors who report that the Roman chant has been corrupted by the natural coarseness of the local cantors, though Metz is better than the rest of the country.

Another version of the same story, about ten years later, comes from Notker the Stutterer.[23] In this story Charlemagne has twelve Roman cantors come to the North. To vex Frankish pride and to prevent the success of their chant in a foreign region, they agree to vary what they teach in different centers. As he travels, however, Charlemagne notices the differences and the pope recalls them and punishes them. The pope invites two of Charlemagne's best singers to go to Rome where they are introduced secretly into the papal *schola*.

We are not concerned here about which of these versions might be correct. The bias of both is obvious: John is a deacon of the papal court and is writing the Life of Gregory to enhance the prestige of Rome and the papacy; Notker, a monk of Saint Gall, is keen to justify the Northern cantors. We are more interested to see how learning, preserving, and correcting a new repertoire of liturgical music took place in the Carolingian period. In this respect, both stories present a coherent picture of the oral dynamic at work.[24] What is surprising for us is not so much the literate change that took place in the twelfth and thirteenth centuries, but the persistence of orality for such a long time in the Middle Ages.

Memorized Texts

Music was not the only part of the liturgy that was executed from memory. The sixth-century Rule of the Master describes how the monk simultaneously learned to read and learned the psalter.[25] This psalms of the divine office, taken always in biblical order, could thus be recited from memory. For the biblical lessons, the Rule is explicit: they are to be recited from memory and not read from the book (except for the all-night vigil on Saturdays); this would ensure that the monks knew the Scriptures and, wherever there was no book, they could recite the text of the lesson by heart.[26] Whether working in the fields or detained by urgent needs in the monastery, whether travelling outside the monastery or praying with the brothers in the monastery chapel, the liturgy is regularly celebrated without any suggestion that a book might be necessary.

The use of a text in liturgy increases with the Rule of Benedict but still seems to be minor.[27] Though the Rule adopts its own weekly cycle for the psalter, the psalms could just as easily be memorized according to their liturgical order and divisions. The Rule adds about twenty hymns and canticles to the psalms, some repeated daily, some weekly; this would not seem an impossible additional burden. Usually the lessons are to be recited by heart, but the amount of reading is increased—at daily vigils in winter and at a weekly vigil in summer. Finally, it is unclear whether liberty is allowed on feast days to select more pertinent texts or whether such proper texts are prescribed; in the latter case it would be necessary to consult some kind of ordo before celebrating the liturgy. Again, those working a distance from the oratory or those travelling are not exempt from the office; while travelling they celebrate as they are able.[28]

The clergy continue to know the psalter and other texts by heart until well into the Middle Ages. The statutes of the vicars of Lincoln of 1236 offer a good example. Before admission as a vicar, the candidate will be examined to see if he can read and sing. During a first probationary year, he must memorize the antiphonary and hymnary; in the second year he must learn the psalter so that it is also known without a book. Then he may be admitted.[29] Dominican novices in Paris at the end of the thirteenth century are given an extraordinary amount to memorize: first they learn the *Salve Regina* and the Hours of the Blessed Virgin, then the psalter beginning with the psalms used most frequently, next a creed and a number of hymns, the Office of the Dead, the texts used at chapter meetings, and prayers for meal times.[30]

The execution of liturgical texts from memory had particular significance for the semi-literate rural clergy. William Durandus, a thirteenth-century bishop of Mende, gave detailed instructions to his clergy about the celebration of the eucharist. According to the new mood of the century, he directs them to look at the book regularly while they are saying the words of consecration even if they know them by heart.[31] He also directs them to memorize certain texts, though it seems this may be more important for those who are less fluent in reading and understanding Latin. "Work to understand the prayers of the Mass, the prefaces and the canon," he writes, "or at least to know them by heart and say them clearly."[32] Is it possible that uneducated clergy memorized a minimum of liturgical texts which they used for their parish celebrations?

The popular *Golden Legend*, a mid-thirteenth-century book of stories about the saints, tells of a village priest who was reported to his bishop for never celebrating any other Mass than that of the Virgin Mary. He confesses that he knows no other and is chastised and suspended by his bishop. That night the bishop has a vision of the Virgin Mary who threatens him with death if he does not restore her servant to his ministry. The bishop apologizes to the priest and orders him never to celebrate any other Mass than that of the Virgin Mary.[33] Although the point of the story is to foster devotion to Mary, one wonders if it could refer to the practice of illiterate rural clergy using only a small number of memorized texts. Certainly it seems some churches possesssed no liturgical books or copies that were far from complete.[34]

Finally, educated lay people also participated in the liturgy using memorized texts. All lay people were encouraged to memorize the Creed, the Lord's Prayer, and later the Hail Mary. But with the rise of a "literacy of recreation" among cultivated nobles and a "literacy of business, administration and law" among the more pragmatic bourgeoisie,[35] the way was opened for a "literacy of devotion" enabling lay people to use the written text in and for the liturgy. *The Lay-Folks Mass-Book* is a late thirteenth-century English translation of a twelfth-century Franco-Norman original. It follows through the Mass liturgy explaining what is happening, indicating the actions and postures to be adopted, and giving prayer texts to be said by the lay person at each moment during the liturgy. But these are not to be read during the Mass. They are to be said from memory.

> How þou at þo messe þi tym shuld spende
> haue I told: now wil I ende.
> Þo rubryk is gode vm while to loke,
> þo praiers to con with-outen boke.[36]

Here, as in the official liturgy celebrated by the clergy, the book is at hand and the people concerned are literate; but the texts are recited from memory rather than read.

Liturgical Legislation and Books

Early monastic customaries remain typically local and "oral" in their particularity. Cluny is a good example. Founded at the beginning of the tenth century, its customaries were revised a number of times by the end of the eleventh century, and each new Cluniac foundation produced its own version of the customaries.[37] Each version represents the usage of one house at a particular time. From the beginning of the twelfth century, statutes replaced the customaries as the main form of Cluniac legislation. They were sent to all the houses in the Cluniac family and produced a greater uniformity of observance.[38] So, for example, a statute of Hugh V of 1200 states that, in every one of their places, what is sung and read should be identical for, since they are one congregation and one order, they ought to conform in everything.[39] It is already significant that in the eighth and ninth centuries written documents appear interpreting the Rule of Benedict and regulating monastic liturgy.[40] It is not until the twelfth century that the full potential of written regulation begins to be realized.

The "new orders" of the twelfth century, founded on a stricter interpretation of the rule, make full use of written text in arranging and celebrating their liturgy. In each Cistercian monastery, according to the *Carta Caritatis*, the customs, the chant, and all the books necessary for the office and the Mass should conform to the customs and books of the monastery at Cîteaux so that, in all their actions, there will be no discordance but instead they will live according to the same charity, the same rule, and the same customs.[41] Subsequent legislation confirms this policy and early statutes of the general chapter give the list of liturgical books which all must have.[42] The municipal library of Dijon has an archetype of this collection of books dating from the end of the twelfth century.[43]

The Order of Preachers under Humbert of Romans takes this evolution a step further. After the General Chapter of 1256, he was able to write to his order announcing the end of liturgical diversity and its unification according to a typical model. He requests the correction of all liturgical books to achieve everywhere a uniform office. He then lists the fourteen new books which contain the common Dominican liturgy.[44] Manuscripts of this model collection still exist.[45] By comparison with the Cistercian books, three additions are especially interesting. Besides a missal for side altars, there is a *libellum processionale*,[46] a *pulpitarium*, and a portable breviary. Each of these three books witnesses to a greater dependence on the written text in the performance of the liturgy.

Processionals begin to form within collections of liturgical texts from the eleventh century. Rarely do monastic customaries of this time mention a cantor's book for processions and, even when they do, there is no indication that they were actually carried and read in the procession.[47] The earliest pictorial representation I have found of a procession where open books are carried dates from 1300.[48] With the Dominican books, not only is the processional officially recognized as an indispensable liturgical book for the cantor, but there are *libelli* without rubrics provided for each brother.[49]

The *pulpitarium* brings together the notated texts from the antiphonary and gradual which are to be sung from the lectern in the middle of the choir. It is a book specifically designed for the practice illustrated in the manuscript illumination of cantors before an open book which we mentioned above.

The portable breviary again makes official and necessary for Dominicans a literate practice which was becoming widespread in monastic and secular circles, that of carrying a breviary while travelling.[50] The Dominican constitutions of 1220 were typical of earlier practice: while travelling, the brothers were to say the office as well as they knew it and were able.[51] Between the eleventh and thirteenth centuries, small sized breviaries begin to appear[52] and progressively, as the memorization of the psalter becomes more uncertain, the entire psalter is copied into the breviaries instead of just the psalm incipits.[53] These Dominican books typify a more general development in the use of liturgical texts in the thirteenth century: memorizing the text gives way to reading the text.

* * * * * *

We have been able to trace an evolution in the role played by the written text in medieval liturgy. A first movement towards a more literate mentality seems to occur at the time of the Carolingian renaissance, but it only takes hold during the twelfth and thirteenth centuries. The advent of the printing press in the fifteenth century will expand the possibilities which will then be used to great advantage in the liturgical reform of the Council of Trent. A phrase from the introduction to the Roman Ritual of 1614 shows where the shift in literate culture of the thirteenth century will lead: "In the administration of the sacraments, the collects and prayers are to be said faithfully and conscientiously; the memory is not to be readily trusted since it generally fails, but everything is to be recited from the book."[54]

This attitude to the book and its use in liturgy is in marked contrast to what we have seen during much of the Middle Ages. At first, the written text was scarcely more than an oral improvised prayer put into writing. Later, the written prayer began to serve as an example and as a model. Progressively, certain models took on the character of a reference and norm, and became the object of memorization. During much of the Middle Ages, the written text remained an aide-memoire. Toward the twelfth or thirteenth century, the liturgy is increasingly regulated by writing and is conceived of in these terms. The book becomes indispensable to the celebration, and the normal dynamic of the liturgical celebration becomes that of reading the text from a page.

Notes

1. C. Vogel, *Medieval Liturgy: An Introduction to the Sources*, revised and translated by W.G. Storey and N.K. Rasmussen (Washington, DC: The Pastoral Press, 1986) 31ff.

2. Hippolytus, *The Apostolic Tradition* no. 9.

3. Albert Lord, *The Singer of Tales* (Cambridge: Harvard University Press, 1960). The literature is vast: see John Miles Foley, *Oral-Formulaic Theory and Research: An Introduction and Annotated Bibliography* (New York: Garland, 1985).

4. Gregory of Tours, *History of the Franks* II, 22. In *Monumenta Germaniae Historica, Scriptores Rerum Merovingicarum* 1a (Hannover: Hahn, 1951) 67.

5. Vogel, *Medieval Liturgy* 37ff.

6. Niels Krogh Rasmussen, "Les Pontificaux du haut moyen âge: Genèse du livre liturgique de l'évêque," Doctoral Thesis, (Paris: Institut Catholique de Paris, 1977) 431-436.

7. Michel Huglo, "Les *Libelli* de tropes et les premiers tropaires-prosaires," in Ritva Jacobsson, ed., *Pax et Sapientia: Studies in Text and Music of Liturgical Tropes and Sequences in Memory of Gordon Anderson,* Acta Universitatis Stockholmiensis 29 (Stockholm: Almquist and Wiksell, 1986) 13-22.

8. As an example, Allan Bouley's book suffers on this account: *From Freedom to Formula: The Evolution of the Eucharistic Prayer from Oral Improvisation to Written Texts,* Studies in Christian Antiquity 21 (Washington, DC: The Catholic University of America Press, 1981).

9. Rasmussen, "Pontificaux" 417-419.

10. Brian Stock, *The Implications of Literacy: Written Language and Models of Interpretation in the Eleventh and Twelfth Centuries* (Princeton: Princeton University Press, 1983).

11. M.T. Clanchy, *From Memory to Written Record: England 1066-1307* (London: Edward Arnold, 1979).

12. Isidore of Seville, *Sententiae de Musica,* no. 1, Martin Gerbert, ed. *Scriptores Ecclesiastici de Musica Sacra Potissimum* (Hildesheim: George Olms, 1963; photo-reimpression of St-Blasien, 1784) vol. 1, p. 20.

13. Amalarius, *Prologus de Ordine Antiphonarii,* in J.M. Hanssens, ed. *Opera Liturgica Omnia,* Studi e Testi 138 (Vatican: Bibliotheca Apostolica, 1948), vol. 1, p. 361.

14. Guido of Arezzo, *Regulae Musicae de Ignoto Cantu (Prologus Antiphonarii Sui),* in Gerbert, *Scriptores* 2, p.35.

15. Aurelian of Réomé, *Musica Disciplina,* ed., Lawrence Gushee, Corpus Scriptorum de Musica 21 (Rome: American Institute of Musicology, 1975) no. 2, p. 61.

16. Hucbald of Saint-Amand, *De Harmonica Institutione,* in Gerbert, *Scriptores* 1, pp. 117-118. Text corrected by Warren Babb, *Hucbald, Guido and John on Music: Three Medieval Treatises* (New Haven: Yale University Press, 1978) 46.

17. Guido of Arezzo, *Regulae Musicae de Ignoto Cantu,* in Gerbert, *Scriptores* 2, pp. 35-36.

18. Guido of Arezzo, *Epistola de Ignoto Cantu,* in Gerbert, *Scriptores* 2, p. 44.

19. Gunter Haseloff, *Die Psalterillustration im 13. Jahrhundert: Studien zur Geschichte der Buchmalerei in England, Frankreich und den Niederlanden* (no publisher, 1938) 110-111, 118-123.

20. David conducting: Paris, BN, ms. lat. nouv. aq. 1392. David at organ: Paris, BN, ms. lat. 11931 and Bib. Mazarine, ms. 12. David at organ with singer: Boulogne, Bib. Mun., ms. 5.

21. From the ninth century, for example, there is a scene on the ivory covers of the Drogon Sacramentary of Metz (Paris: BN, ms. lat. 9428), or a famous pair of ivories showing the liturgy of the word (Cambridge, Fitzwilliam Museum) and the liturgy of the eucharist (Frankfurt, Stadtbibliothek, no. 20).

22. PL 75:91.

23. *De Gestis Beati Caroli Magni* (PL 98:1377).

24. In an eleventh-century version of the quarrel, antiphonaries notated with neumes are introduced: Adémar de Chabannes, *Chronique*, II, 8, Jules Chavanon, ed. (Paris: Picard, 1897) 80-84. (PL 141:27-28)

25. Adalbert de Vogüé, ed. *La Règle du Maître*, Sources chrétiennes 105, 106 (Paris: Cerf, 1964) no. 50.

26. Ibid. no. 44, 9-11.

27. Adalbert du Vogüé and Jean Neufville, eds. *La Règle de Saint Benoît*, Sources chrétiennes 181, 182 (Paris: Cerf, 1972). The liturgical part of the Rule covers nos. 8-18.

28. Ibid. no. 50.

29. *Constitutiones Lincolnienses et Capitula de Residentia* (called "Statuta Vicariorum") 13-16. Henry Bradshaw and Chr. Wordsworth, eds. *Statutues of Lincoln Cathedral* (Cambridge: Cambridge University Press, 1897), vol. 2, pt. 145.

30. Jean de Montlhéry, *Tractatus de Instructione Novitiorum* IV, in J.J. Berthier, ed. *Opera de Vita Regulari* (Rome: Befani, 1889) vol. 2, pp.529-530.

31. J. Berthelé and M. Valmary, eds. *Instructions et constitutions de Guillaume Durand, le speculateur* (Montpellier: Delord-Boehm et Martial, 1900) 69.

32. Ibid. 51.

33. Jacob of Voragine, *Legenda Aurea*, ed., Th. Graesse (Vratislavia: Koebner, 1890) nos. 131.7 and 11, pp. 592-593 and 63.

34. The journals of episcopal pastoral visits often mention the lack of books. For example, for the year 1340, the bishop of Grenoble mentions defective books thirty times: on five occasions there are no books at all; usually he simply notes that they are not sufficient. U. Chevalier, ed., *Visites pastorales et ordinations des évêques de Grenoble de la Maison de Chissé: 14e - 15e siècles* (Lyons: Aug. Brun, 1874) 9-32.

35. M.B. Parkes, "The Literacy of the Laity," *The Mediaeval World*, Literature and Western Civilisation 2 (London: Aldus, 1973) 555-577.

36. Thomas Frederick Simmons, ed., *The Lay-Folks Mass-Book or the*

Manner of Hearing Mass with Rubrics and Devotions for the People, in Four Texts, and Offices in English according to the Use of York from Manuscripts of the Xth to the XVth Century, The Early English Text Society (London: Trubner, 1879) B.622-625, p. 58.

37. Kassius Hallinger, *Consuetudines Cluniacensium Antiquiores cum Redactionibus Derivatis*, Corpus Consuetudinum Monasticarum 7, ii (Siegburg: Fr. Schmitt, 1983).

38. Giles Constable, "Monastic Legislation at Cluny in the Eleventh and Twelfth Centuries" (1972), *Cluniac Studies* (London: Variorum Reprints, 1980) 150ff.

39. Statutes of Hugh V, no. 20. In G. Charvin, ed., *Statuts, chapitres généraux et visites de l'ordre de Cluny*, vol. 1 (Paris: Boccard, 1965) 44.

40. Kassius Hallinger and others, *Initia Consuetudines Benedictinae: Consuetudines Saeculi Octavi et Noni*, Corpus Consuetudinum Monasticarum 1 (Siegburg: Fr. Schmitt, 1963).

41. *Carta Caritatis Prior* III, 2. Jean de la Croix Bouton and Jean van Damme, *Les Plus anciens textes de Cîteaux: Sources, textes et notes historiques*, Cîteaux: Commentarii Cistercienses, Studia et Documenta 2 (Achel: Cistercian Abbey, 1974) 92.

42. *Instituta Generalis Capituli apud Cistercium*, III and XII. Ph. Guignard, ed., *Les Monuments primitifs de la règle Cistercienne publiés d'après les manuscrits de l'abbaye de Cîteaux*, Analecta Divionensia 10 (Dijon: Rabutot, 1878) 250, 253. The list includes the missale, collectaneum, gradale, antiphonarium, regula, hymnarium, psalterium, lectionarium, and kalendarium. Statute 3 adds also the epistolare and textus; statute 12 adds the liber usuum.

43. Dijon, Bib. Mun. Ms. 114 (82).

44. "Litterae Encyclicae Magistrorum Generalium Ordinis Praedicatorum (1253-1376)", no. 8b, *Monumenta Ordinis Fratrum Praedicatorum Historica* vol. 5 (Rome: Polyglot, 1900) 42.

45. The most complete are found in the Dominican archives in Rome (Ms. XIV L 1) and in the British Museum (add. Ms. 23935). The latter was carried by the Master General on his visitations and was used to resolve any doubts.

46. This and other Dominican *libelli* are discussed by Pierre-Marie Gy in his contribution to this volume.

47. For example, see *Constitutiones Hirsaugienses*, II, 33 (PL 150:1073-1074).

48. London, British Museum, Ms. Yates Thompson 11, fo 60v: crossbearer, two candlebearers, deacon with closed gospel book, celebrant, nun with closed book, two groups of two nuns with two open books showing the noted text *Suscepimus Deus*, abbess with crosier and closed book.

49. Dominican Archives, Rome, Ms XIV L 1 fo 60v, quoted in Pierre-Marie Gy, "Collectaire, rituel, processionnal," *Revue des sciences philosophiques et théologiques* 44 (1960) 468.

50. Two examples of monastic legislation can be cited: M.-Anselme Dimier, ed., "Les statuts de l'Abbé Matthieu de Foigny pour la réforme de l'Abbaye de Saint-Vaast (1232)", *Revue bénédictine* 65 (1955) no. 34. p.120; and Charvin, *Statuts chapitres généraux et visites de l'ordre de Cluny*, "Visite de Prieuré de Layrac (1245)", no. 38, pp. 212-213. The provincial council of Trier, probably in the 1270s, makes similar prescriptions for the secular clergy: J.D. Mansi, *Sacrorum Conciliorum* 23, p.33, no. IX, 82. The phrase used, *horas legere*, is also found in synodal statutes during the second half of the thirteenth century.

51. *Constitutiones Antique Ordinis Fratrum Predicatorum*, II, 34:2-4 in A.H. Thomas, *De Oudste Constituties van de Dominicanen: voorgeschiedenis, tekst, bronnen, ontstaan en ontwikkeling (1215-1237)*, Bibliothèque de la Revue d'Histoire Ecclésiastique 42 (Leuven: University, 1965) 365.

52. S.J.P. van Dijk and Hazelden J. Walker, *The Origins of the Modern Roman Liturgy: The Liturgy of the Papal Court and the Franciscan Order in the Thirteenth Century* (London: Darton, Longman and Todd, 1960) 530, 539-540.

53. A survey of manuscript breviaries in the French public libraries shows that none of the remaining books of the eleventh century contain the entire psalter, thirty-nine percent of those from the twelfth- and the first half of the thirteenth-century contain the psalter, while seventy-two percent of those from the second half of the thirteenth century contain the entire psalter. This tendency seems strongest in small breviaries and in secular breviaries. Source: V. Leroquais, *Les Bréviaires manuscrits des bibliothèques publiques de France* (Paris, 1934).

54. *Rituale Romanum* I. 11.

THEOLOGY AND PRACTICE

6

"Holy Things for the Saints": The Ancient Call to Communion and Its Response

Robert Taft

Ta Hagia Tois Hagiois

WITH THE POSSIBLE EXCEPTION OF THE WARNING IN *DIDACHE* 10:6 (CA. 50-70), to which I shall return below,[1] the earliest relatively complete descriptions of the eucharist, like Justin's *Apology* I, 65, 67 (ca. 150),[2] and the *Apostolic Tradition* 22 (ca. 215),[3] pass directly from the concluding "Amen" of the anaphora to communion, without indicating what formulas, if any, accompanied the fraction and communion rites.

From the time of our earliest extant formularies of a complete eucharistic liturgy in the second half of the fourth century, however, *Ta hagia tois hagiois* appears as the pristine exhortation at once summoning to communion the faithful, and warning off the unworthy.[4] We see it in Palestine, in Cyril/John II of Jerusalem (after 390), *Catechesis 5, 19*;[5] in Cyril of Scythopolis (d. ca. 558), *Life of St. Euthymius 29*, a Palestinian monk (377-473);[6] and in the *Oratio de Sacra Synaxi* of Anastasius of Sinai (d. after 700).[7] From Syria, the *Apostolic Constitutions* VIII, 13:12-13 (ca. 380),[8] and Theodore of Mopsuestia, *Homily 16, 22-23* (ca. 388-392),[9] both have it. And John Chry-

sostom's *In Mt hom. 7, 6*,[10] shows he knew it in the liturgy of
Antioch during his ministry there before becoming archbishop
of Constantinople at the beginning of 398, where he will testi-
fy to the same usage.[11] For Alexandria we have the testimony
of Didymus the Blind, *De Trinitate* (ca. 381-392), 3, 13,[12] and
Cyril, *In Johannis Evangelium* (before 429) 4:7; 12.[13] Narsai (d.
502), *Homily 17*, witnesses to it in Mesopotamia, though in the
ancient, variant Syriac redaction of the East-Syrian tradition,
Sanctum sanctis decet in concordia.[14] So by the end of the fourth
century the *Sancta sanctis* had become the common acclamation inviting to communion throughout the Christian East.

An Invitation—and a Warning

In Constantinople, Chrysostom's homily *In Heb hom. 17*, 4-5,
conjures up a scene redolent of the Last Judgment in Matthew
25:31-46. Eucharist is unto judgment as well as salvation, Chrysostom teaches, echoing Paul in 1 Corinthians 11, the oldest extant eucharistic text. The presence of the Lord in table fellow-
ship in not just a sign of the banquet of the Kingdom. It is also
an anticipated judgment against unworthy partakers:

> After the whole sacrifice has been completed . . . with a loud
> voice, with an awful cry, like some herald lifting his hand on
> high, standing aloft conspicuous to all and crying out in that
> awesome silence, the priest[15] invites some and excludes others,
> not doing this with his hand, but with his tongue more clearly
> than with his hand. For that voice, falling on our ears, is like a
> hand that pushes away and expels some, and leads in and
> presents others . . . For when he says, "Holy things for the holy,"
> he is saying this: "If anyone is not holy, let him not approach."[16]

This apotropaic interpretation of "Holy things for the holy"
is standard. Like the *Sursum corda*, it warns away the unworthy,[17] and, indeed, the already cited Cyril of Scythopolis, *Life of
St. Euthymius* 29, and Anastasius, *Oratio de Sacra Synaxi*, explicitly compare the two exclamations.[18]

The more remote origins of such warnings off before the eucharist can be seen as early as ca. 50-70 in *Didache* 10:6, at the
end of the eucharistic prayers in that document: "If anyone is
holy, let him come! If anyone is not, let him repent! Maranatha!
Amen!"[19] I have discussed this text elsewhere, apropos of the

praefatio or warning off of the pre-anaphoral dialogue, in the context of the Pauline conclusion in 1 Corinthians 16:22-24: "If anyone has no love for the Lord, let him be accursed. Our Lord, come! The grace of the Lord Jesus be with you. My love be with you all in Christ Jesus. Amen."[20] Though Audet argues, against Lietzmann, that this *Didache* text is not a precommunion call,[21] *Apostolic Constitutions* VII, 26:6, places it explicitly in the context of the approaching communion.[22] So regardless of its pristine *Sitz im Leben*, it came to be interpreted in that sense, and can be considered an antecedent to the *Sancta sanctis*.[23]

Who Are the Saints?

But who are the *hagioi*, the "holy ones" or "saints" to whom the *hagia*, the "holy things" are reserved? In the Septuagint text of Leviticus 22:14, *hagia* is the meat offered in sacrifice. Matthew 7:6 uses the singular, *hagion*, in the same sense, a text *Didache* 9:5 applies to the eucharist: "But let no one eat or drink of your eucharist except those baptized in the name of the Lord, for the Lord said about this, 'Do not give what is holy to the dogs'."[24] So the "holy thing[s]" are the people's oblations to God, and in Christian Greek, the "holy ones" were initially the baptized faithful, a usage encountered frequently in the New Testament where Christians are simply called "the saints" without further ado.[25]

After the Peace of Constantine in 312, the flood of converts, the development of the category of public penitents, and the spread of the late fourth-century view of the eucharist as a "terrible" mystery,[26] this category of "saints" will become much less inclusive. No longer is any baptized Christian considered "holy," as in the halcyon days when grave post-baptismal sin was presumed a rarity, and post-baptismal penance was a once-in-a-lifetime offer. In the new circumstances, the meaning of "saint" is ultimately refined to designate only those baptized who can approach the altar without fear of condemnation because they are free of grave sin.

But late in the fourth century, the Jerusalem, *Catechesis 5*, 19, and Theodore of Mopsuestia, *Homily 16*, 22-23, still understood the "holy ones" in the Pauline sense: they are the baptized, who are holy because they have received the Holy Spirit.[27] So we can take the original meaning of "Holy things for the holy!" to be the same as the ancient admonition of *Didache* 9:5: "But let no one eat or drink of your eucharist except those who have been baptized in the name of the Lord."[28]

Of course this does not exclude the need for personal worthiness, as Paul himself insists in 1 Corinthians 11:27-29:

> Whoever . . . eats the bread or drinks the cup of the Lord in an unworthy manner will be guilty of profaning the body and blood of the Lord. Let a man examine himself, and so eat of the bread and drink of the cup. For anyone who eats and drinks without discerning the body eats and drinks judgment upon himself.

Not much later, *Didache* 10:6 stresses the same need: "If anyone is holy, let him come! If anyone is not, let him repent!"[29] *Apostolic Constitutions* VII, 26:6 makes this even more explicit in the context of communion: "If anyone is not [worthy], let him become so through penance (*ginesthô dia metanoias*)," undoubtedly a reference to the order of penitents, *hoi en metanoia*, of *Apostolic Constitutions* VIII, 9:2, 11.[30]

This need of personal holiness in order to approach the sacrament is how Chrysostom interprets the *Sancta sanctis* in his homilies *In Mt hom. 7, 6*,[31] from Antioch, and *In Heb hom. 17, 4-5*,[32] from Constantinople. In another of his Antiochene sermons, *In Mt hom. 82 (83), 5-6*, Chrysostom uses especially strong language regarding unworthiness to approach the holy table:

> Therefore it is necessary to be watchful in every way, for no small punishment is in store for those who partake unworthily. Consider how indignant you are . . . against those who crucified him. Watch out, therefore, lest you too become guilty of the body and blood of Christ. They slaughtered the all-holy body, but you receive it with a filthy soul . . . Should not one who has the benefit of this sacrifice be purer than anyone? Should not the hand that severs this flesh, the mouth filled with spiritual fire, the tongue reddened by that most awesome blood, be purer than any sunbeam? Consider . . . what sort of table you are partaking of . . . I say these things to you who receive and to you who minister. For it is necessary to address myself to you [ministers] also, that you may distribute the gifts with much care. There is no small punishment for you, if you are conscious of any wickedness in anyone you allow to partake of the table . . .

So let us not drive away just these [energumens], but absolutely all whom we see coming unworthily. Let no one communicate who is not a disciple; let no Judas receive, lest he suffer the fate of Judas. This multitude is also Christ's body. See to it, therefore, you who administer the mysteries, lest you provoke the Lord by not purging this [ecclesial] body . . . Even if such a one comes to communicate out of ignorance, forbid him. Do not be afraid. Fear God, not man . . . But if someone does not recognize the evil one . . . there is no blame. For these things were said about the obvious [unworthy ones].[33]

Among the Byzantine liturgical commentators, ca. 630 Maximus Confessor, *Mystagogia* 21, 24,[34] refers the *Sancta sanctis* to the whole sacramental economy of Christ, which makes us holy. A century later, Patriarch St. Germanus I of Constantinople, *Historia Ecclesiastica* 42, paraphrases the call into a confession by the priest of his own sinfulness in the face of God's holiness.[35] Symeon of Thessalonika (d. 1429), *Expositio de Divino Templo* 91, interprets the *Sancta sanctis* as a Christological confession like Philippians 2:11, a proclamation that we are one in the communion of the one Lord Jesus and of the sanctity of the one God, who deigns to sanctify us all.[36] Other later commentaries like the *Protheoria* 37 (A.D. 1085-1095) adopt Chrysostom's view,[37] though Nicholas Cabasilas does so with his customary balance, as Arranz has pointed out.[38] In his *Commentary* 36:1-5, Cabasilas carefully distinguishes between venial and mortal sins (*hamartia pros thanaton*). Only the latter exclude one from communion.

On the point of approaching the holy table, and of summoning others to it, the celebrant, who knows that partaking of the sacrament is not permitted to all, does not invite all to Communion. He takes the Bread of Life, and, showing it to the people, summons those who are worthy to receive it fittingly. "Holy things to the holy," he cries, as if to say: "here before your eyes is the bread of life. Let not everyone come to receive it, but only those who are worthy, for holy things are for the holy only." Those whom the priest calls holy are not only those who have attained perfection, but those also who are striving for it without having yet obtained it. Nothing prevents them from being sanctified by partaking of the holy mysteries, and from this point of view being saints. It is in this sense that the whole Church is called holy, and that the Apostle, writing to the

Christian people as a whole, says to them: "Holy brethren, partakers of the heavenly calling" [Heb 3:1]. The faithful are called saints because of the holy things of which they partake, because of him whose Body and Blood they receive. Members of his Body, flesh of his flesh and bone of his bone, as long as we remain united to him and preserve our connection with him, we live by holiness, drawing to ourselves, through the holy mysteries, the sanctity which comes from that Head and that Heart. But if we should cut ourselves off, if we should separate ourselves from the unity of this most holy Body, we partake of the holy mysteries in vain, for life cannot flow into dead and amputated limbs.

And what can cut off the members from this holy Body? "It is your sins which have separated me from you" [Is 59:2], says God.

But does all sin then bring death to man? No, indeed, but mortal sin only; that is why it is called mortal. For according to St. John there are sins which are not mortal [1 Jn 5:16-17]. That is why Christians, if they have not committed such sins as would cut them off from Christ and bring death, are in no way prevented, when partaking of the holy mysteries, from receiving sanctification, not in name alone, but in fact, since they continue to be living members united to the Head.

So when the priest says: "Holy things to the holy," the faithful reply: "One is Holy, One is Lord, Jesus Christ, in the glory of God the Father." For no one has holiness of himself; it is not the consequence of human virtue, but comes to all from him and through him. It is as if we were to place mirrors beneath the sun; each would shine, and send forth rays of light, so that one would think there were many suns; yet in truth there is but one sun which shines in all; just so Christ, the only Holy One, pours himself forth upon the faithful, shines in so many souls, and gives light to many saints; yet he alone is holy, in the glory of the Father.[39]

But despite later nuances and restrictions in the interpretation of "the saints," there can be no doubt that in an earlier period, only major crimes excluded one from communion until public penance had been undergone. Lesser sins were forgiven through contrition and the eucharist itself, which according to universal tradition is received unto the remission of sins, as Eastern anaphoral epicleses explicitly affirm.[40]

The Response

Traditionally, the people responded to the *Sancta sanctis* communion call with the Christological confession: "One [is] holy, one Lord, Jesus Christ, to the glory of God the Father! Amen!" The Greek text of the acclamation literally means "One holy one, one Lord, Jesus Christ . . ." But our earliest commentary, the Jerusalem, *Catechesis 5,* 19, interprets it in the sense I have given it: only one is holy, just as there is only one Lord.[41]

Actually, Cyril/John and, in Asia Minor, Gregory of Nyssa (d. 394), *Refutatio Confessionis Eunomii* 183,[42] cite only "One holy, one Lord, Jesus Christ," with no ending, though this should perhaps be taken as an incipit implying the full text—which, after all, is no more than *heis hagios heis* ("one holy, one") prefixed to 2 Philippians 2:11: *Kyrios Iêsous Christos eis doxan Theou Patros* ("Jesus Christ, to the glory of God the Father") plus a concluding "Amen."[43] That, at least, is certainly how one must understand numerous later liturgical texts, beginning with the sixth-century (?) Egyptian eucharistic formulary in Arabic edited by A. Baumstark,[44] that give a similar incipit. For the full, unelaborated, Christological recension is found before the end of the fourth century: our earliest Alexandrian witness, Didymus the Blind (d. ca. 398), in his *De Trinitate* written between 381-392, cites it several times, once in its entirety, including even the final "Amen."[45] Since it is highly unlikely that it originated in Egypt rather than in the Diocese of Oriens under the liturgical leadership of Antioch, the Alexandrians must have borrowed it as they found it.

The Origins of the Confession

But that is just speculation: we have no direct evidence for the provenance of this text. We do know, however, that such acclamations were part of the *Formelqut* of antique culture. Instructive parallels for the incipit of our acclamation are readily available in both pagan *heis/solus* acclamations and Judeo-Christian "one God/Lord" confessions. And I have already noted that the conclusion is simply Philippians 2:11.

Although "one Lord" (*heis Kyrios*) is frequent in the Septuagint, "one holy [one]" (*heis hagios*) occurs only in the Theodotion recension of Daniel 8:13,[46] cited in *Apostolic Constitutions* VII, 35:3[47] in conjunction with the biblical Trisagion (*Sanctus*).[48]

New Testament parallels are more promising. In 1 Corinthians 8:6, Paul nuances the confession of Septuagint Deuteronomy 6:4 (*"Kyrios ho theos hêmôn kyrios heis estin"*) as follows:

> For although there may be so-called gods in heaven or on earth
> . . . yet for us there is one God, the Father, from whom are all
> things and for whom we exist, and one Lord Jesus Christ (*heis*
> *kyrios Iêsous Christos*), through whom are all things and through
> whom we exist.[49]

And ca. 381-392 Didymus the Blind, *De Trinitate* 3, 10:23,[50] notes resonances with Ephesians 4:4-6: "There is one body and one spirit . . . one Lord, one faith, one baptism, one God and Father of us all, who is above all and through all and in all."

Further, the classical origins of "one god" (*heis theos*) acclamations have been studied in great detail, with innumerable examples, by Peterson. The evidence he has amassed for the use of this acclamation in pagan and Christian inscriptions and texts is massive: further, the use of *heis* formulas in Manichaeism, and of such acclamations as "one Zeus, one Aides, one Helios, one Dionysos" in the mystery cults, is meticulously attested.[51]

Closer to our formula is a prechristian prayer cited by Julius Firmicus Maternus in *Mathesis* V, *praef.* 3, written before May 22, 337, while its author was still a pagan: . . . *solus enim gubernator et princeps, solus imperator ac dominus, cui tota potestas numinum servit . . .*[52] Similar *tu solus* prayers and inscriptions appear in Christian Latin.[53] And in Greek, *heis theos* acclamations in a Christian context are heard, for example, at the Synod of Constantinople in 518: "One God who did this . . . One God, one faith. One peace of the Churches, one peace of the Orthodox."[54]

Development of the Christological Text

The pristine Christological text of the response soon underwent redactional developments. By ca. 380, *Apostolic Constitutions* VIII, 13:13-16, has appended to it early Christian liturgical *Formelgut*:

> Be he blessed unto the ages, amen! Glory to God in highest, and
> peace on earth, good will among men (Lk 2:14)! Hosanna to the

Son of David! Blessed is he who comes in the name of the Lord
(Mt 21:96 = Ps 117:26a)! The Lord is God and has appeared
among us (Ps 117:27a)! Hosanna in the highest (Mt 21:9c)![55]

The relation of this acclamation to the liturgical *Gloria in excelsis* is apparent in the fifth-century redaction of the conclusion
to the *Gloria* found in the *Codex Alexandrinus* Septuagint in the
British Library, London:

For you are alone holy,
you are alone Lord,
Jesus Christ,
to the glory of God the Father.
Amen.[56]

The earlier *Gloria* text in *Apostolic Constitutions* VII, 47:3,
however, does not conclude with this doxology from Philippians 2:11.[57] So perhaps a better paradigm for this added material is its presence in the liturgical *Sanctus*:

Holy, holy, holy Lord . . .
Heaven and earth are full of your glory!
Hosanna in the highest!
Blessed is he who comes in the name of the Lord!
Hosanna in the highest!

The Trinitarian Redaction

From the original *Sitz im Leben* of the *Sancta sanctis* as a call
to communion in Christ's body and blood, the suitability of a
Christological confession as the people's response to it is obvious. And indeed, the early evidence already adduced points to
the Christological redaction as the *Urform*. Today, however,
most liturgies respond to the ancient communion call with a
trinitarian confession: "One holy Father, one holy Son, one
Holy Spirit . . ." Only the Byzantines and the Armenians have
kept the Christological form.
    Like most such changes in liturgico-confessional formulas,
the roots of this shift lie deep in the history of doctrine. In the
turbulent fourth-century climate, Christological formulas were
often suspect, and the response acquired this new trinitarian
shape, undoubtedly in reaction to Arian and pneumatochomi-
an subordinationism, which provoked a levelling of Eastern
doxological formulas in order to affirm without any possible

ambiguity the Nicene teaching of the absolute equality-in-divinity of the Son and Holy Spirit with the Father.[58] The trinitarian recension first appears ca. 388-392 in Theodore of Mopsuestia, *Homily 16, 23*,[59] and thereafter, in Syriac, in Narsai (d. 502), *Homily 17* and *21*,[60] and the later Nestorian commentaries.[61] Among the Jacobites, the situation was still in flux as late as A.D. 708, as James of Edessa tells us in his *Epistle to Thomas the Presbyter*:

> There is also another difference in many churches: instead of "The one Father is holy, the one Son is holy," and the rest, some say "One Lord, one Son, Jesus Christ, to the glory of God the Father. Amen."[62]

But the later Jacobite commentators all give the trinitarian formula,[63] and eventually the new form was adopted for all the liturgies of Syria, Mesopotamia, and Egypt; only the Byzantines and Armenians held out for the older tradition.[64]

As is often true, the Liturgy of St. James is a case apart, manifesting certain peculiarities that are undoubtedly a result of an initial conservatism, then later acceptance of the influence of the trinitarian redaction. One sees this already in the earliest extant manuscript of James, the ninth-century codex *Vatican Greek 2282*, which gives the integral Christological text, then adds before the Amen: "with the Holy Spirit," then, from Galatians 1:5, "to whom [be] glory unto the ages of ages."[65]

The Sitz im Leben of the "One is Holy" Acclamation

In a recent article I discussed the original *Sitz im Leben* of liturgical acclamations in antique culture, apropos of the *Dignum et iustum est* response of the pre-anaphoral dialogue across the traditions.[66] Arguing from the same cultural context, Peterson has proposed that the "One [is] holy" is an "epiphany acclamation" at the appearance of Christ in the sacred gifts at communion, its *Sitz im Leben* akin, therefore, to parallel pagan *adventus* acclamations at the epiphany of the god—Dionysius, for example—at his festival.[67] Further, Peterson stresses the apotropaic sense of many such acclamations in comparison with 1 Corinthians 16:22 and *Didache* 10:6 already discussed above: they serve at once as apotheosis and anathema, both inviting the worthy and warning off the rest.[68]

This, we have seen, is the sense Fathers of the Church like Chrysostom give to the *Sancta sanctis*, which, with its response, rounds off the anaphora by concluding it where it began, with an invitation to grace that is at once a warning against those not ready to receive it.

Notes

Abbreviations Used in the Notes

CPG = *Clavis Patrum Graecorum* I-V (Turnhout: Brepols, 1974-1987).

CSCO = Corpus Scriptorum Christianorum Orientalium.

Dmitrievskij I, II, III = A.A. Dmitrievski, *Opisanie liturgicheskix rukopisej xranjashchixsja v bibliotekax pravoslavnago vostoka*, I-II (Kiev: Korchak-Novitskij 1895, 1901), III (Petrograd: Kirschbaum, 1917).

LEW = F.E. Brightman, *Liturgies Eastern and Western* (Oxford: Clarendon, 1896).

Metzger I, II, III = M. Metzger, ed., *Les Constitutiones apostoliques*, tome I: livres I-II, SC 320 (Paris: Cerf, 1985); tome II: livres III-VI, SC 329 (Paris: Cerf, 1986); tome III: livres VII-VIII, SC 336 (Paris: Cerf, 1987).

OCA = Orientalia Christiana Analecta (Rome: PIO).

OCP = *Orientalia Christiana Periodica* (Rome: PIO).

Peterson, *Heis Theos* = E. Peterson, *Heis Theos. Epigraphische formgeschichtliche und religionsgeschichtliche Untersuchungen*, Forschungen zur Religion und Literatur des Alten und Neuen Testaments, Heft 41 = neue Folge, Heft 24 (Göttingen: Vandenhoeck & Ruprecht, 1926).

PIO = Pontificio Istituto Orientale (Rome).

SC = Sources chrétiennes.

SH = Subsidia Hagriographica (Brussels: Société des Bollandistes).

Taft, "Dialogue" I-III = R. Taft, "The Dialogue before the Anaphora in the Byzantine Eucharistic Liturgy." I: "The Opening Greeting," OCP 52 (1986) 299-324; II: "The *Sursum corda*," OCP 54 (1988) 47-77; III: "Let us give thanks to the Lord—It is fitting and right," OCP 55 (1989) 63-74.

Trempelas = P.N. Trempelas, *Hai treis leitourgiai kata tous en Athênais kôdikas*, Texte und Forschungen zur byzantinisch-neugriechischen Philologie 15 (Athens: Patriarchal Scientific Commission for the Revision and Publication of Liturgical Books, 1935).

ZKT = *Zeitschrift für katholische Theologie*.

1. At note 19.

2. E.J. Goodspeed, ed., *Die ältesten Apologeten* (Göttingen: Vandenhoeck & Ruprecht, 1914) 74-76 = PG 6:428-429.

3. B. Botte, ed., *La Tradition apostolique de S. Hippolyte. Essai de reconstitution*, Liturgiewissenschaftliche Quellen und Forschungen 39 (Münster: Aschendorff, 1963) 60-61.

4. The mid-fourth-century Egyptian *Euchology of Serapion* is an exception (F.X. Funk, ed., *Didascalia et Constitutiones Apostolorum* [Paderborn: F. Schoeningh, 1905] II, 158-203). But this source, like early Greek euchologies in general, gives only the presider's prayers without indicating *diakonika* or other admonitions and short formulas (*Oremus, Sursum corda, Stemus bene*, etc.). For the *Sancta sanctis* in later sources, see J.-M. Hanssens, *Institutiones Liturgicae de Ritibus Orientalibus* II-III (Rome: Gregorian University, 1930, 1932) nn. 1381-1386.

5. Cyrille de Jérusalem, *Catéchèse mystagogiques*, edited by A. Piédagnel, SC 126 bis (Paris: Cerf, 1980) 168. On the problem of authorship, see ibid. 177-187.

6. E. Schwartz, ed., *Kyrillos von Skythopolis*, Texte und Untersuchungen 49.2 (Leipzig: J.C. Hinrichs, 1939) 46.

7. PG 89:841. The authorship of this homily (=CPG 7750) is disputed. S.N. Sakkos places it earlier, under the authorship of Anastasius II, Patriarch of Antioch (599-ca. 609): *Peri Anastasiôn Sinaitôn*, Epistêmonikê Epetêris Theologikês Scholês, Supplement to vol. 8 (Thessalonika: University of Thessalonika School of Theology, 1964) 41; on Sakkos' study confer E.K. Chrysos, "Neôterai ereunai peri Anastasiôn Sinaitôn," *Kleronomia* 1 (1969) 121-144, and the reviews of G. Weiss, *Byzantinische Zeitschrift* 60 (1967) 324-346, and J. Darrouzès, *Revue des études byzantines* 25 (1967) 280-283. Against Sakkos, I believe the liturgical form of the *Sursum corda* in this homily (PG 89:836-837, 841) precludes assigning it an Antiochene provenance (see Taft, "Dialogue" II, 57-61).

8. Metzger III, 208.

9. R. Tonneau, R. Devreesse, eds., *Les Homélies catéchétiques de Théodore de Mopsueste*, Studi e testi 145 (Vatican: Bibliotheca Apostolica Vaticana, 1949) 565-569.

10. PG 57:80.

11. See the following paragraph.

12. Confer also 2:6, PG 39:528, 861.

13. PG 73:700; 74:696.

14. *The Liturgical Homilies of Narsai*, translated into English with an introduction by R.H. Connolly, Texts and Studies 8.1 (Cambridge: University Press, 1909) 26-27; see also *Homily 21*, p. 60, which gives the response, from which one can infer the existence of the call as

well. On the question of the disputed authenticity of *Homily 17*, see the full discussion in S.Y.H. Jammo, *La Structure de la messe chaldéenne du début jusqu'à l'anaphore. Etude historique*, OCA 207 (Rome: PIO, 1979) 13-25. See also the present Assyro-Chaldean liturgical text, LEW 296:30, and the Nestorian commentators cited below, note 61, all of whom report the traditional East-Syrian redaction.

15. The manuscripts of this text assign this invitation to the deacon (see PG 63:132 note b), but later the passage refers to the priest, and since, traditionally, it is the priest who proclaims the *Sancta sanctis* in all sources, this assignment of it to the deacon is undoubtedly a slip of the golden tongue—or of the copyist. See F. van de Paverd, *Zur Geschichte der Messliturgie in Antiocheia und Konstantinopel gegen Ende des vierten Jahrhunderts. Analyse der Quellen bei Johannes Chrysostomos*, OCA 187 (Rome: PIO, 1970) 529-530. The fifteenth-century Byzantine euchology codex *Sinai Gr. 986* (Dmitrievskij II, 612) also assigns the *Sancta sanctis* to the deacon, but in the face of the unanimous testimony of other Byzantine sources, early and late, this can be judged an aberration.

16. PG 63:132-133.

17. See Taft, "Dialogue" II, 49-53, 76-77.

18. Notes 6-7 above.

19. W. Rordorf and A. Tuiller, eds., *La Doctrine des douze apôtres (Didachê)*, SC 248 (Paris: Cerf, 1978) 180-182.

20. Taft, "Dialogue" I, 323-324.

21. J.-P. Audet, *La Didaché. Instructions des apôtres*, Etudes bibliques (Paris: J. Gabalda, 1958) 410-416; H. Lietzmann, *Mass and Lord's Supper*, with Introduction and Further Inquiry by R.D. Richardson (Leiden: E.J. Brill, 1979) 193; see Richardson's commentary, 391-392.

22. Metzger III, 56; see below at note 30.

23. Richardson in Lietzmann, *Mass and Lord's Supper* (note 21 above) 392 note 2.

24. SC 248 (note 19 above) 176, 178. J. Magne has noted, in this context, the relationship between Matthew 7:6, "Do not give dogs what is holy; and do not throw your pearls before swine," and the early Christian use of "pearl" in the Greek (*margaritês*), Latin (*margarita*), and Syriac (*margônitho*) as a term for the eucharistic species. Confer, for example, J. Magne, "Le chant de la perle à la lumière des écrits de Nag Hammâdi," *Cahiers du Cercle Ernest-Renan* 100 (juin 1977) 25-36.

25. E.g., Acts 9:13, 32; Rom 1:7, 8:27, 12:13, 15:25; 1 Cor 1:2, 6:1, 7:14; 2 Cor 1:1; Eph 3:8; Phil 4:22; Col 1:2, 22, 26; 1 Pet 1:15-16.

26. On this shift of mentality and language, see the literature cited

in R. Taft, "The Inclination Prayer before Communion in the Byzantine Liturgy of St. John Chrysostom: A Study in Comparative Liturgy," *Ecclesia Orans* 3 (1986) 43 note 53.

27. Notes 5, 9 above. On this question see M. Arranz, "Le *Sancta sanctis* dans la tradition liturgique des églises," *Archiv für Liturgiewissenschaft* 15 (1973) 32-37.

28. Note 24 above.

29. Note 19 above.

30. Metzger III, 56, 162, 166.

31. PG 57:80 cited above at note 10.

32. PG 63:132-133.

33. PG 58:743. Confer van de Paverd, *Messliturgie* (note 15 above) 370-371.

34. PG 91:696-697, 709.

35. *St Germanus of Constantinople on the Divine Liturgy*. The Greek Text with Translation, Introduction and Commentary by Paul Meyendorff (Crestwood, NY: St. Vladimir's Seminary Press, 1984) 104-105.

36. PG 155:741.

37. PG 140:464.

38. "Le *Sancta sanctis*" (note 27 above) 35.

39. Text in Nicolas Cabasilas, *Explication de la divine liturgie*, eds., R. Bornert, J. Gouillard, and P. Périchon, SC 4bis (Paris: Cerf, 1967) 222-224; trans. from Nicola *Divine Liturgy*, trans., J.M. Hussey and P.A. McNulty (London: SPCK, 1960) 88-89.

40. For instance, the Byzantine Anaphora of St. John Chrysostom prays God to send his Holy Spirit upon the gifts "so that for those who receive them they may be for the forgivenesss of sins." Numerous other examples can be seen in A. Hänggi and I. Pahl, *Prex Eucharistica*, Spicilegium Friburgense 12 (Fribourg: Ed. Universitaires, 1968). On this whole question, see R. Taft, "Penance in Contemporary Scholarship," *Studia Liturgica* 18 (1988) 15-16.

41. Note 5 above.

42. W.W. Jaeger, ed., *Gregorii Nysseni Opera* II (Leiden: E.J. Brill, 1960) 389 = PG 45:549.

43. Peterson, *Heis Theos* 132. A Baumstark, *Comparative Liturgy* (Westminster, MD: Newman Press, 1958) 60, has asked whether the text of the epistle might not be of liturgical provenance.

44. "Eine ägyptische Mess- und Taufliturgie vermutlich des 6. Jahrhunderts," *Oriens Christianus* 1 (1901) 29.

45. 2, 6:6; 7:8; 3, 10:13, 16, 23, PG 39:528, 589, 861, 869, 928; references from U. Holzmeister, "Unbeachtete patristiche Agrapha," ZKT 38 (1914) 128.

46. A. Rahlfs, ed., *Septuaginta* 8th ed. (Stuttgart: Würtembergische Bibelanstalt, 1965) II, 918 (lower text).

47. Metzger III, 76.

48. Confer J. Brinktrine, "Zur Entstehung und Erklärung des Gloria in Excelsis," *Römische Quartalschrift* 35 (1927) 314.

49. A. Baumstark, *Die Messe im Morgenland* (Kempton/Munich: J. Kösel, n.d.) 158, sees here a possible reflection of the liturgical formula, but Peterson, *Heis Theos* 135, opposes this idea.

50. PG 39:924-925.

51. Peterson, *Heis Theos* 139.

52. W. Kroll, F. Skutsch, K. Ziegler, eds., *Iulii Firmici Materni Matheseos Libri VIII*, fasc. 2, Biblioteca Scriptorum Graecorum et Romanorum Teubneriana (Leipzig: B.G. Teubner, 1913) 2.

53. Confer O. Casel, "Literaturbericht. Altchristliche Liturgie bis auf Konstantin d. Gr.," *Jahrbuch für Liturgiewissenschaft* 4 (1914) 299.

54. E. Schwartz, ed., *Acta Conciliorum Oecumenicorum* III (Berlin: W. de Gruyter, 1940) 85.

55. Metzger III, 208.

56. Rahlfs (note 46 above) II, 182. Confer Baumstark, *Comparative Liturgy* (note 43 above) 60; Peterson, *Heis Theos* 134; Brinktrine, "Gloria in Excelsis," (note 48 above) 313; J.A. Jungmann, *The Mass of the Roman Rite* (New York: Benzinger, 1950) I, 349.

57. Metzger III, 112.

58. On this question see J.A. Jungmann, *The Place of Christ in Liturgical Prayer* (New York: Alba House, 1965) part II *passim*, esp. 172-190.

59. Studi e testi 145 (note 9 above) 569.

60. *The Liturgical Homilies* (note 14 above) 27, 60. Confer J. Quasten, "Der älteste Zeuge für die trinitarische Fassung der liturgischer *heis hagios*-Akklamation," ZKT 58 (1934) 253-254.

61. Gabriel Qatraya bar Lipah (ca. 615), unedited: Latin trans. in Jammo (note 14 above) 45; Abraham bar Lipah (7th c.) and Ps.-George of Arbela (9th c.): *Anonymi Auctoris Expositio Officiorum Ecclesiae Georgio Arbelensi Vulgo Adscripta*, accedit Abrahae bar Lipheh *Interpretatio Officiorum*, ed., R.H. Connolly, CSCO 72, 76, Script. Syri Series 2, Tome 92 (Rome: C. de Luigi/Paris: J. Gabalda/Leipzig: Harrassowitz, 1913, 1915) text 76; 179 (bar Lipah); versio 69-70; 65 (bar Lipah).

62. Cited in ch. 3 of Dionysius bar Salibi, *Expositio Liturgiae*, ed., H. Labourt, CSCO 13-14, Script. Syri Series 2, Tome 93 (Paris: J. Gabalda/Leipzig: Harrassowitz, 1943) text 10, 12; versio 39-40; English trans. LEW 492.

63. Dionysius bar Salibi (d. 1171), *Expositio Liturgiae* (see the previous note) text 86-88; versio 94-95; George, Bishop of the Arab Tribes

(d. ca. 724) and Moses bar Kepha (d. 903): *Two Commentaries on the Jacobite Liturgy by George, Bishop of the Arab Tribes, and Moses Bar Kepha, Together with the Syriac Anaphora of St. James and a Document Entitled The Book of Life*. Text and English trans. by R.H. Connolly and W.H. Codrington (London: Williams & Norgate, 1913) 19, 86-87. The ninth-century commentator John of Dara does not mention the *Sancta sanctis* or its response: J. Sader, ed., *Le "De Oblatione" de Jean de Dara*, CSCO 308-309, Script. Syri 132-133 (Louvain: Secrétariat du CSCO, 1970) cf. II, 29-32, IV, 19-20.

64. See Hanssens, *Institutiones* (note 4 above) nn. 1375-1379; for the liturgical texts of the various traditions, see LEW.

65. B.-Ch. Mercier, *La Liturgie de S. Jacques. Edition critique, avec traduction latine*, Patrologia Orientalis 26.2 (Paris: Firmin-Didot, 1946) 228.

66. See note 17 above.

67. Peterson, *Heis Theos* 140. On the *adventus* concept, see S.G. MacCormack, *Art and Ceremony in Late Antiquity* (Berkeley: University of California, 1981) 17-89.

68. Peterson, *Heis Theos* 130ff.

7

"The Unbloody Sacrifice": The Origins and Development of a Description of the Eucharist

Kenneth Stevenson

PATRISTIC SOURCES HAVE FIGURED PROMINENTLY IN THE WORK OF LITUR-gical reconstruction and renewal during the course of this century. Many a new liturgy, official or unofficial, has had recourse to antiquity in the recovery that has been so much of the history of our times. Indeed, one could almost say that the enthusiasm for making use of all this knowledge has only been matched by the extent to which our accumulation of material about the liturgy in the early centuries has grown apace, as fresh editions of manuscripts have appeared, and old texts once lost have been found, only to be milked of as much eucharistic sustenance as they are able to yield.[1]

But there is one aspect of the story over which churches intent on renovating their rites have walked with some care: eucharistic sacrifice continues to be a theme which certain churches tend to handle with large tongs.[2] This may explain why, among the rich repertoire in the sacrificial vocabulary, the somewhat clumsy and archaic, but indubitably rich and resonant expression "the unbloody sacrifice" has not received any rehabilitation, even an attempted one. André Tarby, enthusiast as he is for the Anaphora of St. James, waxes eloquent about its handling of eucharistic offering, including the "unbloody sacrifice" itself, but studiously omits the expression from his suggested text of the anaphora for use today.[3]

And yet, this curious expression, with its offbeat history, which we shall attempt to tell, sift, and reflect upon, is to be found embedded in what was once described as "the first ecumenical liturgy," the nineteenth-century "Catholic Apostolic" (sometimes called Irvingite) eucharist.[4] In that part of the anaphora which corresponds with the anamnesis comes the following prolix sentence:

> Almighty God, we Thy servants, calling to mind the most blessed Sacrifice of Thy Son, showing forth His death, rejoicing in His resurrection and glorious presence at Thy right hand, and waiting for the blessed hope of His appearing and coming again, do present unto Thee this reasonable and unbloody sacrifice which Thou hast instituted in Thy Church, the holy bread of everlasting life and the cup of eternal salvation.[5]

The sweep of the sentence is plain, as it gathers momentum through its description of the eucharistic action; and no one acquainted with the theological problems of the sixteenth-century West will fail to spot the carefully nuanced way in which the sacrifice of Christ (soon to be described as "once offered upon the cross" two sentences further on) stands in relation to the church's celebration. One can see, too, a determination to link the anamnesis with the institution narrative.[6] One thing, however, is clear: the eucharist is a "reasonable and unbloody sacrifice" by virtue of being a "calling to mind" of the one sacrifice of Christ. And it is achieved by a judicious blending of Eastern and Western piety and theology.

To that piety and theology we must now turn. First, the background of the expression will be discussed, which will take us up to the fourth-century Eastern writers. Then we shall look at the Eastern liturgies, starting with the anaphoras, and after that dealing with other prayers. An attempt will be made to suggest some kind of route for the term. A quick look at the West will follow. The story will thereafter leap onwards in time to the Anglican High Churchmen of the eighteenth century, before some concluding remarks are made.

Background

The earliest known occurrence of the term is to be found in no less a book than the *Testament of the Twelve Patriarchs*, a work that tends to be regarded as late second century. Robert Daly[7] identifies among its special features that are already strong in the Apocrypha an interest in "angelic liturgy," a concern with the "spiritualizing of sacrifice," and a fad for priesthood. It is Jewish-Christian in its origins. The *Testament of Levi* becomes the crucial part for our discussion.

> In the heaven next to it are the archangels, who minister and make propitiation to the Lord for all the sins of the righteous; offering to the Lord a sweet-smelling savour, a reasonable and bloodless offering.[8]

As Daly points out, the "sweet-smelling savour" is the technical term for the fact that the sacrifice is acceptable, and the term "unbloody" is the result of the Jewish redactor who rejected the Maccabean priesthood and was developing his own ideas of a spiritualized notion of sacrifice. The context of "propitiation," too, makes the offering by the archangels needful; it is not just a heavenly adjunct, but part of the divine plan.

Athenagoras late in the second century writes extensively about the self-offering of the Christian, a fact which Daniel Waterland,[9] the eighteenth-century Anglican theologian, emphasizes. Thus, what he says about worship and the eucharist must not be taken out of context, a context which indicates very much the kind of sacrifice-lifestyle approach to the liturgy which inspired my own treatment of the overall theme of eucharistic sacrifice in the early centuries.[10] For Athenagoras, then, the "unbloody sacrifice" applies to all worship, not exclusively the eucharist, and the reason why it is "unbloody" is that it is to be contrasted with pagan worship. Both the redactor of the *Testament of Levi* and Athenagoras have Romans 12:1 ("Present your bodies as a living sacrifice") in the back of their minds, but the results are slightly different. The former is describing the perfect cult of heaven, the latter is alluding to the worship of God in Christ, of self-oblation, free from the shackles of paganism. "What need have I of holocausts, of which God has no need? One must rather present the unbloody sacrifice and offer the reasonable service."[11] The juxtaposition of "unbloody sacrifice" and "reasonable service" will be encountered later. Since Athenagoras, as Cuming points out,[12] may have been head of the theological school in Alexandria, this quotation has importance for the discussion of the Egyptian liturgy later on.

Origen, a little later than Athenagoras and also in Alexandria, comes closer to definition in writing of the Christian "making the unbloody sacrifices in [i.e., consisting in] prayers,"[13] which would appear to be an apologetic-based paraphrase of Hebrews 13:15, "Through Jesus let us continually offer up to God the sacrifice of praise, that is, the tribute of lips which acknowledge his name." The same understanding comes across in the *Martyrium Apollonii*: "I send up the unbloody and pure sacrifice . . . which is through prayers."[14] Methodius of Olympus speaks of the "unbloody altar,"[15] thus linking the earthly with the heavenly in the spiritual.

Eusebius, on the other hand, applies the expression unequivocally to the eucharist: "the sacred offerings of the table of Christ, through which we have been taught to offer the unbloody and reasonable sacrifices."[16] Eusebius' sacramental theology is more developed in other respects, so that such an assertion should be no surprise. But when we move well into the fourth century, specifically eucharistic use of the term becomes much more common. Thus Cyril of Jerusalem in the *Fifth Catechesis* describes the move from consecration to intercession in the anaphora: "Then, after the spiritual sacrifice, the unbloody service, has been perfected, we beseech God over that sacrifice of propitiation, for the common peace of the churches, for the stability of the world . . ."[17] John Chrysostom, in a passage cited by Van De Paverd as an eloquent commentary on the eucharistic prayer, refers to "the great high priest, when he stands at this holy table, offering up the reasonable service, presenting the unbloody sacrifice . . ."[18] It is clear from the context that Chrysostom is speaking not about the eucharist in general, but the *Sanctus* in particular; and in that sense, his words hark back to the *Testament of Levi*.

Cyril of Alexandria alludes to the anamnesis, or else the whole anaphora, when he writes: "We proclaim the death, in the flesh, of the only-begotten Son of God, Jesus Christ, and acknowledge his return to life from the dead and his ascension into heaven, and as we do this we perform the unbloody sacrifice in the churches."[19] Gregory of Nyssa refers to "the sacred and unbloody priesthood," clearly meaning the eucharist as the work of the priesthood.[20] Gregory of Nazianzus goes as far as speaking of the breaking of the eucharistic bread as "an unbloody incision,"[21] probably intending an image from surgery.

The cardinal patristic Old Testament text is Malachi 1:10f: "I have no pleasure in you, says the Lord of hosts, and I will not accept an offering from your hand. For from the rising of the sun to its setting my name is great among the nations, and in every place incense is offered to my name, and a pure offering; for my name is great among the nations, says the Lord of hosts."[22] Preaching on that text, Theodoret of Cyrus refers to "the pure and unbloody offering,"[23] presumably employing the extra word as one which was both familiar to his hearers and needful, in order that the eucharistic context might be clearer. Severus of Antioch, writing at the start of the sixth century, uses our term no fewer than four times, as has been noted in a study by Cuming.[24] The epithets vary slightly: "in the hour of the spiritual and unbloody service"; "the reasonable and unbloody sacrifice"; "the cross completes the reasonable, unbloody, spiritual sacrifice"; and "it is Christ himself and his mystical words which are pronounced over the bread and the cup that complete the reasonable and unbloody sacrifice."

The above list is not intended to be exhaustive, but for all its limitations, some conclusions can be drawn.

First, the notion of "unbloody" worship is post-biblical and is derived from the process commonly described nowadays as "the spiritualization of sacrifice" that went on in late Judaism as well as in early Christianity.

Second, the early quotations (e.g., *Testament of Levi* and Athenagoras) indicate that the pure worship is heavenly, and that the proper human response lies in worship that has no need of dead animals, namely, worship backed up by matching behavior. As Daly, Young, and Hanson have all pointed out, such a broadened ethical view of worship mixes well with their kind of approach to the early eucharistic texts.[25] It also contrasts markedly with another patristic theme, the blood of the *martyrs*.

Third, the popularization, if one may call it such, of the

"unbloody" was also due to the need for an apologetic against pagan sacrifices, which was particularly necessary for the Christian minority in the second- and third-century Mediterranean society.

Fourth, the word "unbloody" was used in conjunction with "reasonable" and "pure" to make the essential Christological point, that it is through Christ that the earthly and the heavenly are connected, united, brought together in worship. We are not yet into the era of the *Sanctus* as a universal phenomenon in Christian worship, though this is one of the consequences. Meanwhile, worship that is "unbloody" is *real*, and while the eucharist is the focal point of worship, the epithet properly belongs to all worship, corporate as well as individual, as the texts we have looked at demonstrate.

Fifth, the tale is one of paradox, for it begins by being a corporatist apologetic, to take sacrifice away from Jewish and pagan temple-cult; and it ends, in the fourth century, by bolstering up the strongly cultic vocabulary that surrounds the eucharist, including the role of the ordained ministry at that service. The very same word migrates from an early role, for which it seems specially coined, to a later one, into which it fits along with a growing repertoire of terms for an expanding liturgy. This development, however, is *not* a progression from "primitive" to "complex." In the second century the word was new, but it connoted a highly sophisticated view of the intimate relationship between worship and service, which is what the early understanding of eucharistic sacrifice is partly about.

Eastern Liturgies: Anaphoras

Some of the writers we have looked at so far overlap in time and in eucharistic vocabulary with the eastern anaphoras. It is therefore appropriate that these are examined next. It is still difficult to be precise as to the provenance of the original versions of these prayers, although the advance of liturgical studies has made this more possible than it was. There are two main groupings, Egypt and Syria, as far as this particular exploration is concerned.

Egypt

Cuming's recently published edition and study of the Liturgy of St. Mark has enabled scholars to look afresh at the evolution of this rite.[26] Some years ago Cuming had, in company with others, suggested that the *Strasbourg Papyrus* was no mere fragment, but a complete anaphora in itself.[27] It is not the purpose of this study to enter the lists over this question, save to say that *if* it is complete, and if it *does* go back to around 200 A.D., then we have a very important correspondence between Athenagoras and Origen over "the unbloody sacrifice." For near the start of what resembles the preface, *Strasbourg* opens out into praise:

> You made everything through your wisdom, the light of your true Son, our Lord and Saviour Jesus Christ; giving thanks through him to you with him and the Holy Spirit, we offer the reasonable sacrifice and this unbloody service, which all nations offer you "from sunrise to sunset", from south to north, for your "name is great among all the nations, and in every place incense is offered to your holy name and a pure sacrifice."[28]

One of the peculiarities of *Mark* and its derivative anaphoras is that the offering takes place in the preface. There is a sense of conclusiveness about the quotation from Malachi 1:11, as if it were defining what the eucharist is supposed to be and do. An oft-quoted text among the Fathers, it naturally arises out of the presupposition that the church is offering "this unbloody service." (The later version of *Mark* in Greek reads "this reasonable and unbloody service," though the Coptic keeps "sacrifice" after "reasonable," following *Strasbourg*— probably the more authentic reading anyway.[29]) As if to locate enthusiasm for bloodlessness even more firmly in Egypt, the Anaphora of *Serapion of Thumis* has the following immediately after the *Sanctus*:

> Full is heaven, full also is earth of your excellent glory, Lord of the powers. Fill also this sacrifice with your power and your partaking; for to you we offered this living sacrifice, this unbloody offering.[30]

It will be noted how the *Sanctus* leads naturally into this assertion. The words are slightly different from *Strasbourg/Mark*, the word "living" taken from Romans 12:1, an unusual combination, only found in the East Syrian Anaphora of *Nestorius* and in the pre-anaphoral prayer in *Theodore*, as we shall see.

Strasbourg/Mark posit the offering in the thanksgiving, whereas *Serapion* has it at the point where the prayer moves from thanksgiving to supplication. But that proves the rule that the material within these prayers is determined by the overall shape. Moreover, *Serapion* uses the past tense ("we offered"), probably referring to an earlier action.[31]

West Syria, East Syria, Armenia

The remaining anaphoras have a similar shape. Unlike the Egyptian prayers where the offering of "unbloody" sacrifice takes place in the first part, the Syrian anaphoras vary between the anamnesis-epiclesis and the intercessions. But it must be clear from the outset that our term is by no means universal in these prayers.

The Anaphora of *John Chrysostom* has the expression once—at the start of the epiclesis: "We offer you this reasonable and unbloody service, and we pray and beseech you . . ."[32] From the point of view of euchological structure, the occurrence of this formula here can be compared with *Mark*, for it comes at the juncture between thanksgiving and supplication. It is also a verbatim copy (or the other way around) of *Greek Mark* (*Coptic Mark*, as we saw, has the probably earlier reading of "sacrifice" after "reasonable"). Interestingly, this prayer begins the commemorations of the departed and the living with "we offer you this reasonable service for . . .," omitting "unbloody," but this is likely to be the result of a wish for some verbal variety. The thrust of the threefold repetition serves to bring out the accentuation on supplication in this part of the prayer: the anaphora gives thanks for creation and redemption, and then goes on to plead for the work of the Spirit on the eucharist, and among the departed and the living. It could be maintained, however, that the fact that "unbloody" only occurs at the start of the first of the three petitions is because it refers explicitly to the eucharist, which the epiclesis immediately following it is meant to fulfill. But that may be too precise a kind of explanation, running against the more general notion of the eucharistic sacrifice which the earlier tradition tried to explore.[33]

Is there a correspondence between the Anaphora of *John Chrysostom* and the quotation by him discussed earlier? In view of the fact that the quotation relates to the *Sanctus* and its adjacent material, such a contention would be hard to substantiate, save in the most general of terms. But it is interesting, nonetheless, that the correspondence is there at all, in view of the scanty references there are to the term.

The anaphora in the Liturgy of *St. James* has a similar usage of the term under discussion. As the anamnesis turns into the epiclesis, we read: "We offer you, Master, this awesome and unbloody sacrifice, asking you . . ."[34] The word "awesome" is a favorite epithet in *James*, occurring on two other occasions. The Syriac version also has this expression at the start of the commemoration of the living.[35] (*James* has them in that order and *with* the word "unbloody," unlike *Chrysostom*). Like *Chrysostom*, however, the emphasis remains on supplication in connection with the use of this term.

The other anaphoras all come from the large collection now seldom, if ever, used in the Syrian Churches today. *Twelve Apostles*, like many others, only has "reasonable sacrifice" at the start of the intercessions.[36] *Timotheus of Alexandria* follows the lead of *Chrysostom* in an original juncture between anamnesis and epiclesis.

> Have mercy upon us, O God, Father almighty, and receive from the hands of us sinners this reasonable and unbloody sacrifice, which we offer to you; a contrite and humbled heart do not despise, O Lord, but receive this sacrifice upon your reasonable altar . . .[37]

Here we have the addition of two elements: first, a quotation from Psalm 51:17 and, second, the notion of God *accepting* the offering, so much more prevalent in Western euchology, but nonetheless present in the East, particularly in the Syrian tradition.

Severus of Antioch, which probably dates from the seventh century, introduces another concept, known elsewhere, but not yet encountered in connection with our term. At the anamnesis we read: "Therefore, completing this unbloody sacrifice . . ."[38] And the idea of "completing" we have seen in two of the four quotations from Severus himself.[39]

Gregory John, like *James* (Syriac) has the word both at the anamnesis and the commemoration:

> We offer to your majesty this awesome and unbloody sacrifice . . . Be pleased, Lord, with this mystic sacrifice, awesome and unbloody, which is offered to you for the Church . . .[40]

The influence of *James* in "awesome and unbloody" and in the shape of ideas is apparent. The other Syrian anaphoras either use the term at the anamnesis or at the commemoration. At the anamnesis:[41]

> Therefore we offer to you this reasonable and unbloody sacrifice. (*Celestine of Rome*)

> You have commanded this single sacrifice to be offered by us, not with the blood of goats and bulls . . . but the reasonable and heavenly type of the blood of . . . (*Isaac*)

At the commemoration[42] (intercessions):

> We offer you this awesome and unbloody sacrifice for . . . (*Moses Bar-Cephas*)

> Therefore I offer you this spiritual and unbloody sacrifice for . . . (*Dioscurus*)

> Remember, Lord, over this spiritual and unbloody sacrifice all orders . . . (*John of Saba*)

> We offer you Lord this awesome and unbloody sacrifice. (*James of Seruq*)

> We offer this awesome and unbloody sacrifice. (*John Patriarch of Antioch*)

> Therefore we offer you this spiritual and unbloody sacrifice. (*Philoxenus of Baghdad*)

> We offer you this living, holy, acceptable, awesome, exalted and unbloody sacrifice for all creatures. (*Nestorius*)

Further influence from *James* suggests that, while it was easier to drop than to introduce afresh in the composition of these anaphoras, the word "unbloody" of the sacrifice was common coin. But there is still the sense in which it has to find a home, almost as if imposed from outside on each anaphoral tradition: in *Mark* in the preface; in *Serapion* after the *Sanctus*; in *James* at the heart of the anamnesis; in *Chrysostom* at the start of the epiclesis; and in other prayers at the beginning of the intercessions. The Armenian Anaphora of *Isaac* takes a more original line, using Hebrews 10:4 to refashion eucharistic oblation in another variation of language which skirts the terrain of the original thinking lying behind our term.

One prominent anaphora of the West Syrian family, however, does not use our expression at all (*Basil of Caesarea*); and there are about seventy West Syrian prayers in all. It must not be thought that the "unbloody sacrifice" is popular. Ironically, Cyril of Alexandria seems to quote an anaphora with the term in the anamnesis-epiclesis, when the Alexandrian Anaphora of *Mark* has it in the preface; and Chrysostom seems to quote one with the term near the *Sanctus*, when the anaphora with his name has it at the start of the epiclesis. This later position expresses prayer that is costly, sacrificial, self-oblatory, but the variations probably reflect the wider earlier view of sacrifice itself.

Eastern Liturgies: Other Prayers

In the three main West Syrian liturgies, we find the term in a few places. *Chrysostom*, in the celebrant's prayer during the prayer of the faithful, asks:

> Make us to become worthy of offering to you our needs and supplications and unbloody sacrifices for the whole people . . .[43]

In the Prayer of the Cherubikon, borrowed from *Basil*, reference is made to "this liturgical and unbloody sacrifice."[44] *Basil* also has, in the pre-anaphoral prayer, a passage reminiscent of the *Chrysostom* prayer:

> . . . that we may become worthy of offering to you this reasonable and unbloody sacrifice.[45]

James has a pre-anaphoral prayer which refers simply to "this spiritual and unbloody sacrifice."[46]

Only seven of the large number of Syrian anaphoras have a pre-anaphoral prayer using our term. There is some variety. Hence it is worth listing them.[47]

> Receive from us the oblation of this unbloody sacrifice. (*Twelve Apostles*)

... that you may receive ... this awesome, spiritual and unbloody sacrifice. (*Mark*)

... that we may offer to you the awesome and unbloody sacrifice. (*John*)

... we offer to you the awesome and unbloody sacrifice. (*Dioscurus*)

... we offer to you this awesome and unbloody sacrifice. (*John of Bosra*)

... to offer to you this spiritual and unbloody sacrifice. (*Holy Doctors*)

... we offer to you this living, holy, acceptable, exalted, reasonable, excellent and unbloody sacrifice. (*Theodore*)

What are we to make of this? First, there is no moment of offering, for that is a notion foreign to the Eastern liturgies. The pre-anaphoral prayers are preparatory in their nature, and if they have any sacrificial language, which many of them do, over and above the six that happen to use "unbloody" as a liturgical term, then this is by way of describing the eucharistic action as focused on the anaphora and communion. The "unbloody sacrifice" is the whole of that prayer and action.

Second, as with the anaphoras themselves, the term "unbloody" refers, if it does to any part at all, to the general activity of the church pleading the work of Christ. The prayer of the church is a costly exercise, as is in particular the work of intercession.

Third, the influence of *James* (or its archetype) is perhaps apparent in the six Syrian prayers listed above. The words "awesome" and "unbloody" go together, occasionally accompanied by "spiritual," in a way similar to the anaphoras.

Fourth, East Syrian prolixity is noticeable in *Theodore*, like the Anaphora of *Nestorius*, and both have the unusual "living" (Rom 12:1), first encountered in *Serapion*.

The West: Almost Silence

In his classic introduction, *The Early History of the Liturgy*, J.H. Srawley sets the Roman Canon side-by-side with the corresponding section of Ambrose's *De Sacramentis*, and by the use of italics brings out the main discrepancies between the two.[48] One of them is the use of the word *incruentam* in the anamnesis of the word *hostiam*. He then goes on to note:

> The phrase "unbloody offering" (incruentam hostiam) in the prayer *Ergo memores* is a common phrase in early Greek fathers. It is also found in Serapion, in the liturgies of St James, the Syriac St James, St Basil, St Chrysostom, and in some Gallican forms.[49]

It would seem that Ambrose has *added* the word to the list of epithets, after *immaculatam* and *rationabilem*, or else that he inherited something like it. What is beyond doubt is that he is exceptional in the West. We know that he was well-acquainted with the Greek Fathers and could quote Basil in Greek. The silence of the West at this stage in the discussion is an eloquent one.

It is even more eloquent when one reads through page upon page of variable prayers making up the whole repertoire of Visigothic and Gallican compositions both within the eucharistic prayer and before it. One Gallican prayer has been cited by Lietzmann[50] and Botte,[51] which is clearly based directly upon Ambrose, and this explains why "unbloody" should appear in the *Missale Gothicum*.[52]

Still more surprising is the staggering silence in the later medieval Western offertory prayers. Tirot's recent study[53] of them has revealed diverse influences at work, and there are certain variations in vocabulary. But the word "unbloody" (*incruenta*) is simply nowhere to be found. On reason is that, following Willis,[54] we may fall back on the assumption that these offertory prayers not only came to be regarded as a "mini-canon" but owe their sequence of ideas partly to the Canon. This would suggest that, if the Canon in some sense was a determining influence on the evolution of these offertory prayers, ideas and language foreign to the Canon might stand a smaller chance of entry into this new layer of material. Recent studies of the language of Latin prayers, in the Roman prefaces, by Michael Witczak, and in the *apologiae* of the Missa of Illyricus Flaccus, by Joanne Pierce[55] have shown what a delicate and intricate process the writing of prayers can be. We shall return to this point later. I think that the fundamental reason for *incruenta* never gaining full acceptance in the West is that it lacked the first background of apologetic which its Greek counterpart had in the formative centuries in the East. There was no Athenagoras to provide its root and base in an important center; there was no opportunity for it to develop its own life with evolving eucharistic prayers. It could then be that the term was thought awkward—or even unnecessary. But the Western silence is a loud one. Even Augustine, who must have known the expression from his time in Milan under Ambrose, does not mention it once.

Anglican Reinterpretation

Western liturgical texts were, indeed, silent on the *hostia incruenta*, but the theme recurred among Catholic theologians. At the Council of Trent the matter is defined as a way of expressing the nature of the eucharistic memorial.

> *Et quoniam in divino hoc sacrificio, quod in missa peragitur, idem ille Christus continetur, et incruente immolatur, qui in ara crucis semel se ipsum cruente obtulit.*[56]

This was cited with approval by John Fisher, and Thomas Murner, and already in 1528 articulated much the same approach.[57] Cuthbert Tunstall, who was bishop of Durham in the reign of Henry VIII, in supporting the doctrine of eucharistic sacrifice, looked to the East: "The Greeks call the whole action *anaimaktos thusia*, that is, the unbloody sacrifice.[58] It continued to be employed by Catholic writers down to our own time, for example, by de la Taille,[59] but it was never central, and never given liturgical expression, even at the time when it could have most easily entered the *lex orandi*—after the Second Vatican Council.

The Reformers, however, toyed with the idea. At his trial Nicholas Ridley, in answer to Pie's assertion that the priest "offereth an unbloody sacrifice," replied:

> It is called unbloody, and is offered after a certain manner and in a mystery, and as a representation of that bloody sacrifice; and he doth not lie, who saith Christ to be offered.[60]

A century later, Jeremy Taylor, in his "underground" rite for the eucharist used during the Commonwealth published in 1658, has an opening prayer which includes the following: ". . .to represent a holy, veenrable, and unbloudy Sacrifice . . ."[61] A little later, John Fell, Bishop of Oxford at the Restoration, took up the matter in a more exegetical mode, leaning on that favorite patristic text, Malachi 1:11:

> *Apud Christianos superest rationale et incruentum Sacrificium, quod Malachiae verbis Mincha puro, hoc est, Oblatione farrea cum suo libamine, Pane scilicet et Vino, vero illos semperque duraturo Sacrificio Eucharistico, et precum thymiamate constat.*[62]

Moreover, in his two-volume commentary on Isaiah, the Dutch Calvinist theologian, Campegius Vitringa, took much the same line.[63]

But where is it to be found in the liturgy? We have to travel to the very fringes of Anglicanism to take up the tale again. Our two earliest exponents are Edward Stephens and William Whiston. Stephens was a priest of the Church of England who was critical of its isolation, keen on international cooperation, and enthusiastic for an enriched liturgy. In 1696 he published no fewer than three liturgies, of increasing prolixity, the second and third of which contain this petition at the end of the anamnesis: "that this our Unbloody, Reasonable and Spiritual Sacrifice may be acceptable . . ." And he appends seven "theses" about eucharistic doctrine, the first of which expounds the "unbloody" as antitype of Jewish bloody offerings,[64] along the lines of Fell, among others.

Whiston, on the other hand, was a layman, deposed from his Cambridge Mathematics Chair in 1710 for Arianism, who in 1712 published *The Primitive Eucharist Reviv'd*, in which he discusses the question of the eucharistic sacrifice from the viewpoint of unbloodiness, again with typological concerns. But he does not go so far as to use the expression in his liturgy.[65]

The scene is now set for John Johnson, who was vicar of Cranbrook from 1710 until his death in 1725. He wrote a long treatise, with an awesomely lengthy title which is worth quoting in full:

> The Unbloody Sacrifice and Altar Unvailed and Supported, in which the Nature of the Eucharist is explained according to the sentiments of the Christian Church in the first four centuries, Proving that the Eucharist is a proper material Sacrifice,

that it is to be offered by proper officers, that the Oblation is to be made on a proper Altar, that it is properly consumed by manducation.[66]

In an age that specialized in long titles, this *is* a long one. For here is the most systematic treatment of the overall theme of eucharistic sacrifice so far seen in Anglicanism. The context in which Johnson was writing was the opposite to that of Athenagoras of old. In second-century Egypt, pagan sacrifices were two-a-penny, and organized religion of any kind would probably involve some kind of sacrifice, whether of animals or of cereal offerings. It was necessary at that time to show how the eucharist was *real* but *spiritual*. Johnson's world, however, was (he feared) dominated by an approach to the eucharist that was "a mere mental figurative sacrifice," in other words, a theology influenced by the aftermath of the Reformers. His priority, therefore, was to show that the eucharist was *spiritual* but *real*. Unlike Stephens and Whiston (who both wrote liturgies, though, as we have seen, only Stephens used the term in his rite), Johnson was an ordinary scholar-priest who remained loyal to the Church of England throughout his ministry. His book had a wide influence on traditional High Church Anglican eucharistic faith and practice.[67]

Johnson's book was (partially) answered by Daniel Waterland's *Review of the Doctrine of the Eucharist*.[68] Full of patristic, medieval, and contemporary Roman Catholic authorities, his book emerges as a moderate counterpoint to what he sees as Johnson's Catholicising tendencies, in particular, what he regards as Johnson's excessively *material* view of eucharistic sacrifice, due to sheer overemphasis. But balance, though an admirable concept, is sometimes a little hard to maintain when one is motivated towards writing on an aspect of a subject that the author feels strongly has been neglected or misunderstood.

Johnson's book was widely read by those Anglicans who left the Church of England as a result of the accession of King William in 1688. Refusing to take the oath of allegiance to an unlawful monarch (as they saw it), they formed a separate group which was soon called "Non Juror." Developing High Church tastes, they soon attempted liturgical reform, and in 1718 their first eucharistic liturgy appeared.[69] It contains a pre-anaphoral prayer with the following words:

... may it please thee, O Lord, as we are ministers of the New Testament, and dispensers of thy holy mysteries, to receive us who are approaching thy Holy Altar, according to the multitude of thy mercies, that we may be worthy to offer unto thee this reasonable and unbloody Sacrifice for our Sins and the Sins of the People ...

It is interesting to note the way in which different insights are brought together in a prayer which includes at this point a direct quotation from the pre-anaphoral prayer in *Basil*. It need hardly be added that the eucharistic prayer in this liturgy is the result of considerable reworking of the Book of Common Prayer (1662), though, like *Basil*, it lacks any reference to the "unbloody sacrifice" in its anaphora, possibly out of imitation, perhaps because of the unfamiliarity of the term. The second Non-Juror liturgy (1734) did not contain the *Basil* reference, but this may be explained by the fact that its pre-anaphoral prayer is to be said over the alms, and before the preparation of the bread and wine.[70] But the Scottish Non-Juror liturgist, Thomas Rattray,[71] has "we offer . . . this tremendous and unbloody sacrifice" in the anamnesis of an anaphora already reflecting his predilection for *James*. Both Johnson's book, the two Non-Juror rites, and Rattray's liturgy influenced the production of the Scottish liturgy of 1764 and its accompanying sacramental tradition, which in turn influenced the American Prayer Book of 1789, thus producing an authentic strand of Anglican eucharistic thought and rite that was quite distinct from England, and which is still alive in the Anglican Communion today. But for all the interest in "unbloodiness," the term never found its way into *official* Anglican eucharistic texts.

But Anglicanism was already no stranger to the tradition of that very medieval tendency of creating devotional prayers for use while the liturgy was being celebrated, or else as a more general pious preparation. Thomas Wilson, for many years bishop of Sodor and Man (= the traditional name for the diocese of the Isle of Man, by this time) until his death in 1755, wrote a set of such prayers, one of which he used himself privately as celebrant:

May I atone unto Thee, O God,
by offering to Thee the pure and unbloody sacrifice,
which Thou hast ordained by Jesus Christ.[72]

Such language is a far cry from the other liturgies of the Reformation, and the pieties which they inculcated, and yet it expresses the way in which the doctrine of the eucharistic sacrifice could find a new milieu, in a different theological context from those of antiquity discussed earlier.

But our story is incomplete without taking in the typological interests and proleptic ecumenical aspirations of John Bate Cardale, the leading "Apostle" of the Catholic Apostolic Church, who died in 1877. In the passage quoted at the outset from the 1880 liturgy (but exactly the same as that contained in the 1842 edition of the same rite), one can see three strands:

a) "do present unto Thee this reasonable and unbloody sacrifice" (James);

b) "the holy bread of everlasting life and the cup of eternal salvation" (Roman Canon);

c) a style of English, together with scriptural allusion, in the tradition of the Book of Common Prayer.[73]

Ironically, there are no Non Jurors left (they died out in the course of the eighteenth century); prayers like those of Bishop Wilson, though important for coming generations, are simply not used any more since they belong to a liturgical genre shunned by the cognoscenti of today; and the last Catholic Apostolic priest died in 1971, thus bringing to an end the use of their liturgy. And yet by drawing consciously on the byways of church history for their liturgical and theological concerns, they demonstrate that the collective memory of the Church Universal is far bigger than what is going on and approved by the larger and official bodies. As we are learning to our cost in our own time, minority groups are important, for they frequently say things that the rest of us ignore at our peril.

Conclusion

Is there an abiding lesson to the curious tale of the "unbloody sacrifice"?

In one sense, it is simply a story of one way of describing the eucharist, a story which emerged out of the mists of antiquity and just happened to be around at the right time in the third and fourth centuries to gain admission into three of the main anaphoras of the East (Chrysostom, James, and Mark), thus ensuring that subsequent liturgiographers in the Greek and Syrian world would draw on it for future use. It was this movement of the formula, from an apologetic definition of *worship* to a concise and theological definition of the *eucharist*, adhesive to the tradition, that ensured that it would travel. And travel it did, first to Milan, because that cosmopolitan city had a cosmopolitan and well-read bishop; and from Milan the Gallican rite, ever keen on using other people's ideas, borrowed it.

Then, in a completely different world, that of the Reformation aftermath, the notion of the "unbloody sacrifice" became acceptable in a few quarters for entirely different reasons from those in antiquity. It was still apologetic, but it was of a different kind. The whole sweep of Anglican eucharistic theology in the seventeenth and eighteenth centuries is one of reappropriating the past in order to provide a more balanced picture of everything that the church stood for—not least its understanding of the eucharist.[74] Not for Athenagoras the fine definitions of sacrifice that need not involve death.[75] But one senses here another irony, that in the wake of the biggest and most wide-ranging debate about the eucharist the church had yet seen, focused on the Reformation, this time-honored patristic description of the eucharist only found a direct, devotional, and liturgical expression on the fringes of Western Protestantism.

In our own day, eucharistic sacrifice has come in for detailed examination, both in historical and ecumenical studies. It could be that a generation yet to come, which looks back on the warfare and ecological destruction of our century, might find some use for "unbloody sacrifice." Meanwhile, for all its careful contextualization, tucked away in the minds of early Greek theologians, bursting forth into classical anaphoras of the East, and feeding selected portions of the Christian West, patristic and Post-Reformation, it stands as an eloquent protest against those who, on the one hand, want to make worship so material that it is purely earthly, and those who, on the other hand, want it to be so spiritual that it has no outward form.[76] Once again, when looking at a gem from another tradition, one is led to appreciate the paradox which lies at the heart of the incarnation.

But the eucharist is not only a celebration of the incarnation.

It is a proclamation of the Lord's death until he comes (1 Cor 11:26), and this means it is also a celebration of the atonement. One of the most fruitful developments in the *rapprochement* between the churches of the East and West in this century has been the way in which we have looked again at our roots, and have discovered much in common as we respond to a much-changed world. In the progress towards agreement on eucharistic sacrifice, some of the methods that lie behind the very writers, doctrinal as well as liturgical, whose work has been placed under scrutiny in our survey, have produced remarkable results. But perhaps one reason why the "unbloody sacrifice" remains a bit of a stranger to parts of Western Catholic tradition is that it pulls somewhat in the opposite direction from the Augustinian view of the eucharist, which has always seen our offering united with Christ's offering. The "unbloody sacrifice" by contrast gazes at the uniqueness of Christ's eternal work, only thereby finding a place in heaven—and on earth, But, as these remarks will have shown, the "unbloody sacrifice," once rooted in the very theological tradition which nourished it into a liturgical formula, is a powerful vehicle of praise and prayer for those Eastern Christians who still use these rich and resonant prayers as they gather around that heavenly altar.[77]

In retrospect, it seems almost inevitable that this very Greek term should not quite find its own feet in Latin Christianity, save as a tool for the theologians, especially those with typological interests. And so much Post-Reformation piety is cross-centered (and rightly so), that there would appear to be little space for a way of looking at the eucharist which is, at first sight, potentially confusing. The eucharistic hymns of the eighteenth-century writers Isaac Watts[78] and the Wesleys[79] are so intent on the "bleeding love and mercy" of the crucified Christ, so powerful in their memorial-theology, that there is no room left for another motif, however historic, however orthodox, however vivid. But no one can affirm that the story of eucharistic faith and practice is complete[80] without this fascinating, paradoxical, and undervalued term—the unbloody sacrifice of the church.

The Origin and Development of 'Unbloody Sacrifice'

1. Literary Background

2nd century:	*Testament of Levi*	Athenagoras and Origen (both Egypt)	*all worship*
3rd/4th	Eusebius	Cyril of Jerusalem	Gregory of Nazianzus	*eucharist*
5th/6th	Cyril of Alexandria	Severus of Antioch	

2 Ancient Liturgies

? Strasburg papyrus: **end**   Serapion: **after Sanctus**   James: **anamnesis**   ? 12 Apostles: **interc's**
Chrysostom: **epiclesis.**

Mark: **preface**

Severus
Gregory John
Celestine
Isaac

Timotheus

Ambrose

Missale Gothicum

Moses Bar-C
Diosc
John of S
James of S
John Patr
Philoxen
Nestorius

NB 1 Use of term in such widely differing positions
2 Use of term also in pre-anaphoral prayers, and in earlier parts of liturgy

3 Modern Liturgies

Jeremy Taylor (1658)	: **intro prayer:**	cf James, Chrysostom in general
Edward Stephens (1696)	: **anamnesis:**	cf James
Non Jurors (1718)	: **pre-anaphoral prayer**	cf James, Chrysostom &c...
Thomas Rattray (1744-posthumus)	: **anamnesis:**	cf James
Catholic Apostolic (1842-1880)	: **anamnesis:**	cf James

NB 1 The term common coin in certain theological circles
2 ...but only used in these 'fringe' liturgies

Notes

1. See, for example, the overview by Geoffrey Cuming, "The Early Eucharistic Liturgies in Recent Research," in *The Sacrifice of Praise: Studies on the Themes of Thanksgiving and Redemption in the Central Prayers of the Eucharistic and Baptismal Liturgies*, ed., Bryan Spinks, Ephemerides Liturgicae "Subsidia" 19 (Rome: Edizioni Liturgiche, 1981) 65-69; see also R.C.D. Jasper, *The Search for an Apostolic Liturgy*, Alcuin Club Pamphlet 18 (London: Mowbrays, 1963).

2. An attempt to redress the balance is Kenneth Stevenson, *Eucharist and Offering* (New York: Pueblo Publishing Co., 1986).

3. André Tarby, *La Prière eucharistique de l'église de Jerusalem*, Théologie historique 17 (Paris: Beauchesne, 1972) 138ff (anamnesis), 185ff (suggested prayer).

4. See Kenneth Stevenson, "The Catholic Apostolic Church—Its History and Its Eucharist," *Studia Liturgica* 13 (1979) 21-45; see also Kenneth Stevenson, "The Catholic Apostolic Eucharist," PhD dissertation, University of Southampton, 1975. See also forthcoming section on this rite in *Coena Domini* II. See also David H. Tripp, "The Liturgy of the Catholic Apostolic Church," *Scottish Journal of Theology* 22 (1969) 437-454.

5. *Liturgy and Other Divine Offices of the Church* (London: Pitmans, 1880) 11. See also Stevenson, dissertation 149ff.

6. See the official commentary by John Bate Cardale (anonymously), *Readings upon the Liturgy and Other Divine Offices of the Church*, vol. 1 (London: Bosworth, 1874) 170ff.

7. Robert Daly, *Christian Sacrifice: The Judaeo-Christian Background before Origen*, The Catholic University of America Studies in Christian Antiquity 18 (Washington, D.C.: The Catholic University of America Press, 1978) 147ff.

8. *T. Levi* 3,3-5 (*prospherontes . . . osmên euôdias logikên kai anaimakton thusian*). See Rowan Williams, *Eucharistic Sacrifice: The Roots of a Metaphor*, Grove Liturgical Study 31 (Bramcote: Grove, 1982) 13, n.5 (and, in general, this most useful study).

9. Daniel Waterland, *A Review of the Doctrine of the Eucharist*, ed., Bishop Van Mildert (Oxford: Clarendon Press, 1896) 357ff.

10. See Stevenson, *Eucharist and Offering* 10ff.

11. *Legatio* 15,2 (*ti dei holokautôseon, hôn mê deitai ho Theos? kai toi prospherein deon anaimakton thusian, kai tên logikên prosagein latreian*).

12. Geoffrey J. Cuming, *The Liturgy of St. Mark*, Orientalia Christiana Analecta 234 (Rome: Pontificium Institutum Studiorum Orientalium, 1990) 107.

13. *Contra Celsum* 8,21 (*thuôn tas anaimaktas en tais . . . euchais thusias*).

14. *Martyrium Apollonii* 8. Quoted by Cuming, *The Liturgy of St. Mark* 108 (*thusian anaimakton . . . anapempô . . . tên di'euchôn*).

15. *Symposium* 5, 6 (*thusiastêrion anaimakton*).

16. *Demonstratio Evangelica* 1,10 (*ta semna tês Christou trapezês thumata, di'hôn . . . anaimaktas kai logikas . . . thusias . . . prospherein . . . dedidagmetha*).

17. *Catechesis* 5,8. English translation in R.C.D. Jasper and G.J. Cuming, *The Prayers of the Eucharist: Early and Reformed*, 3d ed. (New York: Pueblo Publishing Co., 1987) 86. (*eita meta to apartisthênai tên pneumatikên thusian, tên anaimakton latreian, epi tês thusias ekeinês tou hilasmou, parakaloumen ton theon huper koinês tôn ekklêsiôn eirênês.*)

18. See *Vidi Dominum* 6,3. For full discussion see Frans Van De Paverd, *Zur Geschichte der Messliturgie in Antiocheia und Konstantinopel gegen Ende des Vierten Jahrhunderts*, Orientalia Christiana Analecta 187 (Rome: Pontificium Institutum Orientalium Studiorum, 1970) 278. (*dia touto kai ho megas houtos archiereus, epeidan epi tês hagias tautês hestêkê trapezês, tên logikên anapherôn latreian, tên anaimakton prospherôn thusia, ouch haplôs hêmas epi tên euphêmian tautên kalei. . .*)

19. *Epistula* 17 (*kataggelontes . . . homologountes, tên anaimakton en tais ekklêsiais teloumen latreian prosimen te houtô tais mustikais eulogiais*). See *De adoratione* 13 (*tês anaimaktou thusias epiteloumenês*).

20. *Oratio catechetica* 18 (*semnên te kai anaimakton hierosunên*).

21. *Epistula* 171 (*anaimaktô tomê*).

22. *Comentarii in XII prophetas*, Mal. 1:10 (*kathara kai anaimaktos*).

23. R.P.C. Hanson, *Eucharistic Offering in the Early Church*, Grove Liturgical Study 19 (Bramcote: Grove, 1979) passim.

24. Geoffrey J. Cuming, "The Liturgy of Antioch in the Time of Severus (513-518)" in *Time and Community: In Honor of Thomas J. Talley*, ed., J. Neil Alexander (Washington, D.C.: The Pastoral Press, 1990) 89-90 (whole essay, 83-103). The cited passages are: *Hymn* 209 (vii.673), *Hymn* 346 (vii.780), *Hymn* 73 (vi.117), *Epistula* 24 (xii. 221), and *Epistula*, Book VI (II.245).

25. See Daly, *Christian Sacrifice*; Frances M. Young, *The Use of Sacrificial Ideas in Greek Christian Writers from the New Testament to John Chrysostom*, Patristic Monograph Series 5 (Philadelphia: Patristic Foundation, 1979); and Hanson, *Eucharistic Offering*. See also R. Albertine, "Selected Survey of the Theme "Spiritual Sacrifice" to Augustine," *Ephemerides Liturgicae* 104 (1990) 35-50.

26. See note 12 above.

27. Geoffrey Cuming, "The Anaphora of St. Mark: A Study in Development," *Muséon* 95 (1982) 115-129.

28. English translation in Jasper and Cuming, *The Prayers of the Eucharist* 53. See also Cuming, *The Liturgy of St. Mark* 21ff. (*panta de epoiêsas dia tês sophias sou tou phôtos tou aletheinou sou huiou tou kuriou*

kai sôteros hêmon Iêsou Christou, di'hou soi kai sun autô sun hagiô pneumati eucharistountes prospheromen tên thusian tên logikên, tên anaimakton latreian tautên, hên prospherei soi panta ta ethnê ap'anatolôn heliou kai mechri dusmôn apo arktou kai en panti topô thumiama prospheretai tô hagiô sou onomati, kai thusia kathara . . .)

29. See Cuming, *The Liturgy of St. Mark* 21f.

30. English translation in Jasper and Cuming, *The Prayers of the Eucharist* 77. See also Anton Hänggi and Irmgard Pahl, *Prex Eucharistica: Textus e Variis Liturgiis Antiquioribus Selectis*, Spicilegium Friburgense 12 (Fribourg: Presses Universitaries, 1968) 131. (*plêrês estin ho ouranos, plêrês estin kai hê ge tês megaloprepous sou doxês, kurie tên dunameôn. Plêrôson kai tên thusian tautên tês sês dunameôs kai tês sês megalêpseôs; soi gar prosenengkamen tautên tên zôsan thusia tên prosphoran tên anaimakton.*)

31. Kenneth Stevenson, "'Anaphoral Offering': Some Observations on Eastern Eucharistic Prayers," *Ephemerides Liturgicae* 94 (1980) 225ff. See also Stevenson, *Eucharist and Offering*, passim; on the Eastern prayers, esp. 30ff and 105ff.

32. English translation in Jasper and Cuming, *The Prayers of the Eucharist* 133. (The editors note: "The ancient phrase 'this reasonable and bloodless service' is prominent in the anamnesis and the intercessions, which it links closely with the offering . . ." [p. 129].) See also Hänggi and Pahl, *Prex Eucharistica* 226. (*eti prospheromen soi tên logikên tautên kai anaimakton latreian.*)

33. In this connection see Bryan Spinks, "Eucharistic Offering in the East Syrian Anaphoras," *Orientalia Christiana Periodica* 50 (1984) 347-371.

34. English translation in Jasper and Cuming, *The Prayers of the Eucharist* 92. See also Hänggi and Pahl, *Prex Eucharistica* 248. (*prospheromen soi, despota, tên phoberan tautên kai anaimakton thusian, deomenoi . . .*)

35. Hänggi and Pahl, *Prex Eucharistica* 271f.

36. Ibid. 267.

37. Ibid. 280. See also H.W. Codrington, A. Raes, A. Rücker, *Anaphorae Syriacae*, vol. 1, fasc. I (Rome: Pontificium Institutum Studiorum Orientalium, 1939) 21.

38. Hänggi and Pahl, *Prex Eucharistica* 283. See also Codrington, Raes, and Rücker, *Anaphorae Syriacae* 69.

39. See note 24 above.

40. O. Heiming and A. Raes, *Anaphorae Syriacae*, vol. 2, fasc. II (Rome: Pontificium Institutum Studiorum Orientalium, 1953) 221.

41. H.G. Codrington, A. Raes, J.-M. Sauget, *Anaphorae Syriacae*, vol. 2, fasc. III (Rome: Pontificium Institutum Studiorum Orientalium, 1972) 253 (*Celestine of Rome*); Hänggi and Pahl, *Prex Eucharistica* 335 (*Isaac*).

42. For *Moses Bar-Cephas*, see E. Renaudot, *Liturgiarum Orientalium Collectio*, vol. 2 (Frankfurt: Baer, 1847) 393. For *Dioscurus*, see A. Raes, W. de Vries, *Anaphorae Syriacae*, vol. 1, fasc. III (Rome: Pontificium Institutum Studiorum Orientalium, 1944) 311. For *John of Saba*, see H.G. Codrington and A. Raes, *Anaphorae Syriacae*, vol. 3, fasc. I (Rome: Pontificium Institutum Studiorum Orientalium, 1951) 97. For *James of Serug*, see ibid. 23. For *John Patriarch of Antioch*, see Renaudot, *Liturgiarum Orientalium Collectio* 477. For *Philoxenus of Baghdad*, see ibid. 402. For *Nestorius*, see ibid. 624.

43. See F.E. Brightman, *Liturgies Eastern and Western* (Oxford: Clarendon Press, 1896) 375. (*poiêson hêmas axious genesthai tou prospherein soi deêseis kai hikesias kai thusias anaimaktous huper pantos tou laou.*)

44. See ibid. 377 (*Chrysostom*) and 319 (*Basil*). On this relationship see Robert F. Taft, *The Great Entrance: A History of the Transfer of Gifts and Other Preanaphoral Rites of the Liturgy of St. John Chrysostom*, Orientalia Christiana Analecta 200 (Rome: Pontificium Institutum Studiorum Orientalium, 1975) 364 ff. The texts of both are as follows: *tês leitourgikês tautês kai anaimaktou thusias tên hierourgian paredôkas.*

45. See note 44 above.

46. See Brightman, *Liturgies* 47 (*soi tên pneumatikên tautên kai anaimakton thusian*).

47. For *Twelve Apostles*, see Renaudot, *Liturgiarum Orientalium Collectio* 170. For *Mark*, see ibid. 176. For *John*, see ibid. 255. For *Dioscurus*, see ibid. 286. For *John of Bosra*, see ibid. 357. For *Holy Doctors*, see ibid. 410. For *Theodore*, see ibid. 611; see added epithets in *Nestorius* n.42.

48. *De sacramentis* 6,27 in Hänggi and Pahl, *Prex Eucharistica* 421f. See J.H. Srawley, *The Early History of the Liturgy*, Cambridge Handbooks of Liturgical Study, (Cambridge: University Press, 1949) 158.

49. Srawley, *The Early History* 161. See also K. Gamber, "Eine Frühreform des römischen Messkanons zur 'Prex Mystica'," *Ephemerides Liturgicae* 103 (1989) 494ff.

50. Hans Lietzmann, *Mass and Lord's Supper: A Study in the History of the Liturgy* (Leiden: Brill, 1979) 48ff.

51. Bernard Botte, *Le Canon de la Messe romaine: Edition critique* (Louvain: Abbaye du Mont César, 1935) 41.

52. L.K. Mohlberg, *Missale Gothicum*, Rerum Ecclesiasticarum Documenta: Series Maior, Fontes 5 (Rome: Herder, 1961) 120 (no. 527).

53. Paul Tirot, *Histoire des prières d'offertoire dans la liturgie romaine du VIIè au XVIè siècle*, Ephemerides Liturgicae Bibliotheca "Subsidia" 34 (Rome: Edizioni Liturgiche, 1985). See also our discussion of this issue: Stevenson, *Eucharist and Offering* 112, which takes into account Tirot's work and builds on it.

54. G.G. Willis, "The Offertory Prayers and the Canon of the Mass," in *Essays in Early Roman Liturgy*, Alcuin Club Collections 46 (London: SPCK, 1964) 107-110.

55. Michael Witczak, *The Language of Eucharistic Sacrifice: Immolare and Immolatio in Prefaces of the Roman Tradition* (Rome: Pontificium Athenaeum Anselmianum, 1987). Joanne Pierce, "Sacerdotal Spirituality at Mass: Text and Study of the Prayerbook of Sigbert of Minden (1022-1036)," PhD Dissertation, University of Notre Dame, 1988.

56. Session XXII, cap. 2, quoted in B.J. Kidd, *The Later Mediaeval Doctrine of the Eucharistic Sacrifice*, Church Historical Society (London: SPCK, 1958) 86. For a discussion of the wider issue of eucharistic sacrifice, see David N. Power, O.M.I., *The Sacrifice We Offer: The Tridentine Dogma and Its Reinterpretation* (Edinburgh: T and T Clark, 1987). It is clear that the "unbloody sacrifice" did *not* loom as a central issue.

57. Quoted in Francis Clark, *Eucharistic Sacrifice and the Reformation*, 2d ed. (Chumley: Augustine Publishing, 1967) 528 and 534.

58. Quoted in Clark, *Eucharistic Sacrifice* 536f.

59. See M. de la Taille, *Mysterium Fidei de Augustissimo Corporis et Sanguinis Christi Sacrificio atque Sacramento* (Paris: Beauchesne, 1921), Elucidatio XX, Sectio II (255ff). On the background to some of the post-Vatican II reforms, see Cipriano Vagaggini, *The Canon of the Mass and Liturgical Reform* (London: Chapman, 1967) for documentation.

60. See *Nicolas Ridley, Works*, ed., H. Christmas (Cambridge: Parker Society, 1841) 250. See also the "anamnetic" use of the term on p. 210.

61. See W.J. Grisbrooke, *Anglican Liturgies of the Seventeenth and Eighteenth Centuries*, Alcuin Club Collections 40 (London: SPCK, 1958) 185. Taylor's rite, though unofficial, was influential. Simon Patrick, for example, uses the expression in *Mens Mystica, or a Discourse Concerning the Sacrament of the Lord's Supper* (London: Tyton, 1660) 18. On Taylor's very original understanding of the eucharist, see H.R. McAdoo, *The Eucharistic Theology of Jeremy Taylor Today* (Norwich: Canterbury Press, 1988).

62. Quoted from John Johnson, *The Unbloody Sacrifice* (London: Knaplock, 1718), (Reprinted: Oxford: Parker, 1847) 351.

63. See Waterland, *A Review of the Doctrine of the Eucharist* 386 for a quotation from Vitringa's *magnum opus*, his two volume commentary on Isaiah (1714, 1720): "oblatio omnis quae fit a credentibus sub Novo Testamento, est incruenta, et vero castissima, et simplicissima, quia spiritualis. Sive quis se ipsum, sive *sôma* suum, affectum, omnesque suas facultates et actiones Deo offerat ut sacrificium; sive alia *schesei*, ministri verbi, qui in nobis convertendis laborarunt, nos offerant Deo; sive preces, *eucharistias* supplicationes nostras feramus

ad Deum, ubique eadem ratio: nullius hic funditur sanguis, nihil committitur violentum; actio tota est spiritualis, et *logikê*." (On Isaiah 65:21)

64. See Grisbrooke, *Anglican Liturgies* 226 and 241 (liturgies) and 47 (theology).

65. See ibid. 59f.

66. See note 62 above. The parish church at Cranbrook is dedicated to St. Dunstan, and contains an oak font-cover, depicting Dunstan, carved by the writer's father, The Reverend Doctor Erik Stevenson.

67. See, for example, R.F. Buxton, *Eucharist and Institution Narrative*, Alcuin Club Collections 58 (Great Wakering: Mayhew-McCrimmon, 1976) 153ff.

68. See note 9 above.

69. See Grisbrooke, *Anglican Liturgies* 286; see also 71ff for discussion of Johnson's influence, though the other antecedents mentioned in our study should not be overlooked.

70. See ibid. 305f.

71. See ibid. 325.

72. Quoted from G.W.O. Addleshaw, *The High Church Tradition: A Study in the Liturgical Thought of the Seventeenth Century* (London: Faber and Faber, 1941) 183. See also C.W. Dugmore, *Eucharistic Doctrine in England from Hooker to Waterland* (London: SPCK, 1942) 151ff on Wilson's eucharistic devotions.

73. See notes 4 and 5 above. See also Stevenson, *Eucharist and Offering* 183ff. and nn.

74. See Buxton, *Eucharist and Institution Narrative*; Addleshaw, *The High Church Tradition*; Dugmore, *Eucharistic Doctrine*.

75. This was one of Johnson's concerns.

76. Charles Gore captures the spirit of what the Greek Fathers were trying to say: "But all this language of disparagement of material sacrifices still leaves them on their own ground recognizing that the worship in spirit and in truth is not a mere inward and individual approach to God, but a corporate and therefore outward thing—a worship which publicly acknowledges God in all His gifts, though He needs them not; and a worship which finds central expression in the eucharist, in which, according to the ordinance of Christ, bread and wine are presented to the Father, in the name of the Son, and in memorial of His passion, with the adoration and prayer and thanksgiving of sins, and blessed by the Holy Spirit to become the Lord's body and blood, and partaken of by the worshippers that they may be bound all together in Him. That was for Christians the chief and central expression of rational service and bloodless sacrifice." Charles Gore, *The Body of Christ* (London: Murray, 1901) 161f.

77. See in general T.F. Torrance, "The Mind of Christ in Worship: The Problem of Apollinarianism in the Liturgy," in *Theology in Reconciliation: Essays towards Evangelical and Catholic Unity in East and West* (London: Chapman, 1975) 139-214, esp. 184, where he waxes lyrical about *Mark*, "unbloody sacrifice" and all, in its Christological sensitivity.

78. See, for example, "When I Survey the Wondrous Cross," usually sung in Passiontide in our day, but originally written "for the Lord's Supper," *The Psalms of David Imitated in New Testament Language: Together with Hymns and Spiritual Songs in Three Books* by the Rev. Isaac Watts, D.D. (London: Haddon, 1862) 163.

79. See J. Ernest Rattenbury, *The Eucharistic Hymns of John and Charles Wesley* (London: Epworth, 1948) 247. There is no mention of the "unbloody sacrifice" in Daniel Brevint, dean of Lincoln from 1682 until his death in 1695, who was so influential on Wesley's eucharistic theology.

80. The ecumenical potential of the theme (it could be argued) has yet to be fully exploited, and might perhaps serve to clarify confusions and misunderstandings surrounding differing perceptions of eucharistic memorial and the "realness" of the eating and drinking in the presence of Christ.

8

The Priestly Prayer: The Tridentine Theologians and the Roman Canon

David N. Power

IN THE TRIDENTINE DECREE ON THE SACRIFICE OF THE MASS, CANON SIX defends the Roman Canon of the Mass against the accusation of error and against the demand of the Reformers for its abrogation.[1] This Canon is also treated in chapter four of the decree, where its origins are described in this way: *Is enim constat cum ex ipsis Domini verbis, tum ex Apostolorum traditionibus ac sanctorum quoque Pontificum piis institutionibus.*[2] Such teaching and discipline were necessary to the preservation of the doctrine and practice of the eucharistic sacrifice because the Reformers' attack on the Canon was integral to their attack on the sacrifice of the Mass. At the same time, the ascription of the prayer to the Gospel, to apostolic tradition, and to certain holy pontiffs looks rather odd to those more familiar with current historical studies on the eucharistic prayer in general and on the Roman Canon in particular. It can be understood only against the background of Reformation dispute and conciliar deliberation. As we pursue those debates, especially what was said during the conciliar sessions, it is of interest to liturgical studies to see the close connection between ideas about this prayer and doctrinal positions. It is an important and concrete

example of the connection often expressed through the phrase
lex orandi lex credendi and of the ambiguities of that connection.

The Canon as Liturgical Unit

Before unfolding the discussion about it, it needs to be kept
in mind what sixteenth-century writers understood the Canon
to be. This holds for Reformers, Catholic controversialists, and
Tridentine theologians alike.

As had been customary for some centuries, a distinction was
made between the minor Canon and the major Canon, the former referring to the prayers of the offertory of the Mass and the
latter to its principal part.[3] The major Canon or the *Canon Ac-
tionis* was that section of the Mass which begins with the *Te igitur*. The authoritative lead, abundantly quoted, was taken from
Isidore of Seville's division of the eucharistic liturgy into seven
prayers of evangelical and apostolic root, the sixth being the
prayer which begins after the *Hosanna in excelsis* and concludes
with the Lord's Prayer, which is the seventh oration.[4] Isidore
was, of course, commenting on the Mozarabic Liturgy, and the
sixth prayer was the *Post-pridie* of that rite, but from the Tridentine debates one has the impression that theologians appear to
have been familiar only with the Roman and Ambrosian rites
in the West, and with those of Basil and John Chrysostom for
Eastern Christians. Consequently, the divisions of Isidore were
applied to the Roman Rite, and the sixth prayer was identified
with the prayer beginning *Te igitur*, identified as the Canon.
The conclusion of the Canon was not so firmly fixed. It could
be said to end with the Lord's Prayer, with the communion rite,
or even with the reading of the prologue of John's Gospel at the
end of the entire Mass.[5] Gabriel Biel, an important authority for
the century, put the end of the Canon at the Lord's Prayer,
quoting the authority of Albert the Great. However, he also
mentioned the opinion of Gulielmus Durandus and of Alexander Halensis who protracted it to the end of Mass.[6]

As is well known, various editions of the Roman Missal
marked off the Canon at the *Te igitur* with appropriate letter-
ing and illustration.[7] Commentaries, including the first popular exposition in German,[8] referred to this as the starting-point

of the priestly prayer, and the habit of its silent recitation had been established. Some medieval missals even introduced private prayers for the priest at the beginning or into the course of the Canon, to enhance his devotion.[9]

In light of the sixteenth-century attack and subsequent controversy, it is however of interest to note that authorities such as Isidore and Biel did not describe the Canon primarily as a prayer of offering. They saw it rather as a consecration of the offerings already proffered. This was how Isidore defined the sixth prayer,[10] now taken as the Canon. Biel had followed him in this, describing the Canon as the essential part of the sacrifice because it is the consecration of the gifts offered, transforming them into the body and blood of Christ. Describing it as the *secreta actio seu sacrificium*, he places it after the illumination of the people and the offering of gifts.[11] This was in effect to take the same understanding of sacrifice as is found in Thomas Aquinas, who in writing of the eucharist, divided its principal parts into offering, consecration, and communion, positin1g the essence of sacrifice as such in *sacrum facere* or consecration.[12]

When, however, controversy arose over the sacrificial nature of the Mass, all attention concentrated on the prominence given to offering in the words of the Canon. In effect, marking the beginning of the prayer at the *Te igitur* separated the prayers of offering and intercession from the thanksgiving expressed in the preface. Since this was still said aloud, it was connected with those parts of the Mass intended for the people's illumination or could even be identified with the sacrifice of thanksgiving that was considered distinct from sacrifice of propitiation. When in his original order for the Supper, Zwingli presented new prayers to precede the memorial proclamation of the Supper narrative,[13] he too was working on the assumption that the Canon began after the *Sanctus* and tried to substitute prayers that bore none of the offending language of sacrifice.

Attack upon the Canon

Starting with his work on *The Babylonian Captivity of the Church* in 1520,[14] through his work on *The Misuse of the Mass* in 1521[15] and on *Receiving Both Kinds* in 1522[16], and finally in *The*

Abomination of the Secret Mass in 1525[17], Martin Luther had made the Canon a central point of his repudiation of the offering of sacrifice. He did not attack it merely in general terms but even instituted a part-by-part criticism. The unfolding of the attack is anticipated in these words of *The Babylonian Captivity*.

> Now there is yet a second stumbling block that must be removed, and this is much greater and the most dangerous of all. It is the common belief that the Mass is a sacrifice, which is offered to God. Even the words of the canon seem to imply this, when they speak of "these gifts, these presents, these holy sacrifices", and further on "this offering". Prayer is also made, in so many words, "that the sacrifice may be accepted even as the sacrifice of Abel", etc. Hence Christ is termed "the sacrifice of the altar".[18]

In due course, the nicest thing that Luther could say about the Canon was that "it is a human word and work."[19] He contrasts it as a human work with the Supper words found in the New Testament, which must again become the form in which the sacrament is celebrated. In his examination of the particular sections of the Canon in *The Abomination of the Secret Mass*,[20] Luther had taken particular exception to the commemoration of the saints in the *Communicantes*, since it turned the Mass into a remembrance of the saints instead of a remembrance of Christ, and made them mediators who effectively replaced the one mediator, Christ. He also objected to the *Memento* for the living since it seemed to infer that an offering of bread and wine could win them salvation. In particularly strong terms he objected to the *Memento* for the dead, as he had elsewhere at some length repudiated the whole idea of Masses for the dead.[21]

The other strong attack on the Canon was that of Ulrich Zwingli in his *An Attack upon the Canon of the Mass* of 1523.[22] In repudiating the Mass as sacrifice and in upholding the evangelical origin of true celebration, Zwingli had marshalled a variety of arguments against the Canon. One of his principal aims was to show that it lacked an evangelical basis but was in fact a composition of relatively recent origin. His arguments in favor of this contention had the flavor of historical criticism. For one thing, he claims, it is a barbarous and rustic composition, one that could readily be attributed to a person such as

Gregory I, but certainly not savoring of any classical antiquity.[23] Zwingli appealed to historical evidence which showed,
according to him, that such authors as Alexander, Leo, Sergius, and Gregory had a hand in composing the prayer. This
meant that he was not prepared to give it that kind of antiquity and authority which would warrant calling it a *canon*.[24] The
Canon as now known can be described as a *congestio* of private
or public prayers put together by pious but not very learned
men.[25] By no means does it have evangelical or apostolic authority. Zwingli was also party to the growing body of
thought that cast doubts on the authenticity of the work of Dionysius the Areopagite, refusing to accept this personage as
the disciple of Paul identified in Acts. He did not therefore accept his work *De Ecclesiastica Hierarchia* as evidence of the apostolic form of celebrating the Mass.[26]

When they argued the point of the sacrifice of the Mass, the
Tridentine theologians were able to have recourse to the writings of the first controversialists who took issue with Luther
and other Reformers, such as Hieronymus Emser, Johannes
Eck, Kaspar Schatzgeyer, Iodocus Clichtovaeus, Johannes Fa-
bri, Johannes Gropper, and Johannes Cochlaeus.[27] As far as the
evangelical and apostolic origins of the Mass Order and Canon in particular were concerned, they were able to take their
lead from the aforementioned, or from the authorities on
whom they largely relied, principally Gabriel Biel's exposition
on the Canon and Thomas Netter's work against Wyclif, *Doctrinale Antiquitatum Fidei Ecclesiae Catholicae*,[28] which although
written a century earlier was brought to print around 1520.

One of the great controversialists, Iodocus Clichtovaeus (or
Clithoveus) had written a Mass commentary, even before the
outbreak of the Reformation controversies, in which he makes
ample use of the work of Gabriel Biel and speaks of the Canon's apostolic institution. In writings that come after Luther's
attacks on the Mass, he used arguments taken from Thomas
Netter to prove its apostolic origins.[29] Clichtovaeus had also
been an ardent defender of the authenticity of the works attributed to Dionysius the Areopagite in his earlier writings
and was ready to use this authority for the defense of the apostolic origins of ecclesiastical institutions, including the Mass,
when he wrote against Martin Luther.[30]

In 1523 Hieronymus Emser had composed his treatise *Missae Christianorum contra Lutheranam Missandi Formulam Assertio* and in 1524 his *Canonis Missae contra Hulricum Zwinglium Defensio*.[31] Emser upheld the idea that the Mass was first celebrated at Antioch by Peter in the way in which it has since been universally observed, with only a few changes. In giving authorities for this position, Emser takes the lead from the Englishman, Thomas Netter.[32] These are the Council of Trullo, which he calls the *sacra sexta Synodus*,[33] a letter of Gregory the Great to Bishop John of Syracuse,[34] Remigius of Auxerre,[35] and Isidore of Seville, as already cited. As further authority for the apostolic origins of the Mass and of the Canon, Emser quotes the words of Paul in 1 Timothy 2:1, as commented upon by Augustine,[36] Ambrose,[37] Haymo of Halberstadt,[38] and Anselm of Canterbury.[39]

For all the different popes who are said to have had anything to do with the Mass, Emser has an explanation. Gregory stipulated that only the priest, rather than all the people, should say the Lord's Prayer. Celestine introduced psalm singing, Leo the kiss of peace, and Alexander and Gelasius their own small modifications.[40] None of this makes them the author of the Mass rite or of the Canon, which have the force of Petrine authority.

Writing his *De Sacrificio Missae Libri Tres*[41] in 1526, Johannes Eck may have taken some of his references from Emser. In any case, he too places the origins of the Mass with Peter at Antioch, quoting along with the authority of Isidore of Seville[42] that of Hugo of St. Victor.[43] Its commitment to writing he ascribes to James, on this quoting the Council of Trullo under the name of *Synodus Quinisexta*. In chapter two of the second book of the treatise, Eck elaborates further on the origins of the Mass, saying that it was first celebrated in Antioch and on the Vatican by Peter, in Jerusalem by James, and in Alexandria by Mark. These celebrations were in Hebrew, but under the Emperor Hadrian it was first done in Greek and then given its more stylized form (*angustior forma*) by Basil of Caeserea, with another version coming from the hand of John Chrysostom. Later the Roman Church celebrated in Latin, and the text received its final expression at the time of Gelasius.[44]

Like Clichtovaeus, both Emser and Eck looked upon the *De*

Ecclesiastica Hierarchia of Dionysius the Areopagite as a witness to the apostolic origin of the Mass order. In the *Missae Christianorum contra Lutheranam Missandi Formulam Assertio* Emser refers to chapter three of this work as witness to the apostolic form of celebration.[45] In his answer to Zwingli's attack, despite Zwingli's rejection of the authority of Dionysius, Emser quotes the Areopagite in support of the apostolic tradition of commemorating the saints[46] and of praying for the dead.[47] Even before the polemic against Luther, Eck had defended the authenticity of the works attributed to the Areopagite in face of its discrediting by some humanist writers. In the Leipzig dispute with Luther in 1519, he quoted them on the apostolic origins of the Petrine primacy.[48] It is therefore not surprising that he would refer to Dionysius in his work on the Mass. In chapter eight of the second book, drawing on Dionysius, he actually sets forth in parallel columns the apostolic form of celebration (the *apostolicus mos*) and the contemporary form (*ecclesiae mos hodie*).[49] Eck's conviction that nothing much had changed since apostolic times shows clearly in his argument for sacrifice drawn from specific sections of the Canon, justifying this procedure by saying that the major part of this prayer had been composed by the apostles and the early martyrs who sat in the apostolic see.[50] In other words, he confirms Luther's reading of the text but takes it as apostolic argument rather than as an offending ecclesiastical composition.

All these authors relied heavily in their works on the Mass, and in particular for their ideas on the origins of the Mass, on Thomas Netter. In his above mentioned work, he treats of the apostolic origins of the Mass in Title IV, chapter 28, and of the Roman Canon in Title IV, chapters 36 to 40.[51] In this work we already find references to the texts of the Synodus Quinisexta, Isidore, Hugo, Remigius, Augustine, Ambrosiaster, and Dionysius used by the sixteenth-century controversialists.[52]

Gabriel Biel expressed ideas similar to those of Netter in his *Canon Misse Expositio*.[53] In broaching the Canon, Biel says that the substantial part of the prayer, that is, the words of consecration, came from Christ. The rest had Peter as its principal author, but it was added to over time until receiving its definitive form under Gelasius. Biel's authorities on this are Innocent III and Gulielmus Durandus.[54] He mentions the treatise of Hugo of St. Victor where it is said that the Mass was first celebrated at Antioch by Peter, with the three prayers beginning with *Hanc igitur oblationem*. He has, however, some trouble with this idea because of the text of Acts 2:42 on the breaking of the bread as this was interpreted by a gloss,[55] and because of the authority of Gratian's decree which mentions the contributions of James and Basil. One solution would be to say that Hugo is talking about Peter's activity in the primatial see after the apostles had parted from Jerusalem and separated. Another solution would be to follow the interpretation of Antoninus in his *Chronica*[56] where he says that it was at Antioch that Peter first celebrated with pontifical solemnity. Given the way in which the text about Antioch was used by controversialists and conciliar theologians, it is interesting to note Biel's hesitations.

The Tridentine Debate

When the theologians of the Council of Trent were asked to address the doctrine of the sacrifice of the Mass,[57] they could not avoid turning some attention to attacks on the Roman Canon, since its repudiation was so central to the positions taken by the Reformers. Since it was the primary priestly prayer, it was also central to their own concerns in defending the power of the priest to offer propitiatory sacrifice for the living and the dead. They were obliged in the first place to defend its theology, which of course they did in the general defense of the doctrine of sacrifice. They were also obliged to say something about its origins and its apostolic authority, both in order to maintain its legitimate use and to be able in turn to use it as an argument from tradition. In establishing this tradition, they drew heavily on the writers already discussed.

In the context of the total argument for sacrifice, the Order of Mass and in particular the Canon received relatively minor mention in the Tridentine discussions. In fact, as much attention was given to the defense of its silent recitation as to its content. This was because the silent recitation fitted into the central point of debate about the power of the priest to make effective offering for the living and the dead, through the action of the Mass which was distinctively his rather than that of the people. The central priestly role was identified with the

Canon which the priest entered to enact the awesome mysteries. In this article, however, the point of inquiry has to do with ideas about the nature of the prayer as such rather than with the way in which it was to be said, though of course the two questions are not adequately separable.

At the first session devoted to the sacrifice of the Mass (Bologna, 1547), two of the articles proposed for debate had to do with the institution of the Mass and with the Canon. As formulated, they appear to have had Martin Luther and his followers in mind, but when virtually the same articles were brought forward in 1551, reference was included to the works of John Calvin and Ulrich Zwingli.[58] Though both Luther and Zwingli had given lengthy attention to the Canon, it is interesting to note that in the conciliar debates their objections were summarized by one speaker under three headings: its pretension to make the Mass a sacrifice and an offering, the commemoration of the dead, and the commemoration of the saints.[59] When the decree on the Sacrifice of the Mass was promulgated in 1563, it included a chapter and a canon on the Canon but absorbed the question of the origin of the Mass as a whole into more overtly doctrinal sections.[60]

In what follows, we shall bear in mind that in the Tridentine debates the Canon as a liturgical unit was understood in the sense already described. We shall see what speakers said about its origins, both to defend it against attacks and to be able to use it to uphold some crucial points of teaching in the understanding of the Mass as sacrifice. We shall then say something about the authorities which were quoted to support its apostolic origins. Finally, we will see how the reading of the Canon fitted into theological interpretations of the Mass as the commemorative representation of the sacrifice of the cross enacted by the ordained priest, for the living and the dead.

Origins of the Canon

In the propositions put to theological debate, the issue of the institution of the Mass, as already mentioned, was distinct from the issue of respect for the Canon. In conciliar discussion, however, the distinction was often unclear since in both cases the interveners were intent to trace the essentials of sacrifice back to Christ, and the important accidentals which corroborated the sacrificial understanding of the Mass back to the apostles. In the words of Christ at the Last Supper, ending with the memorial command, and often quoted in the version in which they were recorded in the Roman Canon, the essentials of offering, consecration, and communion could be found. The other primary rites, though in relation to these described as accidentals, were thought to constitute an apostolic tradition.

The exact extent of this apostolic tradition was not uniformly described and was blurred by vague notions about the actual history of the liturgy and the diversification of rites within the church. In appealing to the liturgical tradition of the Latin Church, the theologians had the Roman and Ambrosian liturgies in mind and considered these as only slightly modified versions of the same rite, all the more so since Ambrose was taken to be one of the authorities who witnesses to the content of the Canon. They were also vague about the relation of Eastern liturgies to the West, and this vagueness was probably increased by the persuasion that the traditional prayer began after the *Sanctus*, since this allowed closer similarities to be drawn between Eastern liturgies, as represented by the liturgies of Basil and John Chrysostom, and the Western liturgies.

In the 1547 theological debate, we find these descriptions of the origins of the Mass and of the origins of the Canon.

Ricardus Vercellensis[61] in supporting the apostolic origin of the Canon ultimately concludes that the words of consecration, together with some expression of thanksgiving, came from the mouth of Christ, whereas the rest of the Mass derived from the apostles or from holy men almost contemporary with the apostles. En route to this conclusion he cites various authorities, such as Dionysius (for him contemporary with the apostles), Gregory the Great, Augustine, and Basil of Caesarea. He also quotes Biel's recall of the tradition that the Mass was first celebrated by Peter at Antioch, but with only three prayers beginning with the *Hanc igitur*. Behind this argumentation there was the notion, common at Bologna, that the Mass, though instituted by Christ at the Supper with the memorial command, was not the same rite as that of the Supper. At the Supper, Christ gave thanks, consecrated the bread and wine, and with the memorial command ordered the apostles to offer the sacrifice which would commemorate his sacrifice on the cross. Though the command could be given at the Supper, the offering could not be done until the sacrifice of the cross had been consummated. The offering of Christ at the Supper only became an issue in the session of 1551.[62]

Listed immediately after Ricardus in the acts of the Council, Thomas Maria Beccatelli gave a later origin to the Canon, ascribing it to those holy men, Gelasius, Leo, and Gregory. For him, such authorship is in itself sufficient guarantee of its authority.[63] This was in fact to address a problem that had to be resolved by other speakers who wished to date it back to apostolic times. How were they to account for what is attributed to these bishops of Rome, and to others, in the registers of papal actions. The problem had been raised in particular by Zwingli, who as has been seen, found in the Canon nothing other than a compilation of prayers taken from different people at different times.

By way of contrast, Nicolaus Grandis of Paris[64] wanted to ascribe a scriptural foundation to the entire Mass and Canon. The essential words by which the consecration and sacrifice are confected are to be found in the Supper account. The other rites of the Mass are prescribed in 1 Timothy 2:1-2 where Paul asks for *obsecrationes, orationes, postulationes* and *gratiarum actiones*. The *obsecrationes* are the prayers said before the consecration; the *orationes* are those said in the consecration; the *postulationes* are the petitions for the people contained in the blessing of the people by the bishop; and the *gratiarum actiones* come as acknowledgment of the benefits received from God in the action. In this part of his intervention, the Canon would seem to be covered by the *orationes* that belong to the consecration. When he specifically addresses the accusations made against the Canon, he says that the words of consecration are obviously taken from the Supper narrative, but he is not content with this for he wants to find other parts of the Canon, which either precede or follow the consecration, in the same account. From Luke 22 and 1 Corinthians 11 he interprets the making of thanks as the prayers and dedication which Christ offered to the Father before the consecration. He then identifies the hymn mentioned in Mark 14:26 and Matthew 26:30

with the prayers which follow the consecration, and says that the text of this is found in John 17. As far as he is concerned, all the priest does in the Canon is to follow the example of Christ at the Supper and to offer similar prayers both before and after the consecration. In using 1 Timothy 2 for the origins of the Mass, his primary authorities are Augustine and Haymo, whereas the authorities on the apostolic origins of the Canon are Augustine, the Areopagite, and John Chrysostom, corroborated as far as content is concerned by the liturgy of John Chrysostom.

Alexander de Bononia follows Hugo of St. Victor in ascribing the first celebration of the Mass to Peter at Antioch. He then takes up the notion, taken from the *Synodus Quinsexta*, that it was committed to writing by James (for the Hebrews) and Basil (for the Greeks).[65] Antonius Ricius cites the same opinion and authority, and adds the names of Isidore and Remigius Antissiodorensis.[66] However, he also tried to account for the additions made by the popes, Anacletus, Alexander, and Sixtus. Against the abrogation of the Canon and in favor of its apostolic origins, he quotes Isidore, Augustine, Ambrose's commentary on 1 Timothy (in fact the Ambrosiaster), and his *De Sacramentis*. In favor of the application of 1 Timothy to the Mass, and thus to the Canon, he quotes at length from Anselmus Laudensis: the *obsecrationes* are whatever comes before the Canon; the *orationes* are the Canon which Anselm continues to the placing of the particle of the host in the chalice; the *postulationes* are the intercession for the people contained in the priest's blessing; and the *gratiarum actiones* are that to which the priest invites the people when they have communicated.

Hieronymus ab Oleastro,[67] Franciscus a Conceptione,[68] Hieronymus de Bononia,[69] and Franciscus Salazar[70] were others who found evidence for the apostolic origin of the Mass or of the Canon, quoting much the same set of authorities, with a couple of additions, such as the *Historia Ecclesiastica Tripartita*.[71]

Ricardus Cenomanus[72] says that the essentials of the Canon are constituted by apostolic tradition, whereas the accidentals come from holy Fathers of the church and from popes. The essentials are the principal words and actions that extend from the *Te igitur* to the Lord's Prayer, inclusively. Isidore is quoted as to its origins with Peter and the *Synodus Quinisexta* for the contributions of James and Basil in committing it to writing. Other authorities for its apostolic origin are Augustine and Hugo of St. Victor, as well as Ambrose (the Ambrosiaster) commenting on 1 Timothy 2. Basil[73] and Origen[74] are quoted in favor of the idea of a distinct unwritten apostolic tradition. To include the commemoration of the martyrs as essential to the Canon (here he reacts to Luther's objection to the mention of the saints) he quotes the *De Ecclesiastica Hierarchia* of Dionysius and the homilies of Augustine on John.[75] Dionysius was also an authority to support prayer for the dead in the action of the Mass.

Ricardus also attempts to deal with the particular problem arising from the alleged attribution of the Canon by Gregory the Great to *quidam scholasticus*. According to Ricardus, Gregory does not attribute the origins of the Canon to a time later than the apostles, but is referring to the work of later popes who made some changes and additions to it. Thus Gelasius added some hymns and prose texts to the preface and the Canon, and Leo the Great added the words *sanctum sacrificium, immaculatam hostiam*. Indeed Gregory himself is responsible for the words *diesque nostros in tua pace dispones*, as Sixtus is for the addition of the *Sanctus*. In this way the speaker could account for the various attributions cited by the Reformers, without derogating from the early apostolic character of the prayer.

Another theologian who tried to deal with the evidence of later composition was Placidus de Parma.[76] He apparently took his authority from the *Rationale Divinorum Officiorum* of Gulielmus Durandus,[77] so that while he ascribed the origin of the Mass to Peter and James, he could attribute large parts of the Canon to later authorities. Thus he ascribes the *Sanctus* to Sixtus, the *Te igitur* to Clement II, the *Hanc igitur* to Leo I, the *Communicantes* to Siricius, the *Qui pridie* to Alexander, the *Agnus Dei* to Sergius, and the kiss of peace to Innocent I.

The two Jesuits, Claudius Iaius and Alphonsus Salmeron,[78] also displayed awareness of historical diversity, and nonetheless quoted ample authorities for the apostolic origins of the Canon. Their main purpose was to quote from the liturgies of the Roman and Ambrosian Rites, and from the liturgies of Basil, Chrysostom, and the Ethiopians, to demonstrate that the

Mass is a sacrifice. Thus they argue from liturgies that are in fact quite diverse, while still holding apparently for one original prayer of apostolic origin. Of this the Roman Canon is the model. When they refer to what historical documents say to be the work of Popes Leo, Gelasius, Sixtus, and Telesphorus, their obvious intention is to see this as a matter of minor modification or indeed of merely highlighting a part of the original prayer which they did not want to see omitted.

In his intervention, the Franciscan Ioannes Consilii[79] demonstrates the problems of dealing with liturgical traditions. While the authority of Gregory and Augustine shows the antiquity of the Canon, he is aware of the differences between the Latin and Greek Churches, as well as of the differences within the respective traditions between the Roman and Ambrosian Rites, and between the liturgies of Basil and Chrysostom. He finds that all corroborate the sacrificial understanding of the Mass. He downplays the difference between the two Latin rites. To deal with the differences between Latins and Greeks, he gives more authority to the Roman liturgy, since it comes from Peter and his successors, whereas the Greek prayers have Basil and John Chrysostom as authors. Whatever their venerability, these two do not equal the apostles, just as the sees that have them as founders or patrons do not equal the Roman.

In these last mentioned four interventions, we see the difficulties of dealing with historical information about the composition of the Canon. Luther and Zwingli were not off target in raising the issue of a post-apostolic composition, and Zwingli had drawn attention to some of the historical sources to be taken into account. However, the matter was complicated by the attachment of the Reformers to the purity of the Gospel and their use of information or questions about the historical origins of the rites and prayers of the Mass as proof against their importance and even against their orthodoxy. The defendants of the Canon were thus privy to a certain amount of historical information, not all of it accurate and too dependent on medieval sources such as Biel and Durandus, that showed them that the rites of the Mass and the Canon did not come as they stood from apostolic times. Yet they wanted to attribute as much of it as possible to the apostles and to support the idea of an unwritten apostolic tradition that demanded assent and attention alongside the authority of the written Scriptures. As a result, they downplayed the difference between one liturgical tradition and another as much as possible, and found ways of fitting their historical information from later times into the tenets of the theory of apostolic origin.

In keeping with the general line of argumentation that supported the early origins of the Mass rite and Canon, one also finds that various speakers corroborate this by quoting what they took to be references to the Canon in some ancient patristic writers, such as Origen, Tertullian, or Ambrose. Naturally, they were most interested in those quotations that supported the understanding of the Mass as propitiatory sacrifice, offered for the living and the dead. As already mentioned, another line of argumentation taken up had to do with the silent recitation of the Canon, something that was also defended from appeal to various authoritative sources. It was defended strongly because silence was seen as appropriate to the prayer which the priest alone could say as Christ's representative, offering this memorial and representative sacrifice and enacting the awesome and sacred mysteries.[80]

In the session of 1551, Ruardus Tapper,[81] Ioannes Orthega,[82] Iohannes Gropper,[83] Iacobus Lainez,[84] and Ioannes Arze,[85] in responding to the vilifications of the rites of the Mass or of the Canon, responded primarily by stating that its essentials derive from the Supper accounts. These essentials are offering, consecration, and communion. There is not much available record of their discourse on the actual origins of the rite or of the Canon, but in general they held to the same views as those expressed in 1547, quoting much the same authorities. A similar approach was adopted in 1562. By way of anything exceptional, one might simply note the genial intervention of Franciscus Torres who ascribes the writing of the Mass to James, Mark, Clement, and Dionysius the Areopagite, thus allowing an apostolic origin to the liturgy in all major parts of the church.[86]

It is from the arguments at these two sessions, however, that one becomes aware of the particular theological problem which arises from identifying the beginning of the Canon with the *Te igitur*. Some of the speakers, particularly Tapper and Gropper, tried to work out a position on the sacrifice of the

Mass more conciliatory to the Reformers.[87] While they held firmly to the Catholic position that the eucharist is a propitiatory sacrifice, they endeavored to connect it with the sacrifice of thanksgiving, more favored by the Protestants, and with Christ's eternal priesthood, exercised in heaven. Had they seen the preface and Canon as one unified eucharistic prayer, they could have pointed to the liturgical evidence of a tradition that joins offering with thanksgiving in keeping the representative memorial of Christ's death. As it was, as far as they were concerned, the central liturgical prayer of the priest was wholly one of memorial offering, even though it was most appropriate that the people present be more attentive to remembrance and thanksgiving than to offering.[88] In these same sessions, the offering of Christ himself at the Supper was generally affirmed, by way of contrast with opinions expressed at Bologna.[89] Here too had the liturgical evidence supported the connection between thanksgiving and offering, the speakers could have more readily found this connection in the actions and words of Christ himself at the Supper. This would not have totally resolved the problem of the propitiatory character of the eucharistic sacrifice. It would have opened the way to better dialogue and would have been of help to the Catholic piety of the Counter-Reformation.

What remains of the ideas about the origins of the Mass rite or of the Canon is found in the sixth chapter of the final decree of 1563, mentioned in the introduction to this article. The antiquity of the prayer, the respect due to it, and its dignity as authoritative source are affirmed in rather generic terms by attributing its authorship to the Gospels, the apostles, and the holy pontiffs.[90] This reflects the tenor of the debate without going into any particulars. No doubt the Gospel is mentioned primarily because of the words of consecration that are at the heart of the prayer. Mention of the apostolic tradition reflects the general persuasion expressed in the appeals to Petrine and Pauline authority, as well as to the testimony of Dionysius, but it stops short of embracing any of the details of this argumentation. The idea of an unwritten apostolic tradition that complemented the Scriptures was important to the Tridentine fathers and theologians and affected their thought about the origins of the Mass as much as anything else. Though it could have been recognized that particular arguments were questionable, the general notion of such tradition was unassailable. The pontiffs are mentioned because the compilers of the decree did not wish to neglect the historical information that shows the hand of the persons mentioned by the Reformers and often quoted in the course of the Council. By referring to them as pontiffs, however, the decree appeals to the authority of the apostolic see and easily joins them with mention of the apostles themselves. While this account of the origins of the Canon in the conciliar decree does not seriously violate historical truth, it certainly shows no great historical acuity except in its relative reserve. It accounts, as was the purpose of the Council, for the respect due the prayer while telling very little about its precise origins or tackling the whole issue of the origin and development of eucharistic prayers. It thus contributed to the excessive reverence shown the Roman Canon in the following centuries and sustained the idea that the central prayer of the eucharist was complete without the preface of thanksgiving and proclamation, now relegated to relatively minor role in the entire celebration.

The Authorities Quoted

More needs to be said about the authorities quoted on the origins of Mass and Canon, in order to see what exactly is said in those texts, and how this relates to the use made of them in controversy. As has been noted, there was considerable reliance at the Council on what a few more recent writers quoted from earlier tradition. When one goes back over the more commonly cited, if not all, authorities for the apostolic origin of the Mass or of the Canon mentioned at Trent, one finds a list that reflects the works of the controversialists and of Biel and Netter.

Ambrose, *De Sacramentis* VI, 5, 22.[91]
Ambrose (in fact Ambrosiaster), *In Epist. I ad Tim.*, 2 1.[92]
Augustine, *Epist. 149.*[93]
Synodus Quinisexta, c. 32 (Council of Trullo).[94]
Dionysius, *De Ecclesiastica Hierarchia* III.[95]
Isidore of Seville, *De Ecclesiasticis Officiis* I, 15.[96]

Remigius Antissidiorensis, *De Celebratione Missae* (= in Migne printed as Pseudo-Alcuinus, *De Divinis Officiis*), c. 40.[97]

Anselmus Laudensis (= Walafrid Strabo), *Glossa Ordinaria in 1 Tim* 2, 1.[98]

Haymo Halberstatensis, *Expositio in Epist. I ad Tim* 2, 1.[99]

Hugo of St. Victor, *De Sacramentis* 11, 14.[100]

As for the references to post-apostolic composition which had to be explained, there is the letter of Gregory to the bishop of Syracuse[101] and the mention now found in the edition of the *Liber Pontificalis*[102] of the liturgical work of Alexander, Telesphorus, Leo, Gelasius, and Gregory, as well as mention, in the pseudo-decretals, of Anacletus.[103]

It is the work of Isidore of Seville which seems to have been the source of the idea that the Mass was first celebrated at Antioch by Peter. In the *De Ecclesiasticis Officiis* Isidore writes that the *Ordo Missae* and the prayers by which the offerings are consecrated to God as sacrifice were instituted by Peter and that since then the celebration has been enacted throughout the world in the same way. Since his commentary is upon the liturgy of the Mozarabic Rite, it is not clear what exactly he had in mind, but in any case as later quoted he became the authority for the Petrine origins of the central part of the Roman Canon, and indeed at times of much more. It was the late ninth-century exposition on the Mass, the *De Celebratione Missae* of Remigius of Auxerre that began to popularize Isidore's attribution in this way, with specific references to the three orations beginning with the *Hanc igitur oblationem*. This was coupled by Remigius with a strongly sacerdotal understanding of the Mass. He views this Petrine prayer as the prayer of the priest (*sacerdos*) who is the mediator through whose ministry the people offer prayers and oblations to God. Both the historical reference and the sacerdotal interpretation were incorporated, in almost identical words, into the *De Sacramentis* of Hugo of St. Victor.[104]

The nuance given to this position by attributing some part to James and to Basil of Caesarea comes to the later medieval world through the reference in Gratian to the *Synodus Quinisexta* or Council of Trullo of 692. Canon 32 of that council is addressed to the mixing of water with wine in the preparation of the chalice to which some had objected. In prescribing the use of water, the council affirms that the written form of the sacrifice has been passed down through the agency of James the brother of the Lord, first bishop of Jerusalem, and Basil, archbishop of Caesarea, a man whose renown and glory have filled the whole world. There is nothing more precise than that, but when the idea is coupled with the attribution of the central part at least of the Canon to Peter, it gives rise to the notion of one common Mass order that has been transmitted with some accidental differences through the principal Latin and Greek liturgies.

A text taken from Augustine appears to have been the principal reason for the use of 1 Timothy as an apostolic authority on the origins of the Mass order. In his letter to Paulinus, commenting on 1 Timothy 2:1, he takes up the problem put to him about differences between the Greek and Latin texts. It is important to note the form of the Latin text used by him. He lists *obsecrationes, orationes, interpellationes, gratiarum actiones.* His solution to the technical question of translation does not matter much to the later use of his commentary. What does matter is that he says that he believes that in this text the apostle is referring to the common usage of the churches in the celebration of the sacraments, that is, the eucharist. The *obsecrationes* are what belong to the celebration up to the point of the blessing of the offerings. The *orationes* are the prayers said in the actual blessing and sanctifying of the gifts and which conclude with the Lord's Prayer. The *interpellationes,* to which he allows the alternate and older name of *postulationes,* are the prayers by which the bishop blesses the people. Finally, *gratiarum actiones* are the prayers to be said when all is done by those who have partaken of this great sacrament. Granted the similarities that always held between the liturgies of Rome, Milan, and North Africa, we are not sure what precise eucharistic order or prayer was used in the church of Hippo. Augustine's division of prayers is however broad enough to fit any liturgy, and he does assert that the order as he describes it is that followed by nearly all, if not all, the churches. It is therefore interesting that he lists the central prayer as one of blessing and sanctification of the Lord's table. When he explains the use of the Greek word *euke* where the Latin has *oratio* even though the usual translation of the Greek would be *votum* (desire and dedication of self), he says that this sacramental offering made to God expresses the participants' desire to remain in Christ as the one body signified in the one bread. The emphasis here is on offering and self-offering and on the sanctification of the gifts, with no mention of thanksgiving. That is placed at the end of the celebration, as thanksgiving for participation in the sacrament. This of course would fit quite well with the tenor of Ambrose's prayer and of what we know about early forms of the Ambrosian and Roman prayer.[105] In other words, though current historical study does assert the unity of the great prayer even in the Roman liturgy as against the medieval separation between preface and canon, an accent on offering is already apparent in the early agglomerate of the North African, Milanese, and Roman Churches, even in the comments of such a strong sacramentalist as Augustine.

Given this application of the text of 1 Timothy by Augustine, speakers at Trent also used the authority of Ambrose to support the idea that these words of Paul refer to the Mass order. It is therefore interesting to note that in his address to the neophytes the author of the *De Sacramentis* actually used this text as a way of interpreting the Lord's Prayer and not the entire eucharist. He also uses a Latin version different from that of Augustine, listing *orationes, obsecrationes, postulationes, gratiarum actiones*. The other supposed Ambrosian text, in fact the commentary of the Ambrosiaster on 1 Timothy, lists *deprecationes, orationes, postulationes, gratiarum actiones*, and has nothing to do with the eucharist.

Walafrid Strabo, whose work was quoted at Trent as that of Anselm of Laon, in his gloss on 1 Timothy followed Augustine's interpretation of the passage as a description of the order of the Mass. Later this was also done by Haymo Halberstatensis in his exposition on the same text, but he is more specific in its application to the Roman Mass. The *obsecrationes* include everything up to the *Te igitur*. The *orationes* are said in the consecration of the eucharist up to the fraction of the host and the placing of the particle in the chalice.

The authority of Dionysius the Areopagite who describes the synaxis in the third chapter of *De Ecclesiastica Hierarchia* was particularly important to support the commemoration of the saints and prayer for the dead in the Mass and in the body of the Canon. The authenticity of this work was generally upheld or supposed in controversy, despite the questions raised by some humanists and adopted by Zwingli and Luther.

The work did indeed support the commemoration of the saints and prayer for the dead at the heart of the liturgy.[106] When the writer treats of the eucharistic prayer, however, by which in obedience to Christ's memorial command the priest or hierarch remembers and proclaims God's sacred works, he says little of offering. The prayer is presented more as praise, revelation, and contemplation.[107] Dionysius was useful to Catholic apologists inasmuch as he presented a Mass order which they found reasonably similar to the current Roman one, and especially for his supposedly apostolic witness to prayer for the dead and the commemoration of saints.

It is then the transmission of the texts of Isidore, the Council of Trullo, and Augustine, in one form or another, to the later medieval world, and the assumed apostolic witness of the Pseudo-Dionysius, whose work was readily available at the time in Latin translation, that were the main Tridentine basis for the apostolic origins of the Roman Mass and Canon, and which provided the principal historical response to the vituperations of the Reformers. Isidore provided a Petrine authority and Augustine a Pauline, and the *Synodus Quinisexta*, as it was called, explained the written transmission of the one order to the Hebrew and Greek worlds through James and Basil. Dionysius was thought to have described the apostolic form of celebration and supported the controverted practices of the commemoration of the saints and of the prayer for the dead in particular.

As for the ways in which speakers accounted for the intervention of later popes, one gets a reasonable summary of what was at issue by looking at Duchesne's edition of the *Liber Pontificalis*. Alexander is said to have added the words *Qui pridie* to the gospel text of the Supper. Telesphorus is accredited with the introduction of the *Gloria*, though if he did, it had to be in a version quite different from the current. Leo is allowed the insertion of the words *sanctum sacrificium* in reference to the offering of Melchisedech in the prayer *Supra quae*, and Gelasius is accredited with the authorship of many prefaces and *orationes*. Finally, Gregory is said to have added the words *diesque nostros in tua pace dispone* into the *Hanc igitur*.

Gregory the Great's much quoted attribution of the Canon to some *scolasticus* comes in fact from a letter in which he explains his rulings on the use of the *Kyrie*, the *Alleluia*, and the Lord's Prayer, since what he has prescribed appeared to contradict the practice of the Greeks. It is an obscure text[108] in which one reading would have him say that the custom of the apostles was to consecrate through the praying of the Lord's Prayer alone, so that it would be odd to pray only the prayer composed by this *scolasticus* over the oblations, omitting the prayer composed by Christ and used by the apostles. Another reading, however, is that he would find it odd to add the prayer of some later writer to the prayer of oblation and not use the prayer of the Lord. In this latter reading Gregory would not be attributing the Canon to some *scolasticus*, but the issue would be the addition of other prayers to it. The epithet would then be a general way of referring to writers of prayers and would simply contrast their work and authority with the work and authority of the Lord himself.

This kind of information, along with other incidental pieces, was available to sixteenth-century theologians in one form or another. None of it is remarkable for historical accuracy and certainly does not tell the whole story of the Roman Mass or Canon. It simply melds into the common puzzle of its formulation and transmission that contemporary authors have not fully solved. The sixteenth-century controversialists were correct in noting that mention of the popes did not accredit any of them with original authorship and that their actions would have to be taken as some modification of something that existed before them. They were rather off target, however, in thinking that a canon of celebration could be dated back to apostolic times. The Reformers, for their part, in suppressing practically everything but the proclamation of the words of institution, did nothing to restore the properly eucharistic form of celebration.[109] Though at times they were willing to speak of the sacrifice of thanksgiving, they did not connect this with the sacramental form of representing the salvific sacrifice of Christ's death.

Theology of the Canon

Enjoying the apostolic authority attributed to it, the Canon was used as witness to the nature of the Mass as sacrifice. Here four things need to be kept in mind.[110] First, since the whole discussion on propitiatory sacrifice had to do with the power and action of the ordained priest, the Canon had the importance of being seen as the specifically priestly prayer. In entering into it, the minister separated himself from the people in order to act for them as priest of Christ. Second, discussion of the issues was dictated by the order in which the articles taken from the writings of the Reformers were presented. Thus speakers first spoke to the general topic of eucharistic sacrifice, and only later to the question of the Mass as application of the fruits of the cross. Third, in fact the two issues were intimately bound together in the prevailing theology of the Mass and in that theology generally followed at the council. Fourth, however limited a way in which the relation was at times seen, it was always clear in the debates that the Mass was seen in relation to the cross and that it was not a meritorious work functioning independently of the cross. This was true even in the first session, despite the tendency to see the offering of the Mass as an offering numerically distinct from that of the cross. It is necessary to keep these four points in mind as we look at the use made of the Canon to support the abundant proofs for sacrifice taken from Scripture and patristic authorities, at the ways in which its words supported notions of application, and at the elements of representation found in it.

Sacrifice in general was proved from the verbs and nouns used in such sections of the prayer as the *Te igitur*, the *Hanc igitur*, and the *Unde et memores*.[111] Particularly in regard to the last, it is shown that the church has always understood the memorial command of Christ to mean that the church must offer the eucharist as sacrifice. This was supported by reference to the anamnesis of the Ambrosian and Greek liturgies.[112]

There were a number of variations on how this sacrifice was understood. In the first session, 1547, these were promoted by the tendency to see the memorial offering as numerically distinct from the offering of the cross, though dependent on it. Ricardus Vercellensis distinguishes four things that are offered in the Mass by the priest. First, there is the offering of bread and wine in commemoration of all God's benefits. Second, there is thanksgiving for all good things, expressed in the preface. Third, after the consecration, there is the offering of Christ and his passion. Fourth, there is the offering of the mystical body.[113] What constitutes the true nature of the Mass and its benefit for the living and the dead is the offering of Christ himself after the consecration. In his reading of the Mass order, Thomas de Sancto Marino also distinguished between offering Christ and offering the church's own service and devotion. The first object is designated by the words *hostiam puram, hostiam sanctam, hostiam immaculatam*, and the second by the words *sacrificium laudis* and *oblatio servitutis*.[114] For both of these speakers the distinctively priestly act is the offering of Christ, and it is this which obtains grace and redemption for the living and the dead. In general, during the session of the council at Bologna, this went along with the notion that the quantity of the fruit was somehow measured by the church's devotion in offering its own service, as well as by the faith and devotion of those for whom the offering was made.[115] The two Jesuits, Claudius Iaius and Alphonsus Salmeron, used the Canon to show that sacrifice has to include offering as well as consecration,[116] and that the Mass fulfilled the sacrifical types of the Old Testament, with the mention in the *Supra quae* of the offerings of Abel, Abraham, and Melchisedech.[117] Referring the words *sacrificium laudis* to the prophecy of Malachai 1:11, they concluded that offering has to be accompanied by praise, though they still held for the customary Tridentine distinction between sacrifice of praise and sacrifice of propitiation.[118]

In the 1551 session a closer relation between the Supper, the Mass, and the heavenly priestly supplication of Christ in their common relation to the cross, made it easier to see the Canon as sacramental representation of the offering of Christ on the cross.[119] Ruardus Tapper and Johannes Gropper were particularly strong in presenting this encompassing notion of the one offering and sacrifice, begun at the Supper, accomplished on the cross, and continuing in heaven, while being sacramentally represented on earth. This made it unnecessary to distinguish formally between the offering of Christ and the offering of the church, for what the priest does is to sacramentally represent the offering of Christ for its application to the living and the dead. Tapper applied this interpretation to the fulfillment of the memorial command expressed in the *Unde et memores*.[120] Gropper saw this idea expressed in the memorial eucharistic offering *pro redemptione animarum, spe salutis et incolumitatis*.[121] This reading of the Canon was generally supported by Franciscus Condelmerius Tranensis who said that in the *Hanc igitur* and the *Supra quae* the priest offered the sacrifice of the cross in a mystic way, acting in the person of the eternal high priest.[122]

In both sessions, the idea of the application of the fruits of the cross for the living and the dead is inherent to the reading of the Mass and of the Canon as memorial offering. Naturally, given the two ways of seeing the link, application was not interpreted in exactly the same way, even though the same words of the prayer were used. In the session at Bologna, Alexander de Bononia said that through the *memento* for the living and the dead the priest expressed the intention to apply the fruits of the passion in the measure of the church's devotion and of the devotion of those for whom it was offered (*quorum tibi fides cognita est et nota devotio*) or who offered themselves (*pro redemptione animarum suarum et pro spe salutis et incolumitatis suae*).[123] A strong supporter of this idea of application in the measure of devotion, Ioannes Antonius Delphinus argued from the Canon for the two ways in which the Mass could benefit the faithful. The first was by the reception of the sacrament and was expressed in the words about *quotquot ex hac altaris participatione sumpserimus*, while benefit *solum per modum sacrificii* appears in the *memento* for the living and in the *memento* for the dead.[124] The *memento* was also read as an expression of the priest's application by Placidus de Parma, who likewise measured the quantity of fruit obtained by the devotion of the one for whom it was applied and for whom the priest prayed saying, *quorum tibi fides cognita est et nota devotio*.[125] In all these cases the memorial offering and application by the church was somehow distinguished from the offering of the cross which it represented and whose fruits it applied. In the session of 1551 the same parts of the Canon supported the notion of application, but in the case of those interveners it was because of the sacramental and mystic representation of the one offering, that of Christ. It was the sacramental understanding of the second session that appeared to be most favored in the words chosen for the final decree on the Sacrifice of the Mass.[126] This harmonized well with a reading of the Canon that incorporates the offering of the church into the offering of Christ, so that the priest prays in the power of Christ and as minister of the church in one and the same act of commemorative and representative offering.

Theologically speaking, one of the things that needed to be explained was the relation between offering and consecration. Since the body and blood of Christ are made present through the consecration, many were content with the explanation that it is Christ himself who is offered. Iaius and Salmeron, however, found it necessary to explain why offering could be expressed even before the consecration, as in the *Te igitur* and *Hanc igitur*. Their explanation had to do with the fulfillment of Old Testament types or figures. Christ, they said, was in fact offered twice, once in the figures of the Old Testament and once on the cross. All that is said about gift and offering before the consecration recalls the offering in types that anticipated the real offering. All that is said after the consecration is an offering of the body and blood now really present and is representative of the real offering on the cross.[127]

Petrus Paulus Arretinus (or Iannarinus), a Dominican, resorted to Thomas Aquinas for an allegorical explanation, not of the priest's words but of the priest's actions during the Canon.[128] He explains the signs of the cross which the priest makes over the oblations as Aquinas explained them.[129] The combination of two, three, or five signs at different words were said by Aquinas to recall such things as the betrayal by Judas, the selling of Jesus to the priests, scribes, and Pharisees, the five wounds suffered in the passion, the three hours that Jesus hung upon the cross, the three prayers which he uttered from the gibbet, and the like. This was very much in line with the allegorical exposition of the Mass that helped people to concentrate their devotion on the passion and to see some representation of it in the Mass, even when unable to follow what the priest was saying. Quite interestingly, in explaining the actual words of the Canon, Petrus Paulus also followed Aquinas in giving a fairly literal interpretation of these words as a prayer in which sacrifice is offered, its fruits petitioned, and their application made.[130]

The intervention demonstrates the problem of explaining the Mass as a representation of the passion, when there is no resort to thanksgiving and praise. Considerable importance was indeed given to the making of thanksgiving within the Mass and to the notion of sacrifice of thanksgiving. A number of speakers said that the Mass fulfilled all the Old Testament sacrifices, including those of thanksgiving.[131] Tapper thought that commemorative thanksgiving was the best way in which participants at Mass could be engaged.[132] Nicolaus Grandis thought that the making of thanks was one of the actions whereby the church continued the actions of Christ at the Supper.[133] As already seen, there were likewise those who in quoting Augustine or Ambrose (the Ambrosiaster) took the meaning of thanks as one of the four kinds of prayer commanded by the apostle Paul.[134] However, because the prayer of the priest, the Canon, began at the *Te igitur*, it was not possible to link memorial representation and the commemorative proclamation of praise in a sacramental way. Hence thanksgiving was taken as a fit thing to do, either in the course of or at the end of the liturgy, but the essence of the Mass as commemorative sacrifice was posited in the action of offering by the priest, and the offering was linked in one way or another with the consecration. The words of the Canon as words of consecration and offering fitted into and indeed fully supported this explanation, once the prefatory thanksgiving was not seen as integral to the prayer as a unit.

* * * * * *

In continuity with the Council of Trent, the church today celebrates the Mass as the sacramental and memorial representation of Christ's passion and death, and thus seeks to enter more fully into this holy mystery, in communion with the living and the dead. In doing so, however, it has been helped by historical studies to renew the understanding and practice of the eucharistic prayer as a unit of proclamation, commemorative thanksgiving, and offering, and to link the benefits of redemption with this total act in which the people join with the priest. In this context, it is of interest to see how the efforts at liturgical renewal fostered by Trent were hampered by the inadequate knowledge of the history of the Roman Canon itself. In this article, it has been shown within the context of the Reformation controversy what some of the prevailing notions were about the content and history of the prayer, and how these were worked into the doctrinal and theological explanations adopted in discussion of the sacrifice of the Mass. I think that this kind of historical investigation is a good way to do honor to the memory of Niels Rasmussen, who always appreciated that one of the best contributions to renewal was to give an accurate account of history.

Notes

1. This is most readily accessible in Denz 1756.

2. Denz 1745.

3. On this, see Josef A. Jungmann, *The Mass of the Roman Rite*, vol. 2 (New York: Benziger, 1955) 100.

4. Isidore, *De Ecclesiasticis Officiis* I,15 (PL 83:752f.).

5. Jungmann, *The Mass* 106.

6. Gabriel Biel, *Canonis Missae Expositio*, vol. 1, eds., Heiko A. Obermann and William J. Courtenay (Wiesbaden: Franz Steiner Verlag, 1963) 120-121. Biel's references are to Albert, *De Sacrificio Missae* III,1; Gulielmus Durandus, *Rationale Divinorum Officiorum* IV,35,2; Alexander Halensis, *Summa Theologiae* IV,37,2,1.

7. See Adalbert Ebner, *Quellen und Forschungen zur Geschichte und Kuntsgeschichte des Missale Romanum im Mittelalter. Iter Italicum* (Freiburg im Breisgau: Herder'sche Verlagshandlung, 1896). Examining a number of codices, the author reproduces some of the illustrations and letterings that mark the beginning of the Canon.

8. This belongs to the late fifteenth century and has been edited as vol. 29 of the Corpus Catholicorum: *Die Älteste Deutsche Gesamtauslegung der Messe (Erstausgabe CA. 1480)*, edited and introduced by Franz Rudolf Reichert (Münster Westfalen: Aschendorffsche Verlagsbuchhandlung, 1967). The exposition on the Canon begins on p. 120.

9. For examples of private prayers for the priest as he enters or during the Canon, see Ebner, p. 301 for an excerpt from a Florentine codex of the eleventh century, p. 304 for a codex of the same century from Lucca, and pp. 329 and 337 for prayers from Roman codices of the eleventh or twelfth century. For Ebner's comment, see p. 396.

10. "Porro sexta exhinc succedit conformatio sacramenti, ut obla-

tio, quae Deo offertur, sanctificata per Spiritum Sanctum, Christi corpori ac sanguini conformetur." (l.c. 753A)

11. "Iste est canon, secreta actio seu sacrificium, pars principalior totius officii misse, in qua premissis populi illuminatione consecrandorumque munerum oblatione agitur de ipsorum munerum consecratione, qua in verum christi corpus et sanguinem substantialiter convertuntur." (l.c. 120C)

12. *Summa Theologiae* III,83,3.

13. *De Canone Missae Epichiresis*, in *Huldreich Zwinglis sämtichle Werke*, vol. 2, Corpus Reformatorum 89 (Zurich: Theologische Verlag Zürich, 1982; reprint of the 1908 edition by Heinsius Nachfolger Leipzig) 605-607. These are readily available in English translation in R.C.D. Jasper and G.J. Cuming, *Prayers of the Eucharist: Early and Reformed* (New York: Pueblo Publishing Company, 3rd edition, 1987) 184-186.

14. *Word and Sacrament*, vol. 2, ed., Abdel Ross Wentz, vol. 36 of *Luther's Works*, eds., Jaroslav Pelikan and Helmut T. Lehmann (Philadelphia: Fortress Press, 1959) 3-126.

15. Ibid. 127-230.

16. Ibid. 231-268.

17. Ibid. 307-328. There is a good summary of Luther's objections in Bryan Spinks, *Luther's Liturgical Criteria and His Reform of the Canon of the Mass*, Grove Liturgical Books 30 (Bramcote Notts: Grove Books, 1982) 29-31.

18. l.c. 51.

19. l.c. 185.

20. l.c. 314-323.

21. *Misuse* 191-193.

22. *De Canone* 552-608.

23. l.c. 565.

24. l.c. 564.

25. l.c. 566.

26. See Karlfried Froehlich, "Pseudo-Dionysius and the Reformation of the Sixteenth Century," in *Pseudo-Dionysius: The Complete Works*, The Classics of Western Spirituality (Mahwah, NJ: Paulist Press, 1987) 33-46. See also Jean-Pierre Massaut, *Critique et tradition à la veille de la réforme en France. Etude suivie de textes inédits traduits et annotés* (Paris: Librairie Philosophique J. Vrin, 1974) 179-187.

27. For a listing of the principal early controversial works, see *Die Confutatio der Confessio Augustana vom 3. August 1530*, ed., Herbert Immenkötter, Corpus Catholicorum 33 (Münster Westfalen: Aschendorffsche Verlagsbuchhandlung, 1979). Many of these works are now edited and published in the collection Corpus Catholicorum under the direction of Erwin Iserloh.

28. Biel, *Canonis Misse* and Thomas Netter (Waldensis), *Doctrinale Antiquitatum Fidei Ecclesiae Catholicae* (Venice: Apud Iordanum Zilettum, 1571), Vol. 3, Title III, cap. 28 and 36-40. The work was first written as a polemic against Wyclif around 1421. It was given a printing at Paris in 1521 (vol. 2), 1523 (vol. 3), and 1532 (vol. 1). Vol. 3 on ecclesiastical rites and institutions was a ready arsenal of argument and authorities for the controversialists. For more on Netter, his notion of tradition, and his style of argument, see Michael Hurley, "A Pre-Tridentine Theology of Tradition. Thomas Netter Waldensis," *The Heythrop Journal* 4 (1963) 348-366.

29. His exposition of ecclesiastical rites, including the Mass, was entitled *Elucidatorium Ecclesiasticum ad Officium Ecclesiae Pertinentia Planius Exponens et Quatuor Libros Complectens*. This was first published in Paris in 1516 and then at Basel in 1517. His treatment of the Mass in polemical works against Luther is found in *Antilutherus*, dated 1524, and *Propugnaculum Ecclesiae Adversus Lutheranos*, dated 1526. See cap. 32, "De Forma Missae." On Clichtovaeus' works on the Mass, see Adolph Franz, *Die Messe im deutschen Mittelalter* (Freiburg im Breisgau: Herdersche Verlagshandlung, 1902) 615-617.

30. As early as 1515, Clichtovaeus was a great defender of the authenticity of the works attributed to Dionysius. See the excerpts from his work *Theologia Vivificans* in Massaut, *Critique et tradition* 188-204, as well as excerpts from his *Antilutherus* 206-229.

31. Hieronymus Emser, *Schriften zur Verteidigung der Messe*, ed., Theobald Freudenberger, Corpus Catholicorum 28 (Münster Westfalen: Aschendorffsche Verlagsbuchhandlung, 1959) 1-37 and 38-93.

32. He explicitly acknowledges his indebtedness to Netter, *Missae Christianorum Assertio* l.c., 8,26.

33. Concilium in Trullo, see Quinisextum (A.D. 692) c. 32 (G.D. Mansi, *Sacrorum Conciliorum Nova et Amplissima Collectio*, vol. 9, 957,8). The use of this reference by Western writers is probably due to the influence of its use in the *Decretum Gratiani*, De consecratione dist. 1 can. 47. It is already mentioned by Netter.

34. *Gregorii I Papae Registrum Epistolarum*, tomus 2, ed., Ludovicus M. Hartmann (Munich: Monumenta Germaniae Historica, 1978) 59,1-60,12.

35. Remigius Antissidorensis, *De Celebratione Missae* (=Pseudo-Alcuinus, *De Divinis Officiis*) c. 40 (PL 101:1246).

36. Augustine, *Epist. 149 ad Paulinum* (CSEL 34, pars 2, 359,12-364,17).

37. There are two references to Ambrose. One in fact is to a work of the Ambrosiaster, *In Epist. I ad Tim.* 2,1 (CSEL 81, pars 3, 259, 15ff.). The other is to *De Sacramentis* VI,5,22 (CSEL 73, 81,20-82,27).

38. Haimo Halberstatensis, *Expositio in Epist. I ad Tim.* 2, 1 (PL 117:788B-C).

39. Anshelmus Canthuariensis [in reality, according to Freudenberger, Herveus Burgidolensis *Commentarium in Epist. 1 ad Tim* 2,1 (PL 181:1413)].

40. *Canonis Missae Defensio*, l.c. 43,18-44,5.

41. Johannes Eck, *De Sacrificio Missae Libri Tres (1526)*, eds., Erwin Iserloh, Vinzenz Pfnür, and Peter Fabisch, Corpus Catholicorum 36 (Münster Westfalen: Aschendorffsche Verlagsbuchhandlung, 1982).

42. *De Ecclesiasticis Officiis*, l.c.

43. Hugo de S. Victore, *De Sacramentis* II,VIII,14 (PL 176:472).

44. Eck, *De Sacrificio* II,1, l.c. 81-85. Quoting Johannes Capnion, Iacobus Stapulensis, and Iodocus Clithoveus, Eck argues that the etymology of *missa* is a derivation from the Hebrew word meaning *munus personale* or personal gift. This argument was repeated several times during the Council of Trent. Eck's idea that in the early church, up to the time of Hadrian, Mass was celebrated in Hebrew, and thus in a language unknown to the people, found its way into the Confutation of the Augsburg Confession; see Immenkötter, *Die Confutatio* 161,6-9.

45. *Missae Christianorum*, l.c. 10,23ff.

46. *Canonis Missae Defensio*, l.c. 63,4-7.

47. Ibid. 87,15-17.

48. See Froehlich, "Pseudo-Dionysius and the Reformation," l.c. 41f.

49. *De Sacrificio*, l.c. 113f.

50. Ibid. 86: "quia canonis maior pars ab ipsis apostolis posita est et a martyribus in sede apostolica positis, ideo ex canone missae liquescit missam esse sacrificium." He then proceeds to each of the units of the Canon, arguing from their language.

51. See above, note 28.

52. The references to Isidore, the Synodus Quinisexta, Hugo, and Remigius on the origins of the Mass are in Tit. IIII, cap. 28, f.60; to Augustine, Ambrose, and Anselm on the meaning of 1 Tim 2,1 in Tit. IIII, cap. 36,f.73, and the use of Dionysius for the commemoration of the saints in Tit. III, cap. 37,f.76).

53. See above, note 6.

54. Innocent III, *De Sacramento Altaris* III,2 (PL 271:840) and Gulielmus Durandus, *Rationale* IV,35,2.

55. His quotation from Acts reads: "Erant autem perseverantes in doctrina apostolorum, et communicatione fractionis panis, et orationibus."

56. *Chronica*, tit. 6, cap. 2, sect. 1.

57. Accounts in vols. VI/1, VI/2, VI/3, VII/1, VII/2, and VIII of *Concilium Tridentinum: Diariorum, Actorum, Epistularum, Tractatuum Nova Collectio*, ed., Societas Goerresiana (Freiburg im Breisgau: Herder & Co., 1901-). Henceforth CT. For the patristic authorities most often quoted in the course of the conciliar debate, see the listing below.

58. See CT VI/1 321-325 and CT VII/1 375-378.

59. Franciscus Senensis, CT VI/2 506,1-11.

60. CT VIII 959ff.

61. For the pertinent parts of his contribution, see CT VI/2 442.

62. On this point, see David N. Power, *The Sacrifice We Offer. The Tridentine Dogma and Its Reinterpretation* (Edinburgh & New York: T & T Clark and Crossroad Publishing Company, 1987) 76-79, 86-88.

63. CT VI/2 447,7.

64. CT VI/2 451f. and 454f.

65. CT VI/2 459.

66. CT VI/2 462 and 465.

67. CT VI/2 495,10-15.

68. CT VI/2 553,1-46 and 555,35-556,9.

69. CT VI/2 579,26-42.

70. CT VI/2 589,10-38 and 591,10-14.

71. *Historia Ecclesiae Tripartita* IX,38,22ff. (CSEL 71, 562,117ff.).

72. CT VI/2 489f.

73. Basil, *De Spiritu Sancto* 27,66 (PG 32:187-188B).

74. Origen, *In Num Hom.* 5,1 (GCS VII, 26,18-24).

75. *In Ioannem* 84,1 (CC 36,537,26-32).

76. CT VI/2 621,10-622-10 and 625,17ff.

77. His use of Durandus is from *Rationale* IV, 36 & 38.

78. Their lengthy contribution is printed in CT VI/3 383-531. For their ideas about the origins of the Canon, see 500-506,27.

79. CT VI/2 540,15-543,12.

80. On this, see Power, *The Sacrifice* 64-66.

81. CT VII/2 373,33-40.

82. CT VII/2 387,37-44.

83. Gropper, as canon of the chapter of the church of Cologne, was author of a response to the Reformers of which a number of Tridentine theologians made use, namely, *Antedidagma seu Christianae et Catholicae Fidei per Rev. et Illust. D. Canonicos Metripolitanae Ecclesiae Coloniensis Propugnatio* (Venice, 1547).

84. CT VII/2 531,38-532,6.

85. CT VII/2 542,5ff.

86. CT VIII 726,5-9.

87. Power, *The Sacrifice* 76-79.

88. Tapper, for example, says that though the priestly prayer is one of offering and is beneficial for those for whom it is offered, the people are best engaged during the Mass in commemoration and thanksgiving. CT VII/2 376,40-377,4.

89. This was strongly affirmed by the bishops who took part in the session of 1562. See Power, *The Sacrifice* 105-114.

90. Chapter 4 of the decree says of the Canon: *Is enim constat cum ipsis Domini verbis, tum ex Apostolorum traditionibus ac sanctorum quoque Pontificium piis institutionibus.* (Denz 1745)

91. See note 35. (72) CSEL 73, 81,20-82,37.

92. See note 35.

93. See note 34.

94. See note 31.

95. PG 3:424C-445C.

96. See note 4.

97. See note 33.

98. Walafrid Strabo, *Glossa in Epist. 1 ad Tim.* 2,1. (PL 114:627B)

99. See note 36.

100. See note 41.

101. *Gregorii I Papae Registrum Epistolarum*, Tomus 2, ed., Ludovicus M. Hartmann (Monumenta Germaniae Historica: Munich, 1978) 59,1-60,12.

102. L. Duchesne, *Le Liber pontificalis, texte, introduction et commentaire*, vol. 1 (Paris: De Boccard, 1955) 127, 129, 239, 255, 312.

103. Paul Hinschius, ed. *Decretales Pseudo-Isidorianae et Capitula Angilrami* (Leipzig, 1963) 70.

104. Remigius, l.c.: "Missa autem dicitur, quasi transmissa, vel quasi transmissio, eo quod populus fidelis de suis meritis non praesumens, preces et oblationes quas Deo omnipotenti offerre desiderat, per ministerium et orationem sacerdotis ad Deum transmittat, quem mediatorem inter se et illum esse cognoscit . . ."; Hugo, l.c.: ". . . quasi transmissio, eo quod populus fidelis per mysterium sacerdotis, qui mediatoris vice fungitur inter Deum et homines, preces et vota et oblationes Deo transmittat."

105. For positions in this regard, see R.C.D. Jasper and G.J. Cuming, *Prayers of the Eucharist* 155-158.

106. PG 3:437B-C for commemoration of the saints. On rites for the dead, see chapter 7 of the work, PG 3:556C-565B.

107. l.c. 425D, 440C-441D.

108. The pertinent part of the texts reads thus: "Orationem vero Dominicam idcirco mox post precem dicimus, quia mos apostolorum fuit, ut ad ipsam solum modo orationem oblationis hostiam consecrarent, et valde mihi inconveniens visum est, ut precem quam

scolasticus composuerat super oblationem diceremus et ipsam traditionem quam redemptor noster composuit super eius corpus et sanguinem non diceremus." It is indeed most likely that the Canon is the first *prex* or the *oratio oblationis,* and the question is whether anything ought to be added over the already consecrated oblation.

109. It seems to have been taken for granted on both sides of the controversy that the Canon began after the *Sanctus.*

110. These points I recall from Power, *The Sacrifice.*

111. For example, Ricardus Vercellensis CT VI/2 440,15; Thomas de Sancto Marino CT VI/2 477,12-17 and 478,1-11; Hieronymus ab Oleastro CT VI/2 493,36; Claudius Iaius and Alphonsus Salmeron CT VI/3 384,16-22; Ioannes Orthega CT VII 2 384,3f.; Iohannes Gropper CT VII/2 442,29-33; Bartholomaeus Carranza CT VII/2 515,15f.

112. Iaius and Salmeron CT VI/3 419,33f. Salmeron repeated this argument in 1562, CT VIII 724,13.

113. CT VI/2 400.

114. CT VI/2 478,1-11.

115. More is said about this in Power, *The Sacrifice* 80-82.

116. CT VI/3 384,16-22.

117. Ibid. 400,21-23.

118. Ibid. 392,40.

119. Power, *The Sacrifice* 76-79.

120. CT VII/2 373,5-40.

121. CT VII/2 442,29-33.

122. CT VII/2 479,5ff.

123. CT VI/2 459.

124. CT VI/2 607,12-23.

125. CT VI/2 620,20-25.

126. Power, *The Sacrifice* 119f.

127. CT VI/3 509,21-510,8.

128. CT VI/2 564,9-565,15.

129. *Summa Theologiae* III,83,5,ad 3.

130. *Summa Theologiae* III,83,4.

131. Ricardus Vercellensis CT VI/2 441,1ff.

132. CT VII/2 376,40-377,4.

133. CT VI/2 454.

134. That is, in 1 Tim 2:1, as commented upon by Augustine and the supposed Ambrose.

9

Sacraments Shaping Faith: The Problem of Sacramental Validity Today

John A. Gurrieri

THE ISSUE OF SACRAMENTAL VALIDITY HAS BEEN A VEXING QUESTION FOR centuries. Seemingly settled by the medieval theological synthesis and the decrees of the Council of Trent in the sixteenth century, in reality the validity of the sacraments has always been an open-ended question, even a problem, when confronted by crises of the magnitude of Anglican Orders, for example, or *episcopi vagantes*.[1] Essentially the problem can be stated in a series of questions. What constitutes a true and authentic sacrament within the Church Catholic? Who or what institutional instrumentality (e.g., a "magisterium"?) can or may make a definitive statement concerning the validity or authenticity of a sacrament? Can such statements be made definitively so as to rule out doubt about the nature of this or that sacramental celebration? What is the relationship between an authentic/valid sacrament and the nature of the church and its structure? Do sacraments shape faith? If so, how? And is the reverse also true or pertinent? Or, perhaps more to the point, is the question of sacramental validity pertinent to contemporary theology and pastoral concerns?

This essay does not intend to respond to any of these questions with definitive answers. For a history of the question, readers are directed to my 1981 essay "Sacramental Validity; The Origins and Use of a Vocabulary" in *The Jurist* (Volume 41). The purpose of this study is to pose some of these questions by examining the question of sacramental validity within the context of the old adage *lex orandi, lex credendi*; namely, that sacraments *do* shape faith and because of this fact it is necessary to have some idea that what the church is "doing" in a given liturgical sacramental celebration will indeed shape its faith according to the apostolic mission the church has received and the Gospel that has been handed down from the Lord through the apostolic chuch. The issue of "validity," therefore, will always be a salient one for the life of the church.

Prolegomena and Consideration of Method

The following statement should be a maxim of sacramental theology: Before it ever becomes the object of theological discourse, a sacrament is a liturgical event, a celebration in word, gestures, signs, affections, and a whole complex of other elements involving signification and effect. In the experience of the church the event always precedes the definition of the event. The event may only be accurately described after it has taken place, not before. Before its celebration, a "liturgy" is only a possibility. When, however, the reverse is true, that is, when a liturgy is defined only from its texts and possible ritual expression, then it is a sign that liturgical decay has set in the body ecclesial. For when a sacrament is primarily the object of theological discourse or of canonical discipline, and secondarily a liturgical event, then it becomes possible to study a sacrament—to create a sacramental theology—without reference to the prior liturgical celebration of the sacrament.[2] Such forms of sacramental theology are ultimately detrimental to authentic worship. It is no surprise to historians of the liturgy to learn that aliturgical theological enterprises occur with greater frequency in the life of the church than is healthy for the continuing good of worship, the liturgical needs of the Christian people, and the demands of sound or right doctrine. In the end such a situation demonstrates "[t]he failure to respect worship as a source of reliable doctrine . . ., one of the severest limitations of theological method since the sixteenth century."[3]

The adage of Prosper of Aquitaine, *legem credendi lex statuat supplicandi* or, as it is usually stated more succinctly, *lex orandi, lex credendi*[4] indicates a theological method as much as it expresses the church's rule of faith as it is linked to its rule of worship. As a method, *lex orandi, lex credendi* obliges the theologian reflecting on the sacraments to use the liturgy as a *locus theologicus*. Frans Jozef van Beeck states the case succinctly:

> To verify Christian worship, witness takes the shape, not only of conduct, but also of *teaching*. Teaching has its roots in the christological narrative as it came to function both in the kerygmatic-missionary and in paraenetic-communal situations. Eventually, it took shape in *rules of faith* generated by the christological narrative; remarkably soon after the end of the apostolic era, therefore, Christian worship turns out to have generated authoritative doctrine. It is not difficult to see why.[5]

In seeking to apply *lex orandi, credendi* as a theological method for sacramental discourse, one must first understand the true origins of the adage and its inherent limitations as an *ancient* rule. While the formula sounds broad and all-inclusive, the *lex orandi* here really refers to the *lex supplicandi*, that is, "the ancient liturgical practice of the *general intercessions*," now restored to the Roman liturgy. The main agenda of the *Indiculus* is the following: to demonstrate that intercessory prayer *proves* the absolute necessity of grace. That is, the constant and universal practice of petitionary and intercessory prayer from apostolic times demonstrates how Christians pray for the grace of conversion of unbelievers and the grace of perseverance for themselves. In this regard, then, the formula owes its inspiration to Augustine's anti-pelagianism.[6]

Augustine, over and over again in his homiletic and tractarian writings, attempted to give doctrinal proof from the liturgy—the eucharist and baptism especially—that grace is necessary for the Christian life or that children are born with original sin, for example.[7] For Augustine, and for Prosper of Aquitaine, the liturgy was a controlling *locus theologicus* of apostolic proportions, since the church's worship was handed down from the apostles and forms the core of the church's structure and life. The doctrinal value of liturgy was just as important for other writers of the patristic age, for example, Cyril of Jerusalem, Ambrose, John Chrysostom, Theodore of Mopsuestia, as it was for Augustine and Prosper. Indeed, one might conclude that the use of the liturgy formed a distinct patristic theological method to demonstrate the most important of Christian doctrines such as grace, the nature of the church, the divinity of Christ, and so on.

Was the liturgy also a source for sacramental theology in the patristic period? Did the liturgy (as *locus theologicus*) serve also as the method of initiating a theology of the sacraments? For Augustine the response is affirmative. Augustine used all aspects of the church's worship to elaborate his theological outlook on the sacraments. Even the liturgical year and church architecture served his theological discourse on Christian sacramental life. Augustine also formulated his understanding of the sacramental authenticity—or, what later theologians named "validity"—from a reflection on worship. In short, while he may not have formulated the adage *lex orandi, lex credendi*, nor restricted its meaning to intercessory prayer, Augustine nevertheless believed that the "deeper norms that govern the Church's prayer—and hence its faith—are apostolicity and universality, which in turn are signs of the deepest and truest law of prayer and faith: Christ at work, in the Holy Spirit, in the Church's worship."[8] Thus, for Augustine it was paramount to establish which liturgy was truly apostolic and universal, that is, authentic and "valid."

While it is true that the "maxim *lex orandi, lex credendi* is not a general norm that can be indiscriminately invoked to draw doctrine from each and every text used in liturgical settings," the formula does "point to Christ, present in the Spirit, as the ultimate authorization of all of the Church's worship"[9] and, therefore, can stand as a general rule for a theological discourse on the sacraments themselves. It is in this sense that *lex orandi, lex credendi* serves as a theological method: the liturgy draws its authorization from Christ; therefore, the liturgy, and not speculation unrelated to the liturgy, draws us to an understanding of what the sacraments truly mean and how an authentic sacrament is constituted. It is the ensemble of texts, the celebration itself, and the tradition and history behind the texts and celebrations which point the church to a genuine understanding of the nature and function of the sacraments in ecclesial life.

Many theologians have considered that its doctrinal context and teaching power oblige the church constantly to review and reform the liturgy, to see to it that worship remains "free from error" or those things which obscure its reality, that is, its power to convert through grace and the power, again through grace, to aid in Christian perseverance and perfection. Thus, reform of the liturgy is nearly as constitutive of the liturgy as the very texts and events which constitute the experience of worship. Augustine understood this when he advised other bishops "to correct any errors that may be present in it [liturgy] and to introduce features that will be profitable."[10] One might rephrase another old maxim in the following manner: *liturgia ecclesiae semper reformanda est.*

The driving force behind the conciliar constitution *Sacrosanctum Concilium* was essentially the same. The document established the theological framework for a contemporary reform of the church's music when it stated the following:

> In order that the Christian people may more certainly derive an abundance of graces from the sacred liturgy, holy Mother Church desires to undertake with great care a general restoration of the liturgy itself. *For the liturgy is made up of unchangeable elements divinely instituted, and of elements subject to change.* These latter not only can be changed but ought to be changed with the passage of time, if they have suffered from the intrusion of anything out of harmony with the inner nature of the liturgy or have become less suitable. *In this restoration both texts and rites should be drawn up so as to express more clearly the holy things which they signify.*[11]

The liturgy is subject to reform precisely because it is simultaneously the "people's work" and a source of doctrine; as such, the liturgy is subject to the "intrusion" of those things which can cause "error." The liturgy must be as free of error as is *humanly* possible since it is the source of teaching as well as grace. However, whence comes the assurance of truth in the liturgy? Mere antiquity does not assure the liturgy's *veritas* or truth. As Cyprian of Carthage once stated, *consuetudo sine veritate vetustas erroris est* ("custom without truth is but old error").[12] If not antiquity, then what?

Against the schismatics, Cyprian considered baptism and the ensemble of baptismal rites unalterable because of their dominical or apostolic origin. If a rite is known or understood to be instituted by Christ himself or through the apostles, then the church is assured of the *veritas* of the rite. What may be changed and what is unalterable hinge upon dominical institution or apostolicity, or both.

Tertullian held the same view and insisted upon the *truth* of sacramental actions in his polemic against heretics, particularly against Marcion who himself kept the eucharist. But, as Tertullian was quite aware, the mere keeping of the eucharist does not assure the church of the truth or authenticity of the eucharist. The Church Fathers believed that the eucharist must be celebrated "precisely" as the Lord instituted it, that is, with the meaning Christ himself gave to that memorial of his body and blood. The *ratio* or *veritas* of the eucharist resides in the words and actions of the Lord rightly handed down from the apostles to the church over the centuries. Thus, against Marcion, Tertullian appeals to dominical institution and *meaning* and not to ancient custom. Even in his montanist period, Tertullian held that old custom is subject to error or heresy though it may have begun well, for in the praxis of the church ignorance and corruption may give new heretical meaning to what once possessed the truth imparted by Christ.[13]

Behind the adage *lex orandi, lex credendi*, therefore, is a concern for truth—the truth of the liturgy as well as the truth of doctrine. The African concern with this truth—Tertullian, Cyprian, Augustine—has its source in the African preoccupation with heresy, apostasy, and schism—all crisis situations—and therefore a preoccupation with orthodoxy. "Preoccupation with orthodoxy as a prerequisite for worship, in turn, found its way back *into the structure of the liturgy itself.* There is evidence, in other words, that the *lex credendi* sometimes does determine the *lex orandi.*[14]

What all this amounts to is the church's preoccupation with the truth of a sacrament, what later centuries would call its *validity*. Validity must be understood not merely as a concern for the proper conditions for the correct functioning of a rite, but rather as that search for what makes a *sacramentum* true or *verum*. The medieval synthesis would insist that a sacrament's *veritas* is to be found in its *substantia* or *essentia* and that a sacrament's substance is that which comes from the Lord. What comes from Christ—dominical institution—is unchangeable. Therefore, the church, which may set conditions for worship and even change many of its ritual and textual elements, has power over the sacraments, *salva illorum substantia* ("except the substance of the sacraments"), as the Council of Trent later stated.

Salva Illorum Substantia: Lex Orandi?

The maxim *salva illorum substantia* was stated at the twenty-first session of the Council of Trent on 16 July 1552 in Chapter Two of the Decree on Communion under Both Kinds:

> [H]anc potestatem perpetuo in Ecclesia fuisse, ut in sacramentorum dispensatione, salva illorum substantia, ea statueret vel mutaret quae suscipientium utilitati seu ipsorum sacramentorum venerationi pro rerum, temporum et locorum varietate magis expedire iudicaret. (DS 1728)

Or, as one English translation cautiously renders it:

> . . . in the dispensation of the sacraments, *salva illorum substantia*, the Church may, according to circumstances, times and places, determine or change whatever she may judge most expedient for the benefit of those receiving them or for the veneration of the sacraments; and this power has always been hers.[15]

From the time this maxim was stated, Catholic theologians have disputed its meaning, since there does not appear to be only one way to interpret the traditional concept *sacramentorum substantia*. The council's adage continues to be open to interpretation. Vatican II's Constitution on the Liturgy, already cited, is itself an expression of the Tridentine teaching that the church has the power to change various elements of the liturgy of the sacraments which do not touch upon the essence of the sacraments. In other words, the church exerts neither authority nor power over those things which, in the Catholic theological tradition, touch the substance of a sacrament, those things which are *de necessitate sacramenti*: matter, form, and intention. This triad makes up the validity of a sacrament, its authenticity, its *divine institution*. All other elements in the complex of rites, texts, and celebration, express a sacrament's *liceity*, its lawfulness or, as Peter Lombard stated those things *"ad solemnitatem pertinent."*[16] Thus, a sacrament *as liturgical event* is divided into two sets of elements: those necessary for validity and those required for liceity (lawfulness or solemnity or both). The church controls the latter, but has no influence over the former. Or does it? That is the controversy. Just what authority does the church have over the rule of prayer, the *lex orandi*?

Today this question is much more important than would at first appear. For Roman Catholics the question or problem of sacramental validity arises in such diverse issues as the matter (bread and wine) used in the eucharist, the role and use of general absolution, the validity of marriages and the question of annulments, new "functional" trinitarian formularies ("Creator, Redeemer, Sanctifier") at baptism, the ordination of bishops and presbyters by the schismatic Marcel Lefebvre, the Roman Catholic position (or positions) on Anglican Orders, ordinations "without title,"[17] and the ordination of women. Sacramental validity is also an ecumenical question for Roman Catholic doctrine: how does the Roman Catholic magisterium understand the ministry and sacraments of Christians separated from itself since the Reformation? These issues are subject to various forms of theological discourse which are not within the purview of this presentation. However, as "problems" of sacramental theology in a *traditional* Roman Catholic interrogation, the principle of sacramental validity can prove to be helpful.

Establishing Terms and Distinctions

Sacramental validity can be understood in three distinct ways: (1) validity is a theological affirmation of sacramental authenticity; (2) validity is a form of canonical discourse for the regulation of the sacraments; or (3) validity is a form of legal minimalism, that is, a concern that in the external rite of a sacrament or in its form, validity is an expression of the minimum necessary *perficere sacramentum* ("to accomplish or effect a sacrament").[18]

Behind these distinctions lies the question of the power (*potestas*) of the church over the substance or essence of the sacraments. The question might be phrased in the following manner: Does the church have the power to impose conditions of validity on each and every sacrament in such a way as to effect a change in the essential elements and nature of a sacrament? The 1983 Code of Canon Law gives a curious response to this question.

> Since the sacraments are the same for the universal church and pertain to the divine deposit [of faith], it is for the supreme authority of the church alone to approve or define those things which are required for their validity; it is for the same supreme authority in accord with the norm of can. 838.3 and 4 to determine what pertains to their lawful celebration, administration and reception and also the order to be observed in their celebration.[19]

This canon, which is derived from canon 68 of the discarded *Lex Ecclesiae Fundamentalis*, says nothing about the Tridentine exception, *salva illorum substantia*. The canon may even give the impression that the church's "supreme authority" does have power over the substance of the sacraments when it asserts it can "approve or define those things which are required for their validity." The canon seems to obscure what was made clear by the Council of Trent and succeeding expressions of the church's "supreme authority."

In 1947 Pius XII, seeking to clarify the exact matter and form of the sacrament of orders, stated the following:

> In the course of centuries the Church did not and could not substitute other sacraments in place of those instituted by Christ our Lord. The reason is that the seven sacraments of the New Law were all instituted by Jesus Christ our Lord, as the Council of Trent teaches, and the Church has no authority over the "substance of the sacraments," that is, over the elements that Christ our Lord himself, according to the testimony of the sources of divine revelation, determined should be kept in the sacramental sign.[20]

Pius XII made it possible for the Latin Church to distinguish between an integral formula and the essential form necessary for a sacrament. Paul VI, responding to the decrees of *Sacrosanctum Concilium* to revise the Roman liturgical books, followed Pius XII in this regard. For example, in his Apostolic Constitution introducing the newly-revised rites of ordination, Paul VI stated:

> In the ordination of presbyters, the matter is . . . the laying on
> of hands on the individual candidates that is done in silence be-
> fore the consecratory prayer, of which the following belong to
> the essence [of the sacrament] and are consequently required
> for validity . . . [the form is then given].[21]

Paul VI makes it clear that the Latin Church does have the authority or *potestas* to "add, delete, or change certain things, in
order either to restore the texts of the rite to the form they had
in antiquity, to clarify expressions, or to bring out more clearly
the effects of the sacraments." Furthermore, the pope was also
moved by other motives: "We therefore think it necessary, so as
to remove all perplexity of conscience, to declare what are to be
held as the essentials in each revised rite."[22]

Pope Paul refers back not only to Pius XII's 1947 Apostolic
Constitution, but also to the conciliar decree of the Constitution on the Liturgy, article 21, already cited above. Likewise,
Paul's work of reform lies behind canon 841 which establishes
the "supreme authority" of the Latin Church that sets the conditions for sacramental validity. It should be noted that Paul
VI also altered sacramental formularies for other sacraments,
namely, penance (new formulary for absolution with "essential words"), the eucharist (the addition of new anaphoras in-
corporating new forms of the epiclesis and a revised form of
the institution narrative), and so on.

Paul VI, Pius XII before him, the Code of Canon Law, and
the norms of the reformed Roman liturgical books present a
new corpus of church law, destined not only for the ordering
of church worship but (more importantly) for the ordering of
the church itself. One is reminded of Karl Barth's remark that
"church law is liturgical in origin; it creates order starting with
worship, renews itself in worship and at the same time assures
the Church its order."[23] Thus the reformed books of the Roman
Rite express the Latin Church's renewed ecclesiology as much
as they do that church's desire to reform or renew its liturgy.

In locating, in a way slightly different from the Council of
Trent, the church's authority over sacramental validity, the
teaching of Paul VI and the 1983 canon 841 determine more
than the merely canonical. For, as Frederick R. McManus
states, canon 841 "is concerned to reserve the approval or definition of what is necessary for the validity, genuineness, or re-

ality of sacraments to 'the supreme authority of the Church'."[24] Does this mean, therefore, that Vatican II, Paul VI (and Pius XII), and the Code of Canon Law have altered the Council of Trent's demurral about the substance of the sacraments (*salva illorum substantia*)?

Historical Underpinnings

The concern of Vatican II and Paul VI for the validity of the sacraments can be traced first to the Council of Trent and before that council to the medieval scholastic synthesis. The Scholastics eventually developed a "general sacramental theology," a *de sacramentis in genere* approach to the sacraments. This approach in turn owes something to the scholastic elaboration of the septenary nature of the sacraments, that there are seven and only seven sacraments of the New Law. Another element of the scholastic sacramental synthesis is the description of the sacraments according to matter, form, and intention: each sacrament consists of matter and form and requires the proper intention on the part of the minister or ministers for its effective celebration.

This *de sacramentis in genere* approach elaborated in the twelfth and thirteenth centuries "made possible the application of terminology, original to one sacrament [marriage, for example], to all other sacraments."[25] What is true of one sacrament, this reasoning goes, must also be true of the other six, for each is made up of matter, form, and intention. What differs from one sacrament to the next is the substance or essence or reality of each and the effect of grace in the recipients. While Augustine did elaborate certain elements of a general sacramental theology, for Augustine and other writers of the patristic age, each sacrament had its own terminology or vocabulary that expressed differences in ritual, grace, and other aspects of the sacrament. Thus, while the Latin Church Fathers could assert such universals about sacraments as divine institution and the gift of grace, they spoke differently about each sacrament and even applied the idea of *sacramentum* more broadly than the Scholastics.[26]

The concern for a sacrament's "validity," that is, its authenticity, varied with each sacrament prior to the scholastic synthesis. Our best examples of this difference are the sacraments of marriage and ordination, "the sacraments not common to all."

Because marriage is a contract between two parties, either the bride and groom or, more likely before the modern period, between the families of the bride and groom, marriage was and is the object of the church's canonical discipline. A specific canonical or legal vocabulary developed around the contractual and consensual nature of marriage. However, marriage was considered a sacrament, a sign of the New Law of divine institution mirroring the relationship between Christ and the church. As a sacrament, marriage is a covenant and, as such, is a sign of the covenant of Christ and the church. Thus, marriage is both contract and covenant. The two vocabularies come into play: a jurisprudential language for marriage-as-contract, and a biblical-theological language for marriage-as-covenant. While these vocabularies were separate in the patristic period, in the medieval period, when canonists were also to some extent theologians, the canonical or legal vocabulary spilled over into the theological discourse of marriage so that, by the fourteenth and fifteenth centuries, marriage's theological vocabulary was primarily a legal or canonical language.

The canon law of marriage required exacting standards for the validity of the contract or consent, for so many other things hinged upon the marriage's authenticity or genuineness or reality, for example, the legitimacy and status of children, inheritance, the societal and economic status of women, and so forth. The problem of canonical validity, therefore, was inextricably linked to marriage's sacramentality. In fact, they were one and the same.

"Because the *cura animarum* was linked to the purpose of ordination, a terminology proper to this sacrament also developed on its own."[27] Hugh of St. Victor (1096-1141), in his *Sacraments of the Christian Faith* (*De Sacramentis Christianae Fidei*) maintained that ordination was constituted as a sacrament of the New Law by Christ "for the sole purpose of somehow preparing and sanctifying the things that are necessary for the sanctification and institution of other sacraments."[28] Thus the validity, that is, the authenticity or reality, of ordination was paramount for the whole sacramental structure and life of the church. Without validly ordained bishops, priests, and deacons there could be no other genuine or "valid" sacrament of the New Law. It was considered part of the divine dispensation that orders, divinely instituted by Christ, were necessary for the sacramental and liturgical life of the church, indeed for the very structure and legitimacy of the church.

Both marriage and orders demonstrate two other important sacramental concerns of the medieval schoolmen: the objective reality of the sacraments and the effect of the sacraments. Alger of Liège (d. 1131/1132) elaborated this distinction principally from the canonical collections (*Decretum, Panormia*) of Ivo of Chartres (1040-1116), works from which Alger and other schoolmen cited Augustine. "In Alger's writings . . . one finds the distinction between sacramental objectivity and the effect of a sacrament. Alger, being both a canonist and a theologian, already formulated (without the language) a concept of sacramental validity: 'in the celebration of the sacraments of Christ' the Church must follow the institution of Christ so that 'what we perform is true to his power and legitimate authority.'"[29]

Sacramental objectivity and sacramental effect demand sacramental validity in the teachings of the medieval canonists and theologians. That is, those things necessary for the authenticity of a sacrament, what is true to its divine institution, must be discovered and codified for the sake of the church, its structure and sacramental life. For the sacrament of holy orders this was paramount. Crisis situations proved this necessary concern for "validity." For the *lex credendi*, the rule of prayer, to somehow assure the *lex credendi*, the rule of faith and be its source, that is, if the sacraments are somehow to shape our faith, then great care and attention for the liturgy is required; not merely an attention to rubrics and ceremonies, but also and more significantly, for the conditions necessary for a sacrament's validity or veracity.

A Few Final Words

In several recent issues of *Periodica*, a journal published by the Gregorian University in Rome, the Spanish Jesuit Marcelino Zalba has written about the question whether the Roman Pontiff possesses the power and authority to invalidate ordinations conferred by a bishop acting without Roman sanction and on his own authority.[30] Zalba's position, which seems to be that of Cardinal Ratzinger and the Congregation for the Doctrine of the Faith, is that history demonstrates that the Roman Pontiff has indeed exercised such authority in a number of celebrated and not so well-known cases. Zalba maintains that irregular ordinations done with the opposition of the pope are invalid, null and void, since opposing the will of the Roman Pontiff (the "Vicar of Christ") who has the care of the church and its unity runs contrary to the principle of *oikonomia* or Economy and, on the analogy of Economy, what may have been properly ("*rite*") done according to the necessary condition of a sacramental rite (Holy Orders) may be invalidated if such an action ran contrary to the good of the church. Thus, the ordination of bishops by Archbishop Marcel Lefebvre, which all acknowledge to have been illicit or unlawful, were also invalid, null and void, precisely because these ordinations tore at the fabric of the church's unity. They were no ordinations, in other words.

This is a curious position for the Roman Church to take, but one not to be rejected out of hand. The use of the principle of Economy to sort out such a vexing problem of sacramental validity reminds one of the Orthodox view of valid and invalid sacraments.[31] Also, the very analogy used to declare invalid the ordinations by Lefebvre, might be used to declare valid Anglican ordinations (or ordinations of other Reformation Churches). For if one judges the validity of a sacrament not solely on the requisite conditions, but also on the basis of the *oikonomia* of the church, then new doors are opened for a reconsideration of questions once thought definitively resolved. But there is a flip side to such a rosy picture. Richard Hooker in the *Laws of Ecclesiastical Polity* stated an important caution on this matter: "Dissolutions and nullities of things done are not only not favoured, but hated, when either urged without cause, or extended beyond reach."[32]

Notes

1. For an interesting discussion of the issue, see Henry R.T. Brandreth, *Episcopi Vagantes and the Anglican Church* (London: SPCK, 1947), especially pp. 6-11; for an equally interesting, albeit often

amusing, account of *episcopi vagantes*, see Peter F. Anson, *Bishops at Large* (London: Faber and Faber, 1964).

2. See John A. Gurrieri, "Sacramental Validity: Ecumenical Questions," *Ecumenical Trends* 15 (May 1986) 71.

3. Frans Jozef van Beeck, *God Encountered: A Contemporary Catholic Systematic Theology*, Volume I: *Understanding the Christian Faith* (San Francisco: Harper & Row, 1989) 225.

4. This rule first appears c. 440 in the pseudo-Celestine *Indiculus* (Capitulum VIII) which is now attributed to Prosper of Aquintaine and dates from between 435-440. For a full consideration of the subject and an extensive bibliography, see Geoffrey Wainwright, *Doxology: The Praise of God in Worship, Doctrine, and Life, A Systematic Theology* (New York: Oxford University Press, 1980) 224-283. For the text of Capitulum VIII, see DS 246.

5. van Beeck, *God Encountered* 224-225.

6. Ibid. 226.

7. See Wainwright, *Doxology* 227.

8. van Beeck, *God Encountered* 226.

9. Ibid.

10. Wainwright, *Doxology* 228. See Augustine, *ep. 54* (PL 33:202-203); *ep. 55* 34-35 (PL 33:221-222).

11. Second Vatican Council, *Sacrosanctum Concilium*, Constitution on the Sacred Liturgy, no. 21, in *Vatican Council II: The Conciliar and Post-Conciliar Texts*, ed., Austin Flannery (Collegeville: The Liturgical Press, 1975) 9.

12. *Ep. 74*, 9, cited in Wainwright, *Doxology* 521, note 551.

13. See Wainwright's considerations of Tertullian, *Doxology* 232-233.

14. van Beeck, *God Encountered* 231.

15. *Canons and Decrees of the Council of Trent*, trans., H.J. Schroeder, O.P. (Rockford, IL: TAN Books and Publishers, Inc., 1941/1978) 133.

16. *Sententiae IV*, 3, 1.

17. For example, the Anglican Divine Richard Hooker (1554-1600) held the view that presbyters and deacons may lawfully be ordained *without title*, that is, to no particular parish or other "restraint." Hooker asserts his position for the following reasons:

1. The apostolic churches (Jerusalem, Antioch, Ephesus, Rome, and Corinth) all had "colleges" of presbyters and deacons who were created and "ordained" by the "Apostles or their delegates Evangelists" (no. 2). It was only in 112 A.D. that Evaristus divided Rome into "precincts" (the forerunners of parishes) for which presbyters were specifically ordained. This usage ("error") spread throughout the church. However, presbyters were specifically ordained. They were

ordained *kata polin* (for the city of Rome), that is, *kata ekklesian* (for the local church of Rome).

2. If presbyters were to be ordained lawfully only for the specific parish or ministry, then the church could not carry on its mission to preach the Gospel to all nations, since these latter do not yet have churches for which presbyters can be ordained. "[T]herefore it seemeth a thing in their eyes absurd and unreasonable that any man should be ordained a minister otherwise than only for some particular congregation . . . Perceive they not how by this means they make it unlawful for the Church to employ men at all in converting nations?" (no. 3). Richard Hooker (1554-1600), *Of the Laws of Ecclesiastical Polity*, Book V, Chapter LXXX (Oxford, 1841).

18. Charles Wackenheim in his essay "Validité et nullité des sacrements: le problème théologique," *Revue de droit canonique* 26 (1976) 15-22 distinguishes among canonical, ecclesial, and theological forms of validity.

19. Canon 841. *Code of Canon Law, Latin-English Edition*, translated by the Canon Law Society of America (Washington, D.C.: Canon Law Society of America, 1983)

20. Pius XII, Apostolic Constitution *Sacramentum Ordinis* in *The Church Teaches* 133 (DS 3857); confer DS 3858.

21. Paul VI, Apostolic Constitution *Pontificalis Romani Recognitio*, July 18, 1968: AAS 60 (1968) 372; DOL 2610. See DOL 2609 and 2611 for the diaconate and episcopate.

22. DOL 2608.

23. See Karl Barth, *Kirchliche Dogmatik* IV/2 (Zurich, 1955) 791.

24. See *The Code of Canon Law: Text and Commentary*, eds., James A. Cordien, Thomas J. Green, Donald E. Heintschel (New York/Mahwah: Paulist Press, 1985) 607.

25. John A. Gurrieri, "Sacramental Validity: The Origins and Use of a Vocabulary," *The Jurist* 41 (1981) 26.

26. Thus, Tertullian and Augustine, "defining" the word *sacramentum* as mystery and/or sign, named such things as Easter or blessed water or incense as *sacramenta*.

27. Gurrieri, "Sacramental Validity" 26.

28. I, 9, 7 (PL 176:327).

29. Gurrieri, "Sacramental Validity" 27. See Alger of Liège, *De Sacramentis* 3, 14 (PL 180:854).

30. See M. Zalba, S.J., "Num ecclesia habeat potestatem invalidandi ritum sacramentalem ordinis ab episcopis exclusis peractum," *Periodica de Re Morali, Canonica, Liturgica* 78:2 (1989) 187-242; see also *Periodica* 77 (1988) 289-328; 425-488; 575-612.

31. According to John H. Erickson, Orthodox theologians began to

use the principle of *oikonomia* or Economy in connection with sacramental theology only in the eighteenth century, "in the context of the controversy over Latin baptism which rocked the Greek-speaking world." Since that time the principle has played an important role in Orthodox statements concerning Anglican orders and other topics of ecumenical importance.

It will be useful to include here Erickson's summary of the common elements found in modern Orthodox presentations of Economy as applied to sacramental theology.

"1. *Oikonomia* is understood as the departure from or suspension of strict application (*akribeia*) of the Church's canons and disciplinary norms, making it in many resepcts analogous to the West's *dispensatio*.

"2. But *oikonomia* is broader than *dispensatio* in that it is not limited to canon law and church discipline but applies to the sacraments as well.

"3. In this context, from the point of view of strictness all sacoutside the Orthodox Church are null and void. (At this point Orthodoxy's adherence to a 'Cyprianic' ecclesiology and sacramental theology is often noted, as distinct from the West's 'Augustinian' approach.)

"4. But the Orthodox Church, as the sole steward of grace and sovereign administrator of the sacraments, can decide to treat sacraments as valid.

"5. This concerns the sacraments of those entering the Orthodox Church; it does not imply the recognition of the validity of non-Orthodox sacraments *per se*.

"6. One corollary of this approach is that the application of 'economy' need not be everywhere and always the same (hence the remarkable variations in Orthodox treatment of Latin baptism) but may change according to circumstances.

"7. These circumstances may include such considerations as (a) the attitude of the non-orthodox group toward Orthodoxy, (b) the well-being of the Orthodox flock, (c) the ultimate salvation of the person or groups contemplating entrance into the Orthodox Church." John H. Erickson, "Sacramental 'Economy' in Recent Roman Catholic Thought," *The Jurist* 48:2 (1988) 653-654; see also Francis J. Thomson, "Economy: An Examination of the Various Theories Held within the Orthodox Church, with Special Reference to the Economical Recognition of the Validity of Non-Orthodox Sacraments," *Journal of Theological Studies*, New Series, 16 (1965) 368-420.

32. Richard Hooker, *Laws of Ecclesiastical Polity* V, lxii, 13 (Oxford, 1841).

10

A Larger Vision of Apostolicity: The End of an Anglo-Catholic Illusion

Louis Weil

THE DISTINCTIVE CHARACTER OF ANGLICANISM HAS, THROUGHOUT ITS history, been connected with special intensity to two aspects of its ecclesial life, namely, its authorized forms for public liturgical worship and its requirement of episcopal ordination for establishing an authentic and continuous pattern of ministerial authority and pastoral care. This emphasis upon these two dimensions of church life has meant that issues related to the evolution of the Book of Common Prayer and to suggested modifications of the inherited model of the episcopate have inevitably become the source of dispute as well as debate as Anglicanism in its various provinces with their diverse cultural and national identities has faced the need to adapt the received tradition to widely divergent social realities. Dispute results because these two elements are so closely related to the identity of Anglicanism that any significant change seems to threaten the integrity and continuity of that identity.

As Anglicanism expanded beyond the narrow cultural confines of the British Isles, adaptation became an imperative from the beginning. In the American colonies, the absence of resident bishops led, for example, to the abandonment of the rite of confirmation for many decades. Those who sought ordination were obliged to risk the dangerous journey back to England to receive episcopal ordination.[1] After the American Revolution, however, the Episcopal Church in the young nation adhered closely to the models of the English Church both in its own Book of Common Prayer and in its fidelity to the continuity of episcopal succession. On the whole, identification with the Anglican Church required as high a degree of conformity as possible to what were seen as the primary marks of that identity. Yet there was adaptation, not only in such obvious ways as the substitution of prayer for the President in place of that for the King, but in more radical ways such as in the inclusion of a eucharistic prayer based upon that of the Scottish BCP of 1764, with its clearly high church eucharistic theology.[2]

It is in the latter half of the twentieth century that the most radical changes have been proposed both by Prayer Book revision in the various Anglican provinces and by important ecumenical and cultural pressures upon the pattern of the episcopate, such as in the formation in the 1940s of the Church of South India.[3] More recently, the participation of the Anglican Communion in both national and international ecumenical dialogues has placed the question of episcopal ministry within new contexts which have required an unprecedented intensity of reflection among Anglicans upon an understanding of the episcopate which had been taken for granted since the Reformation. A major aspect of this development both ecumenically and within the Anglican Communion has been the debate over the admission of women to the ordained ministries of the church. This issue poses a shift of model far more dramatic than merely the changes in the role of the episcopate which may be observed throughout the history of the church. The admission of women to the ordained ministries, and most significantly the admission of women to the episcopate, confronts a great many assumed principles of ministerial leadership. It demands either an expansion of the model of that leadership, or else it marks a crucial defection from the male model whose defenders find established in both Scripture and tradition.

The goal of a short essay must be modest, and so it is my intention here to consider how Anglicanism had come to understand the episcopate in terms of a static model fostered by the aims of the Oxford Movement of the nineteenth century, and how the ecumenical and cultural dynamics of the late twentieth century have obliged Anglicanism to move into a larger room and to see the gift of apostolic succession, which has been so basic to its identity, within an expanded theological framework not as a mechanical aspect of ministerial validity, but as a characteristic of the church as it seeks to live in fidelity to the Gospel.

The Oxford Movement and Apostolic Succession

The impact of the Oxford Movement upon the common interpretation of "apostolic succession" among Anglicans stretched far beyond those who would have described their Anglicanism as "Anglo-Catholic." The origins of a mechanistic understanding of apostolic succession may be easily documented from the writings of early writers within the Oxford Movement, but as ideas do, their teaching trickled down as a rather unreflected expression of how this mark of the church's life was to be understood.

The Swedish scholar Yngve Brilioth, in his study of the Oxford Movement entitled *The Anglican Revival*, saw in the ecclesiology of the movement an attitude which he called "the static view of the Church." We must consider this approach in relation to its shaping of a view of apostolic succession which emerged within Anglicanism. The primary published instrument of the Oxford Movement was a series of documents known as Tracts for the Times. The posture of the Tracts was defensive: they reaffirmed the church's apostolic origins and authority within a society in which the writers felt these had been undermined.

Upon the Tractarian understanding of apostolic succession as the essential foundation of the church's life, the Oxford writers based their claim for the catholicity of the Church of England and the validity of its sacraments. Their understanding involved an appeal to an unbroken continuity between the Church of England and the Church of the Apostles. The appeal itself had been characteristic of Anglicanism from the start of the English Reformation. It was taught that Christ had given authority to the apostles who had in turn commissioned their successors, the bishops.[4] But under the influence of the leaders of the Oxford Movement, the idea of apostolic commission gained not only a new vitality but also a narrowness of interpretation which is not found in earlier Anglican writings on the subject.

The old high church tradition in Anglicanism never spoke of the episcopate as so fundamental to the church's life that those traditions which lacked the historic succession were thereby unchurched. For these earliest writers, the episcopate was valued as an aspect of the authority inherited from the early Christian community, and certainly as a visible sign of the continuity of pastoral oversight from Christ to the present. Bishop William Beveridge (1637-1708) is an important source for the writers of the Oxford Movement, but Beveridge writes that the efficacy of any ecclesiastical office "depends altogether upon the Spirit of God." His concern for the apostolic succession is as the assured instrument of the Spirit's work in which Christ is present. Certainly Beveridge identifies this succession with the continuity of episcopal ordinations, but not in a mechanical sense. The episcopate is rather the sign and instrument of what is truly fundamental to the church's continuity, that is, the promised activity of the Holy Spirit. Among the writers of the Tracts for the Times, however, this seminal idea, as expressed in the writings of William Beveridge, flowered as an exclusive and deterministic aspect of the church's integrity.[5]

An important expression of this narrowing of the concept of apostolic tradition is found in the writings of William Palmer (1803-1885) of Worcester College, Oxford. Palmer's views received their fullest exposition in *A Treatise on the Church of Christ*, published in 1838. In this work Palmer proposes one of the narrowest interpretations of the authority of Christian ordained ministry which can be imagined. In Chapter VIII, "On the Apostolicity of the Church," Palmer links authentic ordained ministry to his view of apostolic succession. The divine commission for sacred office can only be given, he writes, "by means of ministers authorized to convey it to others." Given the title of the chapter, one might have hoped to find here some claiming of apostolic succession as secured by continuity in the life of the church as a whole, but for Palmer the apostolicity of the church appears to be secured only through the sequence of episcopal ordinations. The latter, rather than being a sign and expression of that continuity, had become the full meaning of continuity. This makes of ministerial succession virtually a self-contained reality standing separate from the continuity expressed in the general life of the church in faith, service, and witness.

For Palmer, there are firm restrictions upon the form through which Christ's commission may be authentically conveyed. Palmer writes:

> The mode by which this commission was conveyed must always be essentially the *same*. Now, the apostolic mode of ordination, by which the apostles and their successors, the bishops of the universal church, sent forth the ministers of Jesus Christ, by imposition of hands and prayer—this mode *alone* has *always* existed in the church. For many ages popular elections were unheard of. The apostolic mode of ordination *alone* prevails in all ages, and among all nations. It is therefore evidently the external vocation instituted by God himself. If it be not so, if it be a mode of human invention, it could never have constituted ministers of Christ, and therefore the whole church would for many ages have been without true ministers; it would have been deficient in what is *essential* to the church of Christ, and therefore the catholic church must have *entirely failed*: a position which is directly and formally heretical.

> The great external sign of such a continuance of ordinations in any church, is derived from the legitimate succession of its chief pastors from the apostles; for it is morally certain, that wherever there has been this legitimate succession, the whole body of the clergy have been lawfully commissioned.[6]

The concept of the church upon which this passage is based is that of a hierarchical ministerial structure whose authenticity is not merely promised but secured through tactile succession in ordination. Any group of Christians who live in separation from that specific ministerial structure cannot, for Palmer, be part of the visible church of Jesus Christ. In this view the church is defined in terms of the ordained ministry rather than in terms of the Christian society which is created through baptism. This high view of ministerial authority carried with it an implied inferiority of status for the laity. Thus Anglo-Catholics found it easy to speak without much theological reflection about "the grace of orders" as a special gift which others, namely, the laity, do not possess.

The idea of the special grace connected with ordination was related to the assertion that the validity of the sacraments depends entirely upon their being celebrated only by bishops of the apostolic succession or by other clergy who have been ordained by those bishops. In Tract 74, for example, it is asserted that non-episcopal forms of ministry have no authority to administer the sacraments. By implication, the sacraments are thus the possession of the clergy who have been validly ordained. Clergy are not so much stewards of the sacraments on behalf of the church, leaders of sacramental actions which properly pertain to the whole community, as instead the primary agents in any sacramental act. The important issue is the nature of the church which is expressed in this view. In their concern for ministerial validity, the Tractarians obscured the ecclesial foundation of all sacramental rites. It is the whole church which acts, for example, in baptism and eucharist, in union with the ordained pastoral leader of the community who takes a presiding role which images that pastoral leadership. The clergy receive specific authority for presiding at sacramental rites through delegation from the church at ordination, but for the Tractaritans, that delegated authority was so esteemed that it obscured the theological principle that in any sacramental act the primary actors are the whole baptized people of God.[7]

The reasons why apostolic succession was of such crucial importance to the leaders of the Oxford Movement would require a discussion beyond the limits of this essay.[8] Suffice it to say that by the early decades of the nineteenth century, the Church of England had come to be viewed in English society as little more than a department of the State, an organizational convenience for dealing with the religious affairs of the nation. A fundamental concern for the Tractarians was the need for finding a foundation for their view of the church as a divinely established institution which received its authority not from the State but from Jesus Christ who had delegated that authority to his apostles and their successors. This was seen as the only means by which to defend the integrity of the church against the assaults of the secularism of the time. The principle of apostolic succession was the foundation for Tractarian claims for the independence of the church from the State.

The particular situation of the Church of England, however, led to the isolation of one aspect of the meaning of apostolic succession from the many dimensions of its full significance in the life of the church: tactile succession became isolated from the wider context of meaning of which it is the sign. The Tractarian teaching thus altered the older emphasis upon apostolic commission into a more restricted emphasis upon apostolic succession which in effect meant apostolic transmission.[9] This shift is illustrated in a hymn by John Mason Neale (1818-1866) for Ember days, the usual time for ordinations and special prayer for the ordained. In verses 2 and 3 Neale writes:

> His twelve Apostles first he made
> His ministers of grace;
> And they their hands on others laid,
> To fill in turn their place.
>
> So age by age, and year by year,
> His grace was handed on;
> And still the holy Church is here,
> Although her Lord is gone.[10]

As Michael Sansom wryly comments in the essay mentioned earlier (see footnote 7):

> This has it all—tactual transmission, grace a transmissible "stuff" separable from Christ, and the church linked to her Lord not by cleaving vertically by faith but by being "graced" through the horizontal pipeline of "stuff" from the first bestowal of it upon the apostles by their risen Lord . . . It is embarrassing that J.M. Neale *actually* said what evangelicals have always thought anglo-catholics were saying.[11]

Although the humorous sarcasm of this comment reflects the author's bias as an Evangelical, the fact is that most recent theological reflection upon the meaning of ordination within the whole range of Anglicanism and also within the wider ecumenical perspective would be similarly concerned with the mechanistic image which Neale's verses presume. Our interpretation of apostolic succession surely must be held within the more inclusive framework of the creedal affirmation that the church in every age lives in continuity with the church of the apostles and their proclamation. That continuity includes the continuing delegation of authority from one generation to the next. But continuity equally involves other aspects of apostolicity: witness to the apostolic faith and its proclamation, participation in apostolic service, unity among the local churches, and faithfulness in the celebration of baptism and eucharist.[12] Nothing less than the fullness of apostolic faith and practice may be viewed as constituting the apostolic tradition.

Tragically, the leaders of the Oxford Movement were unable to claim this larger understanding of apostolicity, and by implication reduced it to one of its outward signs, tactile succession or the episcopal laying on of hands. This narrowed meaning left an indelible mark upon the Anglican tradition, clearly upon the presuppositions of Anglo-Catholics, but also upon many Anglicans who would not identify consciously with that movement. One may still find in diocesan and parish offices charts of the succession of bishops which give visible image to John Henry Newman's historically naive claim in Tract 7 that "every link in the chain is known, from St. Peter to our present Metropolitans."

The primitive church seems to have understood the succession not in so mechanistic a sense as that indicated by Newman's statement, but rather as represented in the succession of occupants of the episcopal chair in a given Christian community. This ancient view saw the episcopal office in an organic relation with the ongoing life of the local church, not as a self-contained and self-authenticating basis for ecclesiastical validity. The Tractarians often claimed the undivided church as an ideal, but it was that ideal looked at through the particular vision of nineteenth-century Romanticism, which viewed the church in terms of a static model which had never quite existed in actual history as they had come to imagine it.[13] The consequences of this adherence to an idealized static model of the church deeply influenced the theological presuppositions of a significant number of Anglicans in succeeding generations, and not merely the self-identified Anglo-Catholics.

It should be noted here that, given the influence of the ideas outlined above, the declaration of Pope Leo XIII in 1896 that

Anglican ordinations are "absolutely null and utterly void" came as a severe blow to Anglo-Catholics who were committed to a mechanistic understanding of ministerial succession.[14] Since apostolic succession had become for Anglo-Catholics a kind of idol of ecclesial identity, the papal declaration could not help but create a defensive posture and some degree of panic among those Anglicans for whom a papal decree carried considerable weight. One positive fruit was the development of a more conscious apologetic for the Anglican understanding of ordained ministry.[15] A more unfortunate consequence was, among a small fringe group, a desire for the assurance of validity according to the mechanistic model of the historic episcopate, even in dubious circumstances.[16]

The most serious matter for Anglicanism in all this is not really the problems raised by Leo XIII's denunciation. Recent scholarship has revealed the very problematic context from which the papal decree was issued.[17] In addition to that, the past few decades have seen the publication of a substantial literature on the question of validity as a corollary of a deepened ecumenical reflection on the nature of ordained ministry in relation to a renewed ecclesiology.[18] The problem for Anglicanism lies at the deeper level of how sacramental signs are understood, of a confusion of the signifier with the reality being signified. Although the most dramatic expression of this problem may be seen in the more crass understandings of the eucharistic presence during the later medieval period, the issue is wider in scope and is a matter of supreme importance for claiming the authentic meaning of sacrament in the church's life. Western Christianity as a whole has placed great emphasis upon the importance of continuity, and in Anglicanism, episcopacy has been affirmed as one of its primary signs. But in the interpretation of episcopacy which we have observed in such writers as William Palmer, the sign became the thing signified, and so continuity as a characteristic of the church became linked to a literalization of the sign in the tactile sequence of ordinations. The result is a well-intentioned illusion which in fact makes a caricature of what it sets out to esteem.

Apostolicity: A Larger Vision

Long before the ecumenical movement placed the issue of apostolicity within a larger context, there were Anglican voices which protested the mechanistic understanding of apostolic succession which Anglo-Catholics sought to promote. Early in the twentieth century, for example, John H. Skrine (1848-1923), a priest and theologian of the Church of England, published a booklet titled *Eucharist and Bishop* in which he opposed the view which seemed to isolate the episcopate from its fundamental frame of reference, the church. Skrine wrote:

> The Thing which is continuous with Christ is not the Episcopate, but the Church which created the Episcopate. The Church created by a communion with the Christ the first bishopric or Apostolate, and by her continued communion with the Christ she has maintained this creation. Therefore whatever is done by the bishop she, the Church, doeth it herself . . .

> And it is next submitted that the Church is continuous with Christ not only or even essentially in regard of time, but in regard—and that essentially—of life.[19]

Skrine goes on to say that there is an historical aspect to continuity because the church's life is united with Christ who is historic, that is, who acts in history. But, he suggests:

> . . . this temporal continuousness is not of the essence. The Church has the life unto Christ to-day not because she has had it every yesterday of recorded time back to the day of Jesus, but because to-day she is alive . . . If at this hour she is in actual communion with Him who died, and behold He is alive for evermore, then in communion with Him she is this hour, even if none could assure her that she had held communion in any hour of all the past.[20]

In conclusion, Skrine writes that "the essential idea of [apostolic succession is] defined as that of Continuity with the Historic Incarnation, that is continuity with Jesus Christ. But the continuity [is] not found to be in the person of individual apostles or bishops, but in the whole organism of the holy society."[21]

This ecclesial approach to the understanding of apostolic succession has gained an increasing self-confidence in official Anglican documents in this century. A characteristic example is found in a statement issued by the General Convention of the Episcopal Church in the USA in 1949. In the "Statement of Faith and Order" the following paragraph on the historic episcopate sums up Anglican thinking on the subject:

> The Church as the Body of Christ, sharing His life, has a ministerial function derived from that of Christ. In this function every member has his place and share according to his different capabilities and calling. The Church is set before us in the New Testament as a body of believers having within it, as its recognized focus of unity, of teaching and of authority, the Apostolate, which owed its origin to the action of the Lord Himself. There was not first an Apostolate which gathered a body of believers about itself; nor was there a completely structureless collection of believers which gave authority to the Apostles to speak and act on its behalf. From the first there was the fellowship of believers finding its unity in the Twelve. Thus the New Testament bears witness to the principle of a distinctive ministry, as an original element, but not the sole constitutive element, in the life of the Church.[22]

The "Statement of Faith and Order" reflects an emerging consensus within Anglican theology in the twentieth century that apostolic ministry cannot be identified narrowly with only those ecclesiastical bodies which have preserved one specific model of the historic episcopate. Apostolic ministry pertains to all those who through baptism are members of the church and thus of Christ.

In this perspective, the possession or non-possession of the historic episcopate cannot offer the unique basis for affirming or denying the legitimacy of the ordained ministries of the various ecclesial communities which make up the Catholic Church.[23] The fundamental ministry of that church is ultimately the ministry of Christ expressed through his apostolic commission to the church as a whole. As a sign of the continuity of that commission, the historic episcopate has, for Anglicans, served as a providential expression, but it is not the unique sign of apostolic continuity. It is especially in the ecumenical dialogues in which the Anglican Communion has participated in recent decades that this larger vision of apostolicity has been nurtured. The Anglican-Lutheran dialogue has been especially fruitful in this regard. *The Niagara Report*, which was the result of a consultation on *episcope,* speaks of the symbols of continuity in the canonical Scriptures, in the gifts of baptism and the Lord's Supper, in the confession of the orthodox and apostolic faith, and in the continuity of bishops and presbyters, but then goes on to insist that these "symbols of continuity" constantly require fresh interpretation. The church's concern must not be "the mere preservation of symbols."[24] In retrospect, the teaching of the Tractarians which so deeply influenced Anglo-Catholic attitudes within the Anglican tradition seems often, in spite of the high intent of the writers themselves, to have done just that by identifying the apostolicity of the church with an external, tactile sequence of ordinations rather than with fidelity to the apostolic commission.

Who are the heirs of that commission? All of us: all of the baptized people of God. It is the church which lives in succession to the apostles.[25] Apostolicity, like the other credal marks of the church, unity, holiness, and catholicity, is not a static attribute. Yngve Brilioth was correct in his study of the Tractarians that theirs was a static view of the church. All four of the creedal attributes of the church must be fulfilled again and again in the ongoing life of the church as it seeks to live out its apostolic commission in changing historical and cultural contexts. It is in this perspective that the issue of the ordination of women, and above all the ordination of women to the episcopate, must be addressed, and by as wide a representation of the church as possible.[26] The true test of apostolicity is fidelity to apostolic teaching and mission. The documents of the various ecumenical dialogues indicate a substantial consensus on the fundamental aspects of Christian faith. Does this doctrinal consensus not offer a basis for an ever increasing unity in our apostolic mission in the world? It is in this practical application of the various dialogues that a renewed ecclesiology will find expression in the ordinary pastoral experience of the church.

This enlarged vision of apostolicity is the fruit of intense scholarly reflection on the nature of the church and the understanding of holy orders which has taken place in this century.[27] It is a primary example of how the study of the sources of the common tradition of Christians leads to a rethinking of even a rejection of views which we have complacently held as long as we were content to live with a divided church. Inherited structures do not adapt easily, but our common inheritance of the apostolic commission obliges us to remold those structures if we are to be faithful to that commission in the century ahead.

Notes

1. Confer my doctoral thesis, *Worship and Sacraments in the Teaching of Samuel Johnson of Connecticut* (unpublished dissertation, Paris, 1972). For general social and political background, see Carl Bridenbaugh, *Mitre and Sceptre* (London: Oxford University Press, 1962).
2. The texts may be compared in Paul V. Marshall, *Prayer Book Parallels, Anglican Liturgy in America*, vol. 1 (New York: Church Hymnal Corporation, 1989) esp. 362-367. See also William Sydnor, *The Real Prayer Book* (Wilton, CT: Morehouse-Barlow, 1978) 42-58.
3. The union scheme for the Church of South India posed a direct threat to the Tractarian concept of the episcopate which we shall consider in this essay. For a discussion of its impact upon Anglican identity, confer Stephen Neill, *Anglicanism* (London: Mowbrays, 1958) 379-382, 388.
4. In *Tracts for the Times*, no. 74, we find a long series of quotations from earlier Anglican divines in support of the theory of apostolic succession. See the comments of N. Sykes, *Old Priest and New Presbyter* (Cambridge: The University Press, 1956) 209-213.
5. See Beveridge's full discussion in Sermon I of twelve sermons on "The True Nature of the Christian Church, the Office of Its Ministers, etc." in *Works*, Library of Anglo-Catholic Theology 1 (Oxford: Parker, 1842) 1-25, esp. 10-11.
6. *A Treatise on the Church of Christ*, vol. 1, 3rd ed. (London: Rivington, 1842) 140-142.
7. A useful discussion is offered by Michael Sansom in his critique of Tractarian teaching on the episcopate, "Magnify Your Office" in *Anglo-Catholic Worship*, ed., Colin Buchanan (Bramcote: Grove Books, 1983) 30.
8. See my survey of the background in *Sacraments and Liturgy* (Oxford: Blackwell, 1983) 7-12.
9. Confer John Henry Newman, *Tracts for the Times*, No. 1, 3 (London: Rivington, 1840).
10. *The English Hymnal*, No. 166 (London: Oxford University Press, 1933).
11. "Magnify Your Office" 29.
12. In the Lima Statement we find a more inclusive approach to the meaning of apostolicity which reflects an emerging ecumenical consensus. Confer "Ministry," section IV, "Succession in the Apostolic Tradition."

13. Especially useful for wiping away the Romantic dust from our eyes are two splendid works: Kenneth Clark, *The Gothic Revival* (New York: Holt, Rinehart, and Winston, 1962) and James F. White, *The Cambridge Movement* (Cambridge: The University Press, 1979).

14. Bull "Apostolicae Curae" and "Answer of the Archbishops of England to the Apostolic Letter of Pope Leo XIII on English Ordinations" (London: SPCK, 1943, reissue).

15. An important example is the work prepared under the direction of the Bishop of Oxford, Kenneth E. Kirk, *The Apostolic Ministry* (London: Hodder and Stoughton, 1946). When we consider such often valuable studies from our own perspective, they seem marked by that narrowness of view in which ordained ministry is seen within its own world rather than in reference to its ecclesial basis.

16. The dangers of a concern for valid orders in separation from the normative framework of ecclesial life is set forth in Henry R.T. Brandreth, *Episcopi Vagantes and the Anglican Church* (London: SPCK, 1947).

17. It is not relevant to our subject to discuss here the debate over Anglican Orders. The most useful survey of the circumstances surrounding the decree, and a comprehensive bibliography, may be found in a study by John Jay Hughes, *Absolutely Null and Utterly Void* (London: Sheed and Ward, 1968).

18. See, for example, Daniel J. O'Hanlon, "A New Approach to the Validity of Church Orders," *Worship* 41 (1967) 406-421; Edward P. Enchlin, "The Validity of Anglican Orders," *Journal of Ecumenical Studies* 7 (1970) 266-281; Killian McDonnell, "Ways of Validating Ministry," *Journal of Ecumenical Studies* 7 (1970) 209-265; John A. Gurrieri, "Sacramental Validity: The Origins and Use of a Vocabulary," *The Jurist* 41 (1981) 21-58; Harry McSorely, "Determining the 'Validity' of Orders," *The Jurist* 41 (1981) 371-404.

19. J.H. Skrine, *Eucharist and Bishop* (London: Longmans, Green, and Co., 1914) 24.

20. Ibid. 24-25.

21. Ibid. 27.

22. *Journal of the General Convention of the Protestant Episcopal Church in the United States of America* (San Francisco, 26 Sept. - 7 Oct., 1949) 666.

23. This last phrase should not be interpreted as an attempt to bring through the back door a refurbished version of the branch theory associated with William Palmer and other Anglican apologists. It is rather to affirm that the church is created through baptism, not through ordination.

24. Anglican-Lutheran International Continuation Committee, *The*

Niagara Report (Anglican-Lutheran Consultation on Episcope (London: Church House, 1988) nos. 29-30.

25. Confer Hans Küng, "Apostolicity and Succession," *The Church* (New York: Sheed and Ward, 1967) 354-359.

26. An excellent Anglican perspective to the ecumenical dimensions of this issue is offered by John Halliburton, *The Authority of a Bishop* (London: SPCK, 1987) 85-94.

27. The bibliography suggested by this comment would be vast. The works which have most influenced my own rethinking of these issues would include: Thomas M. Lindsay, *The Church and the Ministry in the Early Centuries* (London: Hodder and Stoughton, 1903); H.B. Swete, ed., *Essays on the Early History of the Church and the Ministry* (London: Macmillan, 1918); Kenneth E. Kirk, ed., *The Apostolic Ministry* (London: Hodder and Stoughton, 1946); Kewnneth M. Carey, ed., *The Historic Episcopate* (London: Dacre Press, 1954); W. Telfer, *The Office of a Bishop* (London: Darton, Longman and Todd, 1962); Peter Moore, ed., *Bishops, But What Kind?* (London: SPCK, 1982).

11

Communion Services: A Break with Tradition?

Gerard Austin

THROUGHOUT THE HISTORY OF THE ROMAN CATHOLIC CHURCH, MISSION areas have experienced a shortage of ordained ministers. As a result, priestless Sunday services, usually led by catechists, played an important part in the religious life and formation of the baptized. In the post-Vatican II era, this dearth of priests has spread even to countries which previously had been themselves suppliers of priests to the missions. As a result, some communities formerly accustomed to the celebration of Mass on Sundays are faced with a new choice: either to have a priestless Sunday service of some type, or not to gather together at all. In the late sixties and early seventies, certain parishes in West Germany and Austria began to copy the practice of the diaspora church of East Germany and to have communion services on Sunday when no priest was available.[1] The customary Sunday celebration of the Mass was replaced by a communion service in which Scripture is read, prayers of thanksgiving are recited, and previously consecrated hosts are distributed.

Although there was no mention of such communion services for Sunday celebration in the absence of a priest in the 1983 revised Code of Canon Law, the practice spread quite rapidly.

In 1987 John Paul II addressed the Congregation for Divine Worship on the topic of "Sundays in Priestless Parishes." He brought up the question of communion services.

> This type of celebration does not replace the Mass, but must cause one to desire it all the more. It is, for a small community of the faithful, a means, although imperfect, of preserving in a concrete manner its cohesion and vitality; it maintains from Sunday to Sunday its bonds with the whole church, which God does not cease to gather and which offers to him, from east to west everywhere in the world a perfect offering.[2]

The following year he approved the Directory for Sunday Celebrations in the Absence of a Priest which stated:

> Among the forms of celebration found in liturgical tradition when Mass is not possible, a celebration of the word of God is particularly recommended and also its completion, when possible, by eucharistic communion. In this way the faithful can be nourished by both the word of God and the body of Christ.[3]

This is a new approach for already evangelized and well established local communities. The customary celebration of Sunday Mass is being replaced with a communion service. The question is whether this is a break with the tradition? Is it a positive development, or is it a regression in our eucharistic tradition? In order to attempt to answer this, I shall first examine the historical evidence, and then turn to a theological analysis of the difference between a communion service and a eucharist.

Practice of the Early Church

The eucharistic practices described by the New Testament do not offer any one set pattern. Robert Taft writes:

> From the New Testament we can conclude nothing certain about eucharistic frequency. All were "assiduous" at the "breaking of the bread" (Acts 2:42), though how often is not indicated: the "daily" of Acts 2:46 refers with certainty only to the Temple prayer. An incipient Sunday rhythm may be implied in Acts 20:7-12 and I Cor. 16:2, and one might infer the same from the meals of the Risen Lord on the "first day", or from the parallelism between "the Lord's Supper" and "the Lord's day" in Apoc. 1:10.[4]

It is frequently asserted that in the early church Christians took the consecrated bread home with them to communicate privately during the week. While incidents of this practice are recorded, it is difficult to determine just how widespread it really was. One author very cautiously states: "Evidence for extraliturgical Communion at any time is very slight, with the exception of viaticum. Before the fourth century the practice of private Communion in the home is attested to in the West only incidentally, and in the fourth century references are not more numerous."[5] This cautious approach is in contrast to the more common opinion that it was customary for the faithful of the early church to take the blessed elements home with them on Sunday in order to communicate privately during the week.

At any rate, the practice certainly existed, and some historians counter-distinguish the private making of one's communion at home with the corporate action of the eucharist to show that it is the latter which constituted the church as such. In the pre-Nicene era no one was put to death for communicating at home. It was the communal gathering for the eucharist on Sunday that was the cause of death in those early days of persecution. The Mass was so important for the early Christians that they risked death rather than not celebrate it. Dom Gregory Dix describes the situation:

> Literally scores of similar illustrations from contemporary documents of unimpeachable historical authority are available of the fact that it was not so much the personal reception of holy communion as the corporate eucharistic action as a whole (which included communion) which was then regarded as the very essence of the life of the church, and through that of the individual christian soul. In this corporate action alone each christian could fulfill for himself or herself the "appointed liturgy" of his order, and so fulfill his redeemed being as a member of Christ . . . What brought him to the eucharist week by week was an intense belief that in the eucharistic action of the Body of Christ, as in no other way, he himself took a part in that act of sacrificial obedience to the will of God which was consummated on Calvary and which had redeemed the world, including himself. What brought him was the conviction that there rested on each of the redeemed an absolute necessity so to take his own part in the self-offering of Christ, a necessity more binding even that the instinct of self-preservation.[6]

This risk of death brings out clearly their awareness of the difference between the receiving of communion versus the act of celebrating the eucharist which had as its source the Last Supper of the Lord with his disciples. It was the eucharist itself that came to be, as Dix puts it, "that rite which was instituted by our Lord Jesus Christ Himself to be the peculiar and distinctive worship of those who should be 'His own'; and which has ever since been the heart and core of christian worship and christian living—the Eucharist or Breaking of Bread."[7]

Whereas the priestly life and witness of each Christian was a personal thing, the eucharistic gathering was by its very nature corporate. The eucharistic action was seen to be the action of the gathered community because its members had become one with Christ in baptism; it was their action because it was the action of Christ, the priest.[8] Granted the bishop-celebrant (later priest-celebrant) played a unique role, this was never to the detriment of the community itself being the proper subject of the liturgical action. In the *epiclesis* of the oldest eucharistic prayer of the West (about the year 215) Hippolytus asks God to send the Holy Spirit upon the offering of the holy church.[9] St. Cyprian in his *De Dominica Oratione* (c. 252) stressed that the eucharist uses the first-person plural: "When we come together and celebrate the divine sacrifices with the bishop . . ."[10]

It was, of course, St. Augustine who most fully developed this *totus Christus* theology of the eucharist.

> If you wish then to grasp the body of Christ hear the words of the Apostle to the faithful: "You are the body of Christ and his members" (I Cor. 12:27). If then you are the body of Christ and his members, it is your sacrament that reposes on the altar of the Lord. It is your sacrament which you receive . . . You answer "Amen" to the words "The body of Christ." Be then a member of the body of Christ to verify your "Amen" . . . Be what you see, and receive what you are.[11]

This type of theology was at the core of true participation of priestly people in the eucharistic action. The Sunday gathering was not merely a time to be fed by the body and blood of Christ, but a time to gather precisely as a corporate body, the body of Christ, to identify with, and participate in, the priestly action of Christ. The church as offering body contextualized the reception of holy communion, and not vice versa.

Augustine did not fail to recognize the role of the ordained celebrant, but placed it in the context of the sacrifice of Christ being the *sacrificium christianorum*: "This is the sacrifice of Christians: 'we being many are one body in Christ.' and this also the church continually celebrates in the sacrament of the altar, so well known to the faithful, that it may be plain to her that in what she offers she herself is offered."[12] This eucharistic theology was based on a baptismal theology whereby the members of the body were joined and made one with the head who was Christ. In light of such theology, presence or absence at the Sunday eucharist does make a difference; the corporate action is impoverished if members are absent; and eucharist itself is experienced as an action more than as a thing, albeit a sacred thing.

How this corporate understanding of the eucharistic action was lost, or at least lessened, is a complex phenomenon. It was part of a shift at the beginning of the seventh century to a more individualistic approach to the eucharist. According to Cyrille Vogel, little by little the Mass was seen as a "good work" to be performed for one's personal, individual salvation, whether that of the priest who celebrates it or that of the layperson who requests its celebration.[13] Influential in this view of the eucharist was St. Isidore of Seville (d. 636). The eucharist was no longer considered to be the corporate giving thanks of the community but a gift of grace given to the one who celebrates it or has it celebrated, by which one's salvation is effected and assured.[14]

Monastic Practice

This way of viewing things arose to a great extent from monastic practice and spirituality, concerned as they were with gaining one's eternal salvation through good works. As to the good work *par excellence*, the eucharist, the early monastic communities found three possible solutions to assure its availability: (1) the monks (and nuns) had no eucharist themselves, but went out to the local church for it; (2) they invited local priests to come in to the monastery to celebrate for them; (3) they had their own eucharist celebrated by one of their own ordained members.[15]

In the Rule of the Master there was a daily communion service (with communion under both species) held at the conclusion of the hour of none before the community meal.[16] De Vogüé comments: "It seems to have been the abbot who, though a layman, distributed the sacred species . . . Reception of the eucharist was normally associated with the meal. It did not ordinarily imply celebration of Mass: there was no Mass except on Sundays, the patronal feast of the oratory, and the blessing of the abbot."[17] The Sunday Mass, in de Vogüé's opinion, would have been celebrated outside the monastery by the diocesan clergy. (The Rule itself is actually silent on the point.) He argues:

> Ordinarily, the Master's community went to the parish church to assist at offices celebrated by the diocesan clergy. This state of affairs seems fairly archaic in all respects. In daily communion, absence of priests in the community, and the necessity of going out for Mass, the Rule of the Master appears to look towards the past rather than the future. In Gaul at almost the same period, communion was less frequent, monks were ordained priests for the service of the community, and Mass was celebrated in the monastery itself.[18]

Due to silence on the matter, the Rule of St. Benedict presents us with little knowledge as to eucharistic practice. De Vogüé contrasts the practices of the two rules:

> We can perceive without too much trouble what was done at the Master's monastery—daily communion outside of Mass in the oratory, and Sunday Mass at the parish church—but the usage in Benedict's [monastery] is less clear. The celebration of a Sunday Mass in the monastery oratory seems certain, but the existence of a daily communion service remains unsure.[19]

The Sunday practice of some communities of women, however, may have only involved the reception of communion.[20] Still, the general monastic norm would have been the celebration of Mass on Sundays. De Vogüé summarizes the early monastic practice: "It seems then that a brief communion service is the daily Eucharistic rite in harmony with the office as Benedict conceived it. Thus Christ is received each day and is offered once a week on the day of his resurrection. In this way both the Mass and the Sunday are set in singular relief."[21] Finally, beginning with the Carolingian era, the monastic practice would have included not only Sunday celebrations of the eucharist as was done in the parish churches, but it would have included even daily Mass.

The common Christian practice, then, with only rare monastic exceptions, was the Sunday celebration of Mass. Although communion services were found on weekdays at some times and in some places, Sunday was characterized by the celebration of Mass. Writing on the question of the frequency of the eucharist throughout history, Robert Taft says: "How much is too much or too little has varied. The extremes are clear: less than every Sunday can lay no claim to be traditional; more than once a day is excessive except in particular circumstances."[22] The weekly celebration of the Lord's Day was marked by the celebration of the Mass, not merely by the reception of communion. Having surveyed the historical data, it would seem helpful to look at the precise theological difference between a communion service and a Mass.

Difference between Communion Service and Eucharist

Receiving a previously consecrated host at a communion service is laudatory, but it is not the same theologically as celebrating the eucharist and communicating in that context. What, then, constitutes the difference theologically? What is lacking in a communion service that should cause church officials to be dissatisfied with them and to do all they possibly can to provide parishes with Mass itself on Sunday? I limit my observations to four areas.

Eucharist as Action

The Mass is an action (*actio*), and as we have seen, it is the action of all those gathered together, priest and people, not just the priest. Under the leadership of the priest-celebrant, all the baptized who have gathered celebrate the eucharist. It is interesting to note that in the 1975 revision of the General Instruction of the Roman Missal, in those places where the priest was referred to as celebrant (*celebrans*), the phrase was changed to priest-celebrant (*sacerdos celebrans*).[23] This was to indicate that the priest was not the only "celebrant" of the eucharist. The eucharistic prayer is offered in the first-person plural: "We come to you, Father, with praise and thanksgiving, through Jesus Christ your Son" as has been expressed down through the centuries in the Roman Canon.

Although a communion service could also be viewed as an action, it is not as the Mass is, the privileged unique act by which Christ gave of himself to the Father for the salvation of humankind. This is of the utmost importance for understanding the unique role of the Mass in the Christian life. Nicholas Lash expresses this well: "It is misleading to say either that 'we offer Christ to the Father,' or that 'Christ offers us to the Father.' The balanced statement is to the effect that, by the grace of Christ, our self-offering to the Father, expressed and sealed by our sharing in the meal, is a participation in his self-offering to his Father on Calvary."[24] Karl Rahner says succinctly: "In the sacrifice of the Mass the Church, in obedience to the Lord's express command, offers to God Christ's sacrifice of death on the Cross as its own sacrifice."[25] Failure to make this absolutely clear has been the cause of the Protestant malaise which fears that Catholics are adding to, or trying to repeat, the once-and-for-all sacrifice of Christ.

Whereas one could certainly unite oneself spiritually to the death of Christ during a communion service, it is not the mandated, communal act of the church as such that has carried out Christ's command to "do this in memory of me." This is what the eucharist is. Jean Tillard writes: "The eucharist is not just the rite at which the individual baptized can receive the body and blood of the Lord. Each eucharist is also the manifestation of the church *as such* in such and such a place, at such and such a moment."[26]

The command "to do eucharist" is a command to take the word "eucharist" not as a noun, but as a verb: to do eucharist. This seems to be more faithful to the root meaning of the word. It is why the medieval missals announce: *Hic incipit canonis actio missae*. A communion service views "eucharist" as a thing, albeit a sacred thing.

The Mass is communal by its very essence; it is the action of the gathered assembly under the leadership of the priest-celebrant. A communion service is more about "eucharist" as a noun, and it is essentially an individual experience with

istic bread."[30] This could be misunderstood to mean that Christians can play their role in the church merely by receiving holy communion. This is not Catholic tradition. The tradition is that the baptized are to receive communion in the broader context of their celebrating (offering) the eucharist under the leadership of the priest-celebrant. To forget this is quite serious; it undermines the traditional notion of the church as a eucharistic church, namely, that the eucharist makes the church.

By reason of baptism the Christian is a priest. And this priesthood is exercised not simply by receiving holy communion, but first and foremost by celebrating the eucharist. St. Peter Chrysologus, fifth-century bishop of Ravenna, stated:

> Listen now to what the Apostle urges us to do. "I appeal to you," he says, "to present your bodies as a living sacrifice." By this exhortation of his, Paul has raised all to priestly status. How marvelous is the priesthood of the Christian, for he is both the victim that is offered on his own behalf, and the priest who makes the offering. He does not need to go beyond himself to seek what he is to immolate to God: with himself and in himself he brings the sacrifice he is to offer God for himself. The victim remains and the priest remains, always one and the same . . . Each of us is called to be both a sacrifice to God and his priest. Do not forfeit what divine authority confers on you.[31]

This type of dynamic eucharistic theology never envisioned itself being limited to the truncated practice of distributing previously consecrated elements. What was envisioned was the activity of a priestly people. The active voice, not the passive voice, constitutes our eucharistic tradition. The unfortunate expression, "the priest offers Mass, the people receive communion," is a distortion of that tradition. If it is the task of the people merely to receive communion it is no small wonder that communion services are gaining ground with so little protest.

The Role of the "Epiclesis"

Another helpful approach to the difference between a communion service and a eucharist is to examine the role of the *epiclesis* in the eucharist. The General Instruction of the Roman Missal describes the "chief elements making up the eucharistic prayer." One of these is the *epiclesis*: "in special invocations the church calls on God's power and asks that the gifts offered by human hands be consecrated, that is, become Christ's body and blood, and that the victim to be received in communion be the source of salvation for those who will partake."[32] The prayer is not only that the bread and wine be turned into the body and blood of Christ, but that even the members of Christ's Body (the baptized) become all the more that which they already are, that is, the Body of Christ. The 1975 Faith and Order Paper, *One Baptism, One Eucharist and a Mutually Recognized Ministry*, in its section on the eucharist, formulated the principle: "The *anamnesis* leads to *epiklesis*."[33] Recalling and proclaiming all that Christ did depends upon the action of the Holy Spirit and so, as the 1982 Lima Statement puts it: "The church prays to the Father for the gift of the Holy Spirit in order that the eucharistic event may be a reality."[34] That eucharistic reality is about a conversion: not only of the elements of bread and wine but of the gathered assembly of the baptized. This is hinted at in the consecratory *epiclesis* of the First Eucharistic Prayer for Reconciliation: "Send forth the power of your Spirit, so that these gifts may become for us the body and blood of your beloved Son, Jesus the Christ, in whom we have become your sons and daughters." St. Augustine often preached on this theme, for example: "If then you are the body of Christ and his members, it is your sacrament that reposes on the altar of the Lord. It is your sacrament which you receive."[35] The intimacy between the Holy Spirit's acting upon both the gifts of bread and wine and the gathered assembly would be far clearer if our eucharistic prayers did not have a split *epiclesis*, that is, if the consecration aspect and the communion aspect of the *epiclesis* were expressed together. At any rate, a communion service, lacking as it does the *epiclesis* over the elements and over the people, is thus not constitutive of the church as is the eucharist.

Nor does a communion service possess the eschatological dimension that a Mass does, for the action of the Mass is precisely about the unity between the baptized (the members of Christ's Body) and Christ (the head of that Body). As to the *epiclesis*, the consecratory *epiclesis* is prayed in terms of the realization of the communion *epiclesis*, the unity of the Body of

Christ. The eucharistic unity is a sign of that perfect unity to be realized only at the time of death. The eucharistic journey both symbolizes and creates that ever-deepening unity. The Fourth Eucharistic Prayer implores: "By your Holy Spirit, gather all who share this one bread and one cup into the one body of Christ, a living sacrifice of praise." This unity is primarily and essentially the work of the eucharistic action of the church, and to reduce it to the domain of a communion service is to impoverish our liturgical tradition, and to rob Sunday, the Day of the Lord, of its paschal significance.

Word-Sacrament Relationship

A final approach to show the theological difference between a communion service and a Mass is through an analysis of word-sacrament relationship.

A number of writers today are lamenting the tacking on of communion to the celebration of the word at a Sunday service in the absence of a priest. Their fear is that the word has its own integrity which could be undervalued by such a practice. For example, Herman Graf writes: "The hurried introduction of these communion services contains an implicit denial of the real and effective presence of the Lord in his word. It seems this presence in his word *has* to be supplemented by the sacrament in order to be sufficient."[36]

My fear is just the opposite. I fear that our people can forget that the word, in the context of the eucharist, has as its ultimate goal the action of the eucharist. The liturgy of the word is an *anamnesis*, a memorial. The wonderful works of God are remembered, especially the wonder *par excellence* Jesus, who the night before he died left his church the sacrament of his body and blood. In the eucharist "the event of God's giving himself to the world and the acceptance of this gift on the cross of the Son becomes actually present among us, sacramentally, in the space and time we live in."[37] This sacrament is not merely the body and blood of Christ, but the gift, the offering of that body. Again, the action of the eucharist contextualizes communion, and not vice versa.

The introduction to the lectionary states:

The Church is nourished spiritually at the table of God's word and at the table of the eucharist: from the one it grows in wisdom and from the other in holiness. In the word of God the divine covenant is announced; in the eucharist the new and everlasting covenant is renewed. The spoken word of God brings to mind the history of salvation; the eucharist embodies it in the sacramental signs of the liturgy. It can never be forgotten, therefore, that the divine word read and proclaimed by the Church in the liturgy has as its one goal the sacrifice of the new Covenant and the banquet of grace, that is, the eucharist. The celebration of Mass in which the word is heard and the eucharist is offered and received forms but one single act of divine worship. That act offers the sacrifice of praise to God and makes available to God's creatures the fullness of redemption.[38]

It should be asked if the present priest shortage is not causing the frustration of the logical completion of the word leading to sacrament. Karl Rahner, commenting on how the eucharist is "the word of God in the Church which supports and conveys all other words," writes that "all other words, sacramental and non-sacramental, must therefore be considered merely as exposition and application, preliminaries and echoes of this word, which makes the crucified and risen Lord and his whole work of salvation present in the Church."[39] Or again:

The efficacious word of the Mass, being the proclamation of the death of Christ, is the primary kerygma. And every other efficacious word becomes so in the Church because it participates in this kerygma in such a way that the whole force of this primary kerygma can already be embodied in the participation, and for this very reason this mere participation is intrinsically ordained to be absorbed into the Eucharistic kerygma, to find there its full manifestation.[40]

The very relationship, then, of word to sacrament offers yet another foundation for distinguishing between a communion service and a Mass.

* * * * * *

Analyzing the eucharistic tradition and the theological differences between communion services and eucharist, we see that the present eucharistic situation in the church is not a good one. We are, perhaps, on the verge of ceasing to be a "eucharistic church" in the traditional sense, at least in many places throughout the world.

Beginning with the late fourth century with abstention from communion on the grounds of awe and unworthiness, the church experienced something new: the split between sacrifice and meal, with people attending the sacrifice but abstaining from the meal. Today we see the opposite: people participating in the meal but not attending the sacrifice. Neither solution is good: both fragment the unified concept of the sacrificial meal.

Since baptism is the gateway to all the sacraments and gives one the right to a sacramental life, is not the proliferation of communion services on Sunday a denial of what is due baptized women and men? It seems hard to deny that "what in fact appears to be most characteristic of the present situation is that less importance is being ascribed to the integrity of the eucharist and to the eucharistic dimension of the local community than to the maintaining of a male celibate ordained ministry."[41]

A solution to the situation must come by focusing first and foremost, not on the person of the one to be ordained, but on the baptized community: its gifts, its mission, and its needs. This demands that eucharistic presiders come from the ranks of the community and not be foreign missionaries imposed from on high. Rather than praying for vocations, we should pray for the renewal of the church, because with grass-roots renewal will come a variety of ministries.[42]

Finally, in searching for a solution the church must never forget the ancient adage that the salvation of souls is the supreme law of the church.[43]

Notes

1. See H.J. Graf, "Priestless Sunday Services with Communion and Resulting Problems," *East Asian Pastoral Review* 18 (1981) 175-189.

2. *Origins* 17:8 (July 16, 1987) 127.

3. *Origins* 18:19 (October 20, 1988) 305.

4. Robert Taft, "The Frequency of the Eucharist throughout History," *Concilium* 152 (1982) 13.

5. David Callam, "The Frequency of the Mass in the Latin Church ca. 400," *Theological Studies* 45 (1984) 615-616.

6. Gregory Dix, *The Shape of the Liturgy* (London: Dacre Press, 1960) 153.

7. Ibid. 1.

8. See Yves Congar, "L'Ecclesia ou communauté chrétienne, sujet intégral de l'action liturgique," in *La Liturgie après Vatican II*, Unam Sanctam 66 (Paris: Cerf, 1967) 241-282.

9. "And we ask that you would send your holy Spirit upon the offering of your holy church." Translation from Geoffrey J. Cuming, *Hippolytus: A Text for Students* (Bramcotte Notts: Grove Books, 1976) 11.

10. PL 4:538.

11. Sermon 272. Translation by Thomas Halton in *The Mass: Ancient Liturgies and Patristic Texts*, ed., André Hamman (Staten Island, NY: Alba House, 1967) 207-208.

12. *De Civ. Dei*, X, 6 (PL 41:284).

13. Cyrille Vogel, "Une mutation cultuelle inexpliquée: le passage de l'eucharistie communautaire à la messe privée," *Revue des sciences religieuses* 54 (1980) 247.

14. See Ibid. 248-249.

15. See Adalbert de Vogüé, "Le prêtre et la communauté monastique dans l'antiquité," *La Maison-Dieu* 115 (1973) 62-63.

16. *The Rule of the Master*, trans., Luke Eberle; intro. by Adalbert de Vogüé; trans., Charles Philippi (Kalamazoo, MI: Cistercian Publications, 1977), see chapter 21.

17. Ibid. 31.

18. Ibid. 33.

19. Adalbert de Vogüé, *The Rule of Saint Benedict: A Doctrinal and Spiritual Commentary*, trans., John Baptist Hasbrouck (Kalamazoo, MI: Cisterican Publications, 1983) 159.

20. See R. Kevin Seasoltz, "Monastery and Eucharist: Some American Observations," in *Living Bread, Saving Cup*, ed., R. Kevin Seasoltz (Collegeville: The Liturgical Press, 1987) 264.

21. *The Rule of Saint Benedict* 163.

22. Taft, "The Frequency" 20.

23. See nos. 34, 42, 109, 244, 246, 248.

24. Nicholas Lash, *His Presence in the World* (London: Sheed & Ward, 1968) 61.

25. Karl Rahner and Angelus Häussling, *The Celebration of the Eucharist* (New York: Herder and Herder, 1968) 85-86.

26. J.M.R. Tillard, "The Apostolic Foundation of Christian Ministry," *Worship* 63 (1989) 297.

27. Edward Schillebeeckx, O.P., "Transubstantiation, Transfinalization, Transfiguration," *Worship* 40 (1966) 335.

28. *Summa Theologiae* III, q. 73, a. 3.

29. Schillebeeckx, "Transubstantiation" 335.

30. *Origins* 18:19 (October 20, 1988) 307.

31. Sermo 108 (PL 52:499-500).

32. No. 55 (c).

33. *One Baptism, One Eucharist and a Mutually Recognized Ministry*, Faith and Order Paper 73 (Geneva: World Council of Churches, 1975), "The Eucharist," no. 14.

34. *Baptism, Eucharist and Ministry*, Faith and Order Paper 111 (Geneva: World Council of Church, 1982), "Eucharist," no. 14.

35. Sermon 272.

36. Graf, "Priestless Sunday Services" 182.

37. Karl Rahner, *Theological Investigations*, Vol. 4 (Baltimore: Helicon Press, 1966) 281.

38. *Lectionary for Mass: Introduction* (Washington, D.C.: U.S. Catholic Conference, 1982) 16 (no. 10).

39. Rahner, *Theological Investigations* 282.

40. Ibid. 286.

41. William Marrevee, "'Priestless Masses'—At What Cost?" *Eglise et théologie* 19 (1988) 220.

42. See David N. Power, *Gifts That Differ: Lay Ministries Established and Unestablished* (New York: Pueblo Publishing Co., 1980) 113.

43. See 1983 Code of Canon Law, canon 1752.

12

Fons Vitae:
A Case Study in the Use of Liturgy
as a Theological Source

Mark Searle

WHILE THE COMPLAINT IS COMMON THAT THEOLOGIANS RARELY USE LIT-
urgy as a theological source, it is equally true that many liturgical scholars—and Niels Rasmussen was an outstanding example—are often quite sceptical concerning what passes for
"liturgical theology" or "theology of liturgy." Liturgists, especially those who are historians, are inclined to distrust theological approaches to worship and sacraments grounded more
in general ideas of the liturgy than in actual liturgical tradition
and practice. Theologians, for their part, while accepting the
lex orandi in principle, mostly seem to look at the liturgy as a
townsman might look at a milk cow, uncertain at which end to
begin to exploit its potential.

A refreshingly honest statement of some of the unease felt
by the dogmatician about the use of liturgy as a theological
source is to be found in Herbert Vorgrimler's 1986 article, "Die
Liturgie als Thema der Dogmatik."[1] While welcoming and en-
couraging collaboration between liturgists and theologians,
Vorgrimler confesses to a series of misgivings about how liturgy has been used historically, about the theological positions
seemingly implied in certain liturgical practices, and about

certain commonplaces of liturgical and sacramental theology. In partial response to his call for dialogue, it seems worthwhile to take up just one of his misgivings—concerning claims made for the efficacy of the sacraments—and attempt to test its validity by taking one liturgical practice as a case study.

The Problem

It is commonly said that the liturgy consist of a double movement, from God to the gathered church (descending or *katabatic*) and from the gathered church to God (ascending or *anabatic*) and both these dimensions are usually rooted in the mediatorship of Christ as the outreach of God to us and humanity's response to God. The problem, as Vorgrimler sees it, lies in the claim that the liturgy possesses an efficacy beyond any other kind of divine-human transaction, and that the movement of God to humankind is in some sense more particularly reliable in the liturgy than elsewhere.

> The dogmatic theologian has problems with the kind of talk about the katabatic dimension of the liturgy as act of God which seems to suggest that there is something automatic about it, as if it were the liturgy that somehow 'gets God going' and ensures that God performs some specific activity. This, of course, means that God's sovereignty is no longer respected.[2]

While not using the phrase *ex opere operato*, this is clearly what he has in mind as he goes on to point to the use of the indicative formula,[3] the tendency to focus on the words of institution at the expense of the epiclesis, and the theory of character as an indelible mark printed on the soul by baptism, confirmation and holy orders.[4]

Against this, Vorgrimler asserts—presumably on broader theological grounds—that sacramental efficacy cannot be thought of except in the framework of faith.

> All Christian existence, even prayer, even the sacraments (*sacramenta fidei!*), even the liturgy—all are grasped and sustained through faith; and the only thing of which faith can be certain is that it is itself the product of God's unattainable grace.[5]

Does the liturgy in fact give grounds for thinking that there is an anabatic and a katabatic dimension, and that the latter is somehow automatic? What place do the rites make for faith, and what is its role in the sacramental liturgies themselves? How are institution narrative and epiclesis related? Instead of exploring these questions in the abstract, I propose to take, as a test case, a classic text of the Roman liturgy: the blessing of baptismal water at the Easter Vigil. To this text we shall pose the more general question of what is actually going in the ritual performance in the hope that a closer look at what is said and done might offer new ways of posing these traditional theological questions.[6]

A Note on Method

The only way in which a genuine dialogue between liturgists and theologians can take place is on the basis of a close study of the liturgy itself. Here we immediately run into problems, since one of the characteristics of liturgy which poses difficulties for using it as a theological source is that it uses a number of codes—verbal, iconic, proxemic, visual, and the like— simultaneously and cannot be reduced to liturgical texts. One of the advantages of semiotics, as a general theory of signification, is that it applies in principle to all signifying systems and should provide a way of taking seriously the multi-dimensionality of ritual behaviour. For the purposes of this exercise, however, we shall restrict ourselves to the examination of the text and rubrics of the blessing of water, since it is the normative meaning projected by the script that engages us here, rather than the specific meanings that may be operative in a particular blessing of a particular font at a particular time and place.

Semiotics is the study of how meaning is produced. It developed out of linguistics and carries over from linguistics two convictions that undergird the whole enterprise: first, that meaning is produced by difference and, second, that differences are found on different levels. The import of the first axiom is that a significant whole can be broken down into contrastive units whose meaning-value derives from their opposition to each other: a classic example is that of the pieces on a chessboard. The significance of the second axiom is that it is essential to compare things on the same level. It is not only the chessboard that is a sign-set: the room in which the game is being played, the clothes the players and onlookers are wearing, and so on, also consist of sign-units in contrast with each other: chair vs. table, spotlight vs. subdued lighting, uniforms vs. civil clothing, and the like. But it would be a mistake to contrast the pawn to the light fixture: they operate on different levels of signification.

Within a text, too, there are different levels at which contrasts and oppositions are operative. In the method we will use here—that of the Paris School, associated with A.J. Greimas,[7]— it is customary to distinguish the form of the signifier from the form of the signified and to focus on the latter. (In other words, we shall not examine the presentation and lay-out of the blessing, but the form of its semantic content). Within the form of the content, there are three levels: that of the discourse (the images employed by the text), that of the narrative which underlies the images and organizes them to reflect a certain logical sequence, and that of the "deep structures" or underlying values that account for the fact that this text says what it says.

The study that follows does not attempt to provide a complete analysis of the text of the blessing. Instead, trying to respond to Vorgrimler's misgivings, we shall operate mainly at the narrative level, drawing on the imagery of the discoursive level only as much as may be necessary. This is somewhat less than satisfactory from an analytical point of view, but it will allow us to focus on the question that most interests us: what is going on in the text?

The Text[8]

Blessing of Water[9]

(A)   R1. *The priest then blesses the baptismal water. With hands joined, he says or sings the following prayer:*

    1. Father, you give us grace through sacramental signs,
       which tell us of the wonders of your unseen power.
    2. In baptism, we use your gift of water,
       which you have made a rich symbol
       of the grace you give us in this sacrament.

(B)   3. At the very dawn of creation
           your Spirit breathed on the waters,
           making them the well-spring of holiness.
      4. The waters of the great flood
           you made a sign of the waters of baptism,
           that make an end to sin and a new beginning of
           goodness.
      5. Through the waters of the Red Sea
           you led Israel out of slavery,
           to be an image of God's holy people,
           set free from sin by baptism.

(C)   6. In the waters of the Jordan
           your Son was baptized by John
           and anointed with the Spirit.
      7. Your Son willed that water and blood
           should flow from his side
           as he hung upon the cross.
      8. After his resurrection he told his disciples:
           "Go out and teach all nations,
           baptizing them in the name of the Father
           and of the Son and of the Holy Spirit."

(D)   9. Father, look now with love upon your Church,
           and unseal for her the fountain of baptism.
     10. By the power of the Holy Spirit
           give to the water of this font
           the grace of your Son.
     11. You created man in your own likeness:
           cleanse him from sin in a new birth of innocence
           by water and the Spirit.

(E)   R2. *The priest may lower the Easter candle into the water
           either once or three times, as he continues:*

     12. We ask you, Father, with your Son,
           to send your Holy Spirit upon the waters of this
           font.

     R3. *He holds the candle in the water:*

     13. May all who are buried with Christ
           in the death of baptism
           rise also to him with newness of life.

14. We ask this through Christ our Lord.

(F)   15. **R.** Amen.

(G)   R4. *Then the candle is taken out of the water as the people sing the acclamation:*

16. Springs of water, bless the Lord.
Give him glory and praise for ever.

R5. *Any other appropriate acclamation may be sung.*

Semiotic Analysis

The text under study exists in the pages of the Rite for the Christian Initiation of Adults as the script for an act of prayer. Two levels must therefore be distinguished: that of the *script* which pre-scribes an event of communication, and that of the *performance* of the communication. Here we are studying the script rather than the performance, but as a script it has to be studied precisely as something to be enacted.

Moreover, thinking of the performance itself, we must also distinguish the act of saying (in semiotic terms, the enunciation) from what it is that is said (the utterance). The "saying" is a verbal act of communication that transpires in the doing of the rite between a Speaker (the priest speaking in the first person plural in the name of the community) and a Hearer addressed as "Father." The "utterance," on the other hand, is what is said: an implicit narrative[10] referring to events of the past and to further events hoped for in the immediate future. The "saying" (enunciation) is thus an event which occurs between the past which is remembered and the future which is prayed for, both of which are figured more or less concretely in the utterance (what is said).

A prayer is clearly not a narrative, a recounting of events. Yet it seems almost inevitable that any prayer beyond the shortest ejaculation contain narrative elements. And not just random elements, but elements belonging to an implicit narrative sequence or syntax. In Greimassian semiotics, this syntax consists in part of what is called the "canonical narrative schema." What this means is that the temporal clues given in the surface discourse (verb tenses, temporal adverbs like "yester-day," "meanwhile," "henceforth") suppose an underlying log-ical and temporal structuring or schema. This schema, com-mon to all narratives, and without which narratives would lapse into absurdity, consists of four phases, each one of which logically supposes the others: mandate - competence - performance - sanction.[11] Any performance logically supposes a Subject of the performance who is mandated or motivated for it and who has the necessary resources and know-how ("competence") to carry it out. After the performance is com-pleted, the sanction phase consists of the recognition of the Subject's performance and of the new state of affairs which it brings about.

In the text we are studying, we have to distinguish different levels of narrativity. At a first level, the enunciation, or act of saying the prayer, corresponds to the "mandate" phase (phase 1) of an unfolding timeline in which the praying community is itself a participant: the community tries to "motivate" God to undertake a proposed performance (phase 3) for which he is recognized to be already competent (phase 2). This recognition of God's competence, an integral factor in the persuasive force of the prayer, is at the same time a very positive sanction on God's previous performances and on God himself (phase 4 of a prior timeline). These past performances, however, not only prove God's competence: they also constitute a mandate to the community to baptize (cfr. esp. v.8). Finally, the praying com-munity (PC) speaks for itself in sanctioning the performance of the priest ("Amen") and then itself mandating a new pro-gram (v.16). There are thus three narrative levels operating here:

future act of God: mandate [>competence>performance>sanction]

prayer offered: ...> performance > sanction ("Amen")

past acts of God: ...> sanction

At each of the three levels, the same fourfold schema is logically supposed. The past acts of God were performances for which God was motivated and competent and which reach their final stage (sanction, or acknowledgement of what has transpired) in the liturgy itself. The future acts of God presume the same motivation and competence and will in turn be sanctioned. Between past and future narrative sequences (both of which, note, are only alluded to in fragmentary fashion in many prayers) there intervenes the ritual present and the unfolding timeline in which the praying community (PC) acts as as a subject mandating a new performance or series of performances from God. The importance of all this is that it shows how the narrativity of the rite goes far beyond its allusions to stories past and future (the utterance, or *what* is said) to incorporate the community itself into a larger or higher level narrative line. By prayer, then, the praying community (PC) enters into salvation history.

Such, in very broad terms, is what is going on in the act of communication (or "blessing of the font") which takes place at this part of the baptismal liturgy. This account will have to be elaborated and refined in light of a closer study of the text and rubrics.

> *The priest then blesses the baptismal water. With hands*
> *joined, he says or sings the following prayer:*

1. Father, you give us grace through sacramental signs,
    which tell us of the wonder of your unseen power.
2. In baptism, we use your gift of water,
    which you have made a rich symbol of the grace
    you give us in this sacrament.

These first two verses are rather complicated, both in their syntax and in their allocation of roles, but if we ask what is going on here, the following can be identified as the main performances:

> A. God gives grace to "us" in baptism.
> B. "We" use water in baptism.

Now, when two performances occur together in a text like this, it is usually the case that one is subordinated to the other as means to end or that the two are in conflict. In this instance, however, they are presented as two performances related to one another in such a way that one (B) is the signifier and the other (A) the signified. The semiosis between the two is assured by two subordinate performances, one past and one present:

a. God established water as a "rich symbol";
b. sacramental signs "tell us" of God's power.

Two other things are worth noting about these opening verses. One is the use of "Father" as a vocative. The vocative always presumes *and enacts* some sort of relationship: in this case the particular kind of relationship which must be presumed already to exist between the Praying Community (PC) and God is one which is appropriately expressed by calling God "Father." We shall have to look for further clues in the prayer to what makes this particular appellation appropriate. The other thing worth noting is the absence of all temporal and spatial constraints on the various activities predicated of God and us. Apart from the use of the past tense with reference to the "institution" of baptism, the utterances are made in a sort of gnomic present, as if sanctioning an arrangement that is always and everywhere valid: namely, that sacramental activity is a joint program of such a kind that the performance of the praying community is always and everywhere the signifier of the performance of God in giving grace. Note that the sacrament is not the sign posited by the church, but the signifier (ritual) conjoined with the signified (grace) and that these are not things, but performances.

3. At the very dawn of creation
      your Spirit breathed upon the waters,
      making them the well-spring of holiness.
4. The waters of the great flood
      you made a sign of the waters of baptism,
      that make an end to sin and a new beginning to
      goodness.
5. Through the waters of the Red Sea
      you led Israel out of slavery,
      to be an image of God's holy people,
      set free from sin by baptism.

In contrast to the universally valid principle stated in the opening verses, the text now reverts to specific events of the past. Three successive utterances sanction three successive achievements with only a semantic, as opposed to a narrative, connection between them: not one story, but three stories involving "you" and "water." God establishes water as "the wellspring of all holiness"; God sets the flood up as a sign of baptism's role in making an end of sin and a new beginning of holiness; after its liberation by God, Israel becomes a sign of the community of the baptised, liberated from sin. Note that these are "anaphorizations"—cryptic references to stories presumed familiar to the PC—in which only those aspects of the original stories are retained which link them to baptism.

6. In the waters of the Jordan
   your Son was baptized by John
   and anointed with the Spirit.
7. Your Son willed that water and blood
   should flow from his side
   as he hung upon the cross.
8. After his resurrection, he told his disciples:
   "Go out and teach all nations,
   baptizing them in the name of the Father
   and of the Son and of the Holy Spirit."

With this section a new character moves to center stage as "Father" yields to "your Son." Here again, we have three statements, each an anaphorization of a story presumed familiar and each relating a distinct performance. In this case, however, the three incidents are narratively linked and correspond to the "canonical syntax" of narrative grammar: competence, performance, and recognition or sanction.[12] This is confirmed by the fact that, whereas in verses 3-5 each incident resulted in some abiding value, in this instance the new state of affairs which is an abiding effect of the Son's performance is only manifest at the end: "after his resurrection."

Note, too, that traces of the subjects of the enunciation, or act of communication, while serving to maintain continuity in verses 6 and 7 ("*your*" Son), disappear entirely in verse 8. In verse 8, direct address cedes to impersonal narrative, creating the meaning-effect of "objectivity" characteristic of institution myths. (One thinks especially of the institution narrative in the eucharistic prayer.)

9. Father, look now with love upon your Church,
   and unseal for her the fountain of baptism.
10. By the power of the Holy Spirit,
    give to the water of this font
    the grace of your Son.

11. You created man in your own likeness:
    cleanse him from sin in a new birth of innocence
    by water and the Holy Spirit.

In contrast to the impression of "objectivity" given by verse 8, verse 9 immediately reverts to direct address—"Father" and "your Church" (i.e., the PC)—as the partners in the act of communication surface again in the text. There is also a temporal engagement of the enunciation in the use of "now," negating the "not-now" of the previous time frame ("after his resurrection"). This represents a major turning point in the trajectory of the discourse. Up to this point it was not clear where the prayer was going; now it appears that all the previous utterances were acts of sanction and veridiction[13] subordinate to the PC's larger program of "manipulation."[14] On the basis of what has been recalled and reaffirmed, the PC is now attempting to persuade God to do two things, one cognitive ("look . . . upon your Church") and one pragmatic ("unseal . . . the fountain of baptism"). The pragmatic performance is "for her," so that the community can carry out here and now the mandate given the disciples unrestrictedly.

It is characteristic of ritual in general and prayer in particular to be marked by "intentionality," by a tension between a virtual state (having to and wanting to baptize in accordance with the mandate) and a realized state (successful completion of the performance in the endowment of the candidates with the values intended by the Trinity as ultimate sender of the mandate). Such motivation and finality give the whole liturgy its semantic unity, unite all its parts into a single "line of action."[15] But among all those parts, the water-rite ("baptism") is the climax: it lends its name to the whole liturgy. By a similar synechdoche, "water" refers not just to the liquid, but stands for the ritual action in which it is used, (much as "tea" may mean the meal and not just the drink). Hence it is referred to in verses 9ff precisely as "the fountain of baptism" and "the water(s) of this font." The implication of this, as we shall see, is that the Spirit is invoked not to transform the waters, but to ensure the connection (semiosis) between the rite and what it signifies.

What is signified by the rite of baptism is spelled out in the very dense series of statements in verses 10-11. Here we see again how a whole series of narrative allusions tend to be compacted into a very small space in Christian prayer and they really require a rather more detailed analysis than is possible here.[16] Such analysis would attempt to identify the basic building blocks of narrative, namely states of affairs and transformations of those states of affairs. In our own case, analysis reveals that two sets of transformations are envisaged, each consisting of the negation of one state of affairs and the affirmation of a new state of affairs.

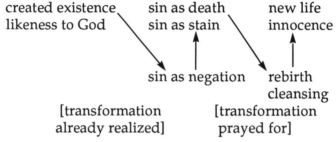

created existence · sin as death · new life
likeness to God · sin as stain · innocence

sin as negation · rebirth
cleansing

[transformation · [transformation
already realized] · prayed for]

The story-line, in other words, is this. The unbaptized represent humanity which, having been made originally in God's likeness, has suffered a transformation in the form of a negation of that original life and likeness (act of sin), so that their state is one of "death" and "disfigurement" (state of sin). A second transformation is therefore sought, a negation of the first negation (rebirth from death, cleansing from sin), which will result in a new mode of existence, figurativized as "new life" and "innocence." The desired transformation from death to life, from stain to innocence, is to be achieved jointly by God and the PC by means of water (which the PC already has) and the Spirit. In the unpacking of verse 11, then, we can see how the logic of the "canonical schema" enables us to fill in what the text presumes when it jumps from creation in God's likeness to cleansing from sin.

> R.2 *The priest may lower the Easter candle into the water either once or three times, as he continues:*

> 12. We ask you, Father, with your Son,
> to send your Holy Spirit upon the waters of this font.

The gesture of "lowering the candle" seems on the face of it to be one of dramatizing the petition, "We ask you . . . to send the Holy Spirit upon the waters of this font." However, this creates a semantic problem, for the candle is figuratived in the rubrics (and would have been visually figurativized for those taking part in the opening of the Vigil) as "the Easter candle," an iconic metaphor of Christ. Out of this ambiguity we retain only the isomorphism between the /descent/ of "lowering the candle" and the /descent/ of "send the Holy Spirit upon the waters of this font".[17]

R.3 *He holds the candle in the water:*

13.　May all who are buried with Christ
　　　　in the death of baptism
　　　　rise also with him to newness of life.
14.　We ask this through Christ our Lord.

Here at last the (proposed) main performance appears to which all other (proposed) performances (opening the font, giving the water the grace of the Son, sending the Spirit) are merely ancillary. The candle is held *in* the water as the priest prays: "May all who are buried with Christ in the death of baptism rise also with him to newness of life." There are three things to note here: the candle is ceremoniously lowered and held in the water; the prayer uses the optative, "May . . . ", so that the addressee is not identified (though from the context it must be God); there is no explicit subject of the performance.

In actual fact, not one but two performances are envisaged here: "baptismal burial" and "rising to new life." The prayer is that those who undergo the (signifying) ritual performance of which the PC is the subject will all be beneficiaries of the other (signified) performance of which Christ is the operative subject. Praying for the descent of the Spirit upon the waters is a figurative way of expressing the hoped-for correlation between the two performances, so that those who participate in the rite may also participate in the paschal experience of Christ. The figure "Christ" is obviously a reference to something outside the text presumably known by all potential readers or hearers. If the hearers make the link between "Christ" and "your Son," then there is also internal referenciation, pointing back to verses 7 and 8 which speak precisely of *his* death and resurrection.[18]

But to return to the two performances, and specifically to that of the PC. The church's prayer that God will effect what the ritual performance signifies—figurativized in the prayer that the Spirit be sent upon the waters of the font, etc.—seems to imply that "burial with Christ in the death of baptism" is as far as the church can go. In terms of the diagram given above, the immersion-burial signifies on the part of the candidates and the church a desire to negate the previous negation: the ritual act of washing and bringing to birth signifies a negating of the previous state of death and stain brought about by sin. But it cannot *achieve* it. It is a ritual mimesis of Christ's death and burial, but it cannot of itself achieve the rising with him to new life which is sought. The church has the rite and the mandate, but remains radically powerless to achieve the values they are meant to realize because what the ritual performance signifies is precisely a performance of God.

The candle rubric, for all its ambiguity, is not without interest either. "Burial" carries the values of /below/, plus /conjunction/ and /duration/, precisely the semic values[19] of the candle held in the water. An isomorphism is thereby created between the baptized and Christ (the candle) *resting* in the water, as opposed to the earlier isomorphism between the *movement* of the Spirit and the *movement* of the candle. (This in turn corresponds to previous patterns of immersion: the baptism of Christ (v.6) and his burial (implicit in vv.7-8).) There is thus a certain "duplicity" in the meaning-effect created by the lowering of the candle into the water. On the one hand it accompanies (and is isomorphic to) the utterance of the virtual program of "sending (down) the Spirit" in verse 12, which repeats the "breathing" of the Spirit upon the waters in verse 3 and the "anointing" of Christ with the Spirit in verse 6. On the other hand, as symbol of Christ, the immersion of the candle figurativizes the descent of Christ into death and his *resting* in the tomb, a pattern which the baptizands will ritually enact in their immersion in the waters of the font.

In the last verse (v.14) of the prayer, the PC invokes the name of the one who delivered the original mandate to baptize, thus providing a concluding (and conclusive?) move in this manipulative or persuasive discourse.

15. R. Amen.

The "Amen" marks a shift at the level of the enunciation or communication. The PC no longer addresses God though the priest as its spokesman, but speaks directly to sanction both the performance undertaken by the priest in its name and the contents (values) of that prayer-performance.

R.4 *Then the candle is taken out of the water as the people sing the acclamation:*

16. Springs of water, bless the Lord.
Give him glory and praise for ever.

R.5 *Any other appropriate acclamation may be sung.*

It is only at this point ("then") that the candle is removed, after the completion of the prayer and its sanctioning by the people. The use of the passive voice ("the candle is taken out of the water"), plus the fact that the move is made without any verbal accompaniment, being done under cover of the people's singing, indicates that it is purely a practical move, devoid of signification. Thus, in comparison with the /descent/, the /ascent/ is neutralized, perhaps because, while the church can "baptize," it cannot "raise."

The acclamation raises a number of interesting problems, but only two of them are pertinent to our investigation of what is going on in the text.

First, the rubric mandates the PC to mandate the waters to bless "the Lord." In the context of the whole discourse, it seems that "the Lord" here is the "Father" to whom the prayer was addressed and who, "with your Son," was asked to send the Spirit upon the waters. The acclamation is an act of sanction or recognition which, in the canonical schema,[20] can only follow the completion of a mandated program by a subject of the performance. The question, therefore, is whether the sanction relates to past activities of "the Lord", or to the performance just completed in its name by the priest, or whether there is something more at stake. Certainly it is an assent to the prayer of the priest, both in its acknowledgement of God's past deeds and in its attempt to persuade God to act again now. What more could be going on?

Could the acclamation be an act of sanction on God's present performance? And which present performance? Is it the sending of the Spirit on the waters (an auxiliary program to the conjoint main performances of "baptizing as ritual death and burial" and "raising to life")? Or is God being sanctioned proleptically for his performance of "sanctification of the baptizands," even though the baptism of the candidates has not yet taken place, and God is not yet a realized Subject of this performance? In either case—but especially in the latter—the enunciation of this acclamation represents a remarkable act of *croire interpretatif* on the part of the enunciator (the church). The proleptic "recognition" of God as realized Subject rests on an interpretation not only of the past acts of God but of the situation of the enunciation itself. In other words, God is acclaimed already for giving new life to the candidates in a sacramental performance which has has still to take place—an acclamation which implies both confidence in God's saving activity and in the validity of the present ritual to signify it. Moreover, the fact that the subject of the performance of enunciation is here the community and not the priest alone seems to lend it additional weight.

The second problem concerns what sort of performance is indicated by the mandate to "bless the Lord"? Since the issue touches on the nature of the prayer itself—identified as "The Blessing of the Water"—we will hold discussion of it over until the next section.

Summary

As we noted above, ritual is characterized by its intentionality, that is, by the fact that it represents a stage in the development of action between its conception (virtuality) and its realization, an intentionality which lends semantic unity to all its parts. In the overarching program of passing from outside the church to inside the church, from not sharing the new life of Christ to sharing it, the main phases are as follows:

Manipulation	Competence	Performance	Sanction
Christ's mandate to baptize	acceptance of mandate, tradition[21]	act of baptism	Eucharist

But this program of baptizing undertaken by the church is simply an instrumental program (signifier) in relation to the program of which God is the subject of performance (signified). In the blessing of the font, then, which takes place *immediately* before the act of ritual immersion, the PC asks God to ensure that what is signified by the ritual of baptism will, in fact, occur: that the baptized will experience an end to sin and a new beginning of goodness, will become part of a liberated people, will be raised to new life with Christ, and so on. This seems to reflect a rather clear understanding of the limitations of ritual even while expressing total confidence in the God who mandated baptism in the first place.

The Meaning of "Blessing"

The term "bless" occurs in two rather different contexts: first in the title and the first rubric, then in the acclamation. Can we identify the meaning of the term simply in the context of this text? The text of the "Blessing of Water" is essentially an act of manipulation or, rather, a hierarchical series of manipulations:

A. The text "manipulates" the community that uses it by laying down what is to be said and done and how it is to be said and done.

B. The Praying Community (through its priest) manipulates "Father" to a proposed course of action: to carry out the performance which is signified by the rite.

C. The Praying Community (directly) manipulates "springs of water" to another course of action: sanctioning God.

According to R.1, "the priest blesses the baptismal water", but the text of the blessing turns out to be an act of manipulation, persuading God to act in regard to the water (or, metonymically, the water-rite). In the acclamation there is also an act of manipulation, in the form of the imperative, "bless." Here "blessing" is not the act of manipulation, but the "doing" proposed to the "springs of water," a "doing" which is synonymous with giving glory and praise, thus with an act of sanction in which God (and God's performance) is recognized.

The differences between the two can be set out as follows:

	Prayer	*Acclamation*
Level of Enunciation:		
Speaker/Hearer:	Priest/God	PC/springs of water
Performance:	manipulation	manipulation
Level of Utterance:		
Proposed subject:	God	springs of water
Proposed performance:		
auxiliary	-send Spirit, etc.	sanctioning (bless-
main	-raise baptizands	ing) God

In the case of the acclamation, the verb "to bless" denotes a benediction in the literal sense of the term: a speaking well of someone (positive sanction); in this instance, God. The prayer is more complex, since the text to be spoken is a communication in the form of a manipulation to action. If we situate both in the canonical narrative schema, this is how they appear:

cognitive level:	(1) PC manipulates God	(4) waters sanction God
	(mandate)	(sanction)
pragmatic level:	(2) God sends Spirit	(3) God raises candidates
	(competence)	(performance)

If we ask what the two cognitive/communicative performances have in common (so that they can both be said to be a "blessing"), we can say that the acclamation is a sanction, while the prayer-manipulation contains elements of sanction. We saw that the "argument" of the prayer consists in a recognition of God's competence as manifested in previous *mirabilia*. On these grounds, it might be suspected that the elements of benediction, while actually subordinate to the petitionary intentionality of the prayer, nonetheless give grounds for calling the prayer a "blessing."[22] An analogous situation seems to have occurred with the eucharistic prayer, in which *eucharistia* or acknowledgement of God by no means exhausts its content or intentionality. Nevertheless, as early as Justin Martyr, reference to "eucharist" gave rise to calling the bread and wine over which it was spoken the "eucharistized gifts" or simply "the eucharist." In similar fashion, the term "blessing" refers both to acknowledgment of God and to the whole petitionary prayer of which it is often part, and to the effects of such prayer when they are realized. In that sense, we may count our blessings.

While this accounts for certain features of the text, it does justice neither to the expression "blessing [of] water" in title and rubric, nor to the convention (expressed, *inter alia*, in the reverence accorded the "blessed" water) that the status of the water is altered as a result of the prayer pronounced over it. And, indeed, there is a semiotic distinction between blessed and unblessed water, expressed precisely in terms of the corresponding *uses* to which each is or is not put, which may account for what the term "bless" means. The question remains, however, whether the water is "blessed" (in the conventional sense of "transformed") *for* use in baptism, or "blessed" *by* its use in baptism.

The place of the blessing in the rite, coming as it does immediately before the central rite of immersion, does seem on the face of it like a preparation of the water, in the form of a dedication of the water to sacred use. In fact, however, the text of the prayer in its present form does not support this interpretation. We have already suggested that the ritual water referred to in verses 10-12 of the blessing functions, unlike the other water(s) referred to in verses 3-5 and 6-8, as a metonymic figure of the whole water-rite about to be undertaken by the PC (as "bread" is metonymic for all that one needs to survive). We have also seen that main point of the prayer is to ask that the water-rite as signifier might be linked to the divine action which it signifies (the link being figurativized by "the Holy Spirit"). The focus of the petition, then, is not the water but the water-rite. The "Blessing of water" is a prayer for the fruitful celebration of the rite which is about to follow, a prayer whose main theme is precisely that the divine activity accompany the ritual activity which signifies it. In that sense, it might be more precise to speak of "a prayer for the blessing of the water-rite", where "blessing" is understood precisely as the "katabatic" dimension of the rite, as opposed to the "anabatic" dimension represented by the blessing of God by the PC.[23]

Conclusion

The purpose of studying the blessing of water at the baptismal vigil of Easter was not so much to harvest all its insights but to try to determine what is going on in a sacramental liturgy. The effort was prompted by the recognition that sacramental theology commonly discusses the katabatic dimension of the liturgy in such a way as to suggest that the divine action is somehow guaranteed once the ritual is performed. This, Vorgrimler objected, is an affront to God's sovereign freedom. The question is whether the view of sacramental efficacy to which Vorgrimler objects is really to be found in the texts of the liturgy, or whether he may not be jousting at windmills created by sacramental theologians dealing with the issue in abstraction from the liturgy itself. A text, of course, is not the whole liturgy, and one must be willing to concede the influence of sacramental theology on liturgical practice and sacramental discipline. The very way theologians have posed the question of how the sacraments "work" has contributed to a minimalizing of the sacramental signs in practice. Nonetheless, the faith of the patristic church is preserved in such older prayers as the one we have studied and must claim a larger authority than theological speculations over matter and form, efficient causality, instrumental causality, and so forth.

1. Liturgical prayer is an act of communication between a collective actant we have called the "praying community" and God, whom it confidently calls "Father." The intentionality of the prayer as a whole makes it an act of persuasive manipulation in which units commonly identified as "anamnesis," "institution narrative," and "epiclesis" each have a subordinate and logical place. The performative character of the text, indicated by the "empty slots" ("we," "your Church," "now," "this font"), implies that relations between God, community, and baptizands are intended to be altered as a result of the ritual performance of baptism, for which the saying or singing of the "blessing of water" is a necessary presupposition.[24]

2. Semiotically speaking, all communication implies a "veridictory contract" between the partners concerning the truthfulness of what is said, that is, some degree of mutual trust. In the case of manipulation, the communication can only be successful in virtue of a "fiduciary contract" or some agreement between the parties concerning the values to be sought in the program proposed. In the case of prayer, this involves the necessary anthropomorphism of treating God as a partner who is to be persuaded. If this sounds theologically unacceptable, there is more to it than at first appears. For in fact, in the inevitable guise of persuading God to be present and to act—so that the signs are not rendered deceitful—the Praying Community is at the same time persuading *itself* that the signs are to be trusted, that the ritual stands to the divine operation as signifier to signified. The prayer is not merely a repetition of old "facts," but an exercise in auto-manipulation in view of the rite to follow.

3. The key issue for sacramental theology, as Vorgrimler indicates, is that of the semiosis—or signifying function—between ritual signifiers and the transformation they signify in relationships between God and the participants. Further analysis of the "deep structures" of this text reveals that this is precisely what the prayer of blessing is about: the relationship of signifier to signified, of "seeming" to "being." In the final analysis, (again, semiotically speaking), that is the point of recalling the past performances of God, the baptism, death, and resurrection of Jesus, and the mandate to baptize. Not only does the Praying Community affirm the truthfulness of the narratives it has inherited, and thus the truthfulness and competence of the God who features in them, but, on the basis of such conviction, persuades *itself* that the semiosis between the "rich symbol" and the grace of participation in Christ's paschal mystery can be relied upon. Far from manipulating God (in the usual sense of that term), the text shows by its "empty slots" (cfr. above) that the community gathered for the ritual is obediently submitting itself to the production of signifiers which incorporate it into the history it recalls and which should result in its being conjoined with those values proposed by the Trinity in the divine mandate to baptize.

4. Greimassian semiotics brackets off all questions of extra-textual referents and ontological truth, restricting itself instead

to the study of referentialization as an intratextual process and to "truth-effects" produced in and by the text. This agnosticism is inherent in a discipline which sees everything in terms of signs, where the relation of signifier-signified is always a matter of belief rather than knowledge. Trust between persons establishes trust in their speech and, ultimately, trust in the things about which they speak.[25] In that sense, the prayers of the liturgy are not only expressions of faith, but rehearsals of faith, establishing a relationship of trust between the believers and God on the basis of which the sacramental signs may be taken seriously as effecting what they signify.

5. The problem with deception in ritual signs, then, lies less in the uncertainty about whether God can be relied upon to cooperate than in uncertainty about whether the human participants can be relied upon to enter into the relationship mediated by the signs. This was recognized early on in the life of the church, in the controversy over Donatism which gave rise to the distinction between valid and fruitful celebration of the rites. From a semiotic perspective, however, one is prompted to ask whether the distinction is not identical with that between the church's program of sacramental ritualization and God's program of self-communication in grace. If this were so, then "character" need be nothing more mysterious than the ecclesio-social consequences of celebrating the rite, namely, that X is now a member of the church, an ordained minister, and so forth, much in the same way that a ceremony of naturalization results in a person becoming a citizen, or inauguration makes someone an office-holder. The fact that the processes of baptism, confirmation, and ordination are not repeatable seems a matter of church discipline[26] which could have been different, just as some nations practice irrescindible citizenship while other citizenships may be lost or withdrawn. In either case, "character" is the inherently public fact of having been made a Christian, or confirmed, or ordained, and thus assuming a wealth of rights and responsibilities within and without the community of the church. It is a *res et sacramentum*: a *res* because it is the ecclesial meaning of the rites; a *sacramentum* because the ecclesial dimension of the rite is at the same time a signifier of a signified which is an interaction with God. This is true of both the ritual celebration and of its lasting effects.

The ecclesial status resulting from the rite is a sign of (and ought thus to be correlated with) an intersubjective relationship with God, just as the ritual celebration of the church is a sign of (and ought therefore to be correlated with) the forging of that relationship with God.

The problem is simply that, while the issue of socio-ecclesial status can be resolved juridically, the relationship to God, like any interpersonal relationship, rests on its own inherent qualities and above all on faith. For semiotics, all relationships are based on a certain measure of trust (the "fiduciary contract"). A certain minimal level of mutual trust must exist between the community and the candidates, in the form of a willingness to baptize and a willingness to be baptized. Such minimal trust, at least a willingness to observe the convention and to abide by its social consequences, is expressed by the very fact of participation[27] and is usually sufficient to ground the new conventional relationship created between the participants and the church in the rite. On the other hand, the relationship with God, while signified by the convention of becoming a member of the church, is not identifiable with it any more than the church is identifiable with the Kingdom of God.

It is precisely this more-than-conventional quality of the relationship (expressed as "grace" or "participation in the divine life") which requires a faith that transcends simple belief in the conventional efficacy of the rite, a faith that opens the participants (community and candidates) to an intersubjective relationship with God. It is for this reason that the "blessing of baptismal water" comes where it does in the liturgy: preceded by the readings of the word of God in the Vigil and followed by a collective renunciation of Satan and a personal profession of faith in the Father, the Son, and the Holy Spirit, in the holy church, the communion of saints, the forgiveness of sins, the resurrection of the body, and life everlasting.

Notes

1. Herbet Vorgrimler, "Die Liturgie als Thema der Dogmatik," in *Liturgie—eine vergessenes Thema der Theologie?*, ed., Klemens Richter (Freiburg: Herder, 1986) 113-127.
2. Ibid. 124.

3. "Ego te baptizo . . .", "Ego te absolvo. . .", "Conjungo vos . . ."
Vorgrimler reports that one archbishop (now a cardinal) at the time of
Vatican II wanted the words of consecration altered to something like
"Ego dico tibi, pane, tu es corpus Christi" for the sake of being sure.

4. Already it is worth noting that, of the three issues cited, the last
is purely a theological view with no direct foundation in the liturgy
as such, while the first and second became common in liturgical
practice under the direct influence of theological and canonical efforts to define precisely what a sacrament was at a time when the liturgy itself was not well understood.

5. Vorgrimler, "Die Liturgie" 124-125.

6. One of the characteristic features of liturgy which makes it difficult to use as a theological source is its syncretic character, namely,
the fact that it uses several "codes"—verbal, visual, proxemic, iconic,
etc.—simultaneously, and none of them, not even the verbal code,
independently. It is the fact that Greimassian semiotic theory provides a general model for the production of meaning by both linguis-
tic and non-linguistic semiotic systems which makes its application
to liturgy so promising. In this essay, however, we shall be content
to analyze the text of the rite in terms of the codes of word and gesture alone.

7. See J.C. Coquet, *Sémiotique: L'Ecole de Paris* (Paris: Hachette,
1980). The standard works of this school include: A.J. Greimas, *Sé-
mantique structurale* (Paris: Larousse, 1968) ET *Structural Semantics*
(Lincoln and London: University of Nebraska Press, 1983); *Du Sens I*
(Paris: Seuil, 1970); *Du Sens II* (Paris: Seuil, 1982); ET of selected es-
says from these two collections in *On Meaning: Selected Writings on
Semiotic Theory* (Minneapolis: University of Minnesota Press, 1987).
See also A.J. Greimas and and J. Courtès, *Sémiotique: Dictionnaire rai-
sonné de la théorie de langage, I* (Paris: Hachette, 1979) ET *Semiotics and
Language: An Analytical Dictionary* (Bloomington: Indiana University
Press, 1983); idem., *Sémiotique: Dictionnaire raisonné de la théorie de
langage. II* (Paris: Hachette, 1986).

8. The text as presented here includes the rubrics, the prayer, and
the response and acclamation of the people, and is divided into seven
segments. This segmentation is based on different "scenes" created in
the text by changes of time (tense), place, and actors. It is less a case
of strict disjunction between parts than a hypothesis as to how the
text is organized, and may have to be rethought as analysis proceeds.

9. The English text of the International Committee on English in
the Liturgy is studied here since, unlike the Latin text, it is actually
in use and is in that sense normative for a theology of the liturgy.
Semiotically speaking, the English and Latin texts are two expres-

sions of the same content. Thus while comparison of the two raises interesting questions of intersemioticity (i.e., how do the different versions differ in the way they represent the content), the English text is not considered a translation of the Latin, but a translation of the *content* of the Latin. In any case, the English text creates its own "meaning-effects" independently of any reference to the Latin.

10. Implicit because it is in the form of a prayer.

11. See A.J. Greimas, *Structural Semantics*, chapter 10, and Greimas and Courtès, *Semiotics and Language*, s.v. "narrative schema."

12. The baptism and anointing of Jesus correspond to his becoming competent, his sacrificial death to the main performance, and the resurrection to the sanction phase. The contractual phase, the sending of Christ by God, while logically implied, does not appear in this version of the narrative, although it may be hinted at in "your Son."

13. "Sanction" is an act of judgment upon the behavior and narrative program of a performing subject. See Greimas and Courtès, *Semiotics and Language* 267. "Veridiction" is an act of judgment concerning what seems to be true or seems not to be true (ibid. 367-369).

14. The term "manipulation," while having dysphoric connotations in ordinary language, is used here in the technical sense of a "making to do or not to do," which may be either positive (persuasion) or negative (coercion). See Greimas and Courtès, *Semiotics and Language* 184-186.

15. The concept of "line of action" is borrowed from symbolic interactionism. See Herbert Blumer, *Symbolic Interactionism: Perspective and Method*, [1969], 1986, 1-60.

16. In particular, only very careful semantic analysis can untangle the apparent inconsistencies between verse 10 ("By the power of the Holy Spirit give to the water of this font the grace of your Son") and verse 12 ("We ask you, Father, with your Son, to send the Holy Spirit upon the waters of this font").

17. The use of slashes /. . ./ is to indicate a seme, or minimal unit of meaning. In this instance, the one seme /descent/ is figurativized in two different ways, in words ("send . . . upon") and in gesture.

18. This presents a quandary at the level of discoursive syntax. On the one hand, the death and resurrection of Christ were reported in verses 7 and 8 as past events relating to an individual subject. As such they are marked by the semic values /punctual/, /complete/, and /individual/. Now, however, the text reconfigures the events so that they become /durative/ and /collective/. In other words, Christ's death and resurrection are somehow rendered contemporary with the baptizands, so that "all who are buried with Christ in the death of baptism [might] rise with him to newness of life."

19. A seme is a minimum unit of meaning; its contribution to the semantics of the whole text is its semic value.

20. See what I have written under "Semiotic Analysis" above and note 12.

21. Acceptance of any mandate logically presumes faith in the mandator and in the values of the progam proposed. Consequently, "competence" in the broad sense includes the whole life of faith; in the narrow sense it refers to the will and know-how required for baptizing.

22. It is presumably this understanding of the liturgical act in question which led to its being re-titled *Benedictio et invocatio Dei super aquam* in the *Ordo Baptismi Parvulorum* (Rome: Typis Polyglottis Vaticanis, 1978), although the General Instruction accompanying the same document still speaks of the celebrant "blessing the water of baptism" (no. 18).

23. This seems to hold true even when baptism does not immediately follow, or when the water is used in connection with the renewal of baptismal promises. In the latter case, the sprinkling symbolizes baptism, again by metonymy.

24. "Necessary" in the sense that the logic of performance in the canonical schema requires previous motivation ("manipulation") and competence.

25. See the important article of A.J. Greimas, "Knowing and Believing: A Single Cognitive Universe," in *On Meaning*, 1987, 165-179.

26. The discipline itself may be a further signifier, denoting the faithfulness of the church to its own as an appropriate reflection of the fidelity of God to the church.

27. See Roy Rappaport, "The Obvious Aspects of Ritual," in *Liturgy, Ecology and Meaning* (Richmond, CA: North Atlantic Books, 1979) 173-222.

Bibliography of
Niels Krogh Rasmussen, O.P.
(1935-1987)

1. "Bénédictions de matines attribuées à Réginald de Cantorbéry," *Classica et Medievalia* 25 (1964) 215-224.
2. *Saint Thomas et les rites de la messe.* Dissertation for the ST Lic et Lect., 150pp. Unpublished: La Saulchoir, 1965.
3. "Les rites de préparation du pain et du vin," *La Maison-Dieu* 100 (1969) 44-58.
4. "Une *cartula missalis* retrouvée," *Ephemerides Liturgicae* 83 (1969) 482-484.
5. "Le 'pontifical' de Beauvais," *Studia Patristica* 10, Texte und Untersuchungen 107 (Berlin, 1970) 413-418.
6. "Some Bibliographies of Liturgists," *Archiv für Liturgiewissenschaft* 11 (1969) 214-218; "A First Supplement," ibid. 15 (1974) 168-171; "A Second Supplement," ibid. 19 (1978) 134-139. "Bibliographies of Liturgists: A Third Supplement" (with cumulative index), ibid. 25 (1983) 33-44. "Bibliographies of Liturgists: A Fourth Supplement," ibid. (forthcoming).
7. "Les préfaces pascales du 'Pontifical de Poitiers'," in *Mélanges liturgiques offerts au R.P. Dom Bernard Botte, O.S.B.* Louvain, 1972, 461-476.
8. [*The Catholic Church after Vatican II*] (in Danish), together with Oluf Bohn. Copenhagen, 1975.
9. [*Scandinavian Translations of Patristic Writings: A Bibliography*] (in Danish), together with H. Villadsen, *Lumen* 18 (1975) 73-97.
10. "Unité et diversité des pontificaux aux VIIIe et Xe siècles,"

in *Liturgie de l'église universelle et liturgie de l'église particulière* = Conferences Saint-Serge 1975. Rome, 1976, 393-410.

11. "Liturgie et vie spirituelle. II. Liturgie et vie spirituelle dans les églises chrétiennes. B. Liturgies occidentales. 6. Liturgies occidentales non catholiques," in *Dictionnaire de spiritualité*, vol. 9 (Paris, 1976), cols 912-914. Reprinted separately in P. Grelot and others, *Liturgie et vie spirituelle*. Paris, 1977, 83-87. Italian translation appears in *Liturgia e pietà*. Torino: Marietti, 1980.

12. *Les Pontificaux du haut moyen âge. Genèse du livre liturgique de l'évêque*. Doctoral Dissertation, Institut Catholique de Paris, 1978. 50 copies printed; accepted for publication in the Spicilegium Sacrum Lovaniense with additions. Final preparations have been assumed by Pierre-Marie Gy.

13. ["The Contribution of Scholarly Research to Contemporary Liturgical Practice"] (in Danish), Private publication: Aarhus, 1977; Spanish translation in *Liturgia* 7 (Buenos Aires, 1977) 53-60; Danish re-translation in *Lumen* 20 (1977) 177-193.

14. "The Chrism Mass: Tradition and Renewal" and "The Chrism Mass: Practical Ideas," (the second of these together with Thomas Ryan) in *The Cathedral: A Reader* (Washington, D.C.: USCC, 1979) 29-36.

15. "*Maiestas Pontificia*: A Liturgical Reading of Etienne Dupérac's Engraving of the Capelle Sixtina, 1578," *Analecta Romana Instituti Danici* 12 (Rome, 1983) 109-149.

16. "Quelques réflexions sur la théologie des tropes," in *Research on Tropes: Proceedings of a Symposium Organized by the Royal Academy of Literature, History and Antiquities and the Corpus Troporum, Stockholm, June 1-3, 1981*, ed., Gunilla Iversen, Konferenser 8 (Stockholm, 1983) 77-88.

17. "An Early *Ordo Missae* with a *Litania Abecedaria* Addressed to Christ (Rome, Bibl. Vallicelliana, Codex B.141, XI Century)," *Ephemerides Liturgicae* 98 (1984) 198-211.

18. "Nos professeurs, les pères Dalmais et Jounel," *La Maison-Dieu* 158 (1984) 7-13.

19. "Liturgical Formation in the United States," *Notitiae* 20 (1984) 570-571.

20. "The Liturgy at Saint-Denis" in *Abbot Suger and Saint-*

Denis, ed., P.L. Gerson. New York: The Metropolitan Museum of Art, 1986.

21. "Iconography and Liturgy at the Canonization of Charles Borromeo," *Analecta Romana Instituti Danici* 15 (1986) 119-150.

22. C. Vogel, *Medieval Liturgy*, translated and revised by William G. Storey and Niels Krogh Rasmussen, O.P., with the assistance of John K. Brooks-Leonard. Washington, D.C.: The Pastoral Press, 1986.

23. "Célébration épiscopale et célébration presbytérale: un essai de typologie," in *Segni e riti nella Chiesa altomedioevale occidentale, Settimane di studio del Centro Italiano du studi sull'alto Medioevo XXXIII, 11-17 Aprile 1985*, vol. 2. Spoleto: Presso La Sede del Centro, 1987.

24. "Liturgy, Liturgical Arts," in *Early Modern Catholicism (1540-1700): A Guide to Research*, ed., John W. O'Malley, S.J. St. Louis: Center for Reformation Reserach, 1988.

25. "Messes privées, livre liturgique et architecture. A propos du ms. Paris Arsenal 610 et l'église abbatiale de Reichenau-Mittelzele," *Revue des sciences philosophiques et théologiques* 72 (1988) 77-87.

Contributors

Gerard Austin, O.P., a member of the U.S. Southern Province of the Dominican Order, has taught liturgy at The Catholic University of America, Washington, D.C., since 1969. A doctoral student at the Institut Catholique de Paris with Fr. Niels Rasmussen, he is the author of *Anointing with the Spirit: The Rite of Confirmation, the Use of Oil and Chrism* (New York: Pueblo Publishing Co., 1985).

Paul Bradshaw, an Anglican priest, is Professor of Liturgy at the University of Notre Dame, editor of *Studia Liturgica*, and a member of the Council of Societas Liturgica. He is the author of several books and numerous articles on early Christian liturgy. His most recent publications include *Ordination Rites of the Ancient Churches of East and West* (New York: Pueblo Publishing Co., 1990) and a volume of essays co-edited with Lawrence Hoffman, *The Making of Jewish and Christian Worship* (Notre Dame: University of Notre Dame Press, 1991).

Tom Elich, priest of the Archdiocese of Brisbane, Australia, studied liturgy and sacramental theology in Paris. As director of The Liturgical Commission in Brisbane, he is involved in teaching, publishing, and liturgical consultation. He is also executive secretary of the National Liturgical Commission and a member of ICEL's Advisory Committee.

John A. Gurrieri, a priest of the Diocese of Brooklyn, is the former Executive Director of the NCCB Bishops' Committee on the Liturgy (1978-1988). He is presently the Los Angeles Archdiocesan Consultant for Liturgy, Lecturer in Liturgical Studies at Mount St. Mary's College of Los Angeles, and Adjunct Professor of Liturgy at St. John's Seminary, Camarillo, California.

Pierre-Marie Gy, O.P., served as director of the Institut Supérieur de Liturgie of the Institut Catholique de Paris from 1964 to 1986. During that time he directed the doctoral dissertation of Niels Rasmussen. Fr. Gy, author of *La Liturgie dans l'histoire* (1990) and over 140 scholarly articles in liturgical studies, continues to teach at the Institut Catholique de Paris. He is also a consultor to the Congregation for Divine Worship and for the Discipline of the Sacraments.

Joanne Pierce earned her Doctorate in Theology (Liturgical Studies) from the University of Notre Dame in 1988. She specialized in medieval liturgy and church history, and studied for many years with Niels Rasmussen, O.P. Dr. Pierce is currently Assistant Professor of Theology at Barry University in Miami Shores, Florida.

David N. Power, O.M.I., internationally known as a sacramental theologian, author, and lecturer, teaches in the Department of Theology at The Catholic University of America in Washington, D.C. His *Worship: Culture and Theology* (1991) is published by The Pastoral Press.

Mary M. Schaefer is Associate Professor of Christian Worship and Spirituality Studies, Atlantic School of Theology, Halifax, Nova Scotia and former Chair of the National Council for Liturgy, Canada.

Mark Searle was a colleague of Niels Rasmussen at the University of Notre Dame where he is an associate professor of theology and coordinator of the graduate programs in Liturgical Studies. He is a former president of the North American Academy of Liturgy.

Kenneth Stevenson, a lecturer and prolific author on liturgical studies, is rector of Holy Trinity and St. Mary's, Guilford, England. His *Jerusalem Revisited: The Liturgical Meaning of Holy Week* (1988) is published by The Pastoral Press.

Robert F. Taft, S.J., is Professor of Oriental Liturgy at the Pontifical Oriental Institute in Rome and Visiting Professor of Liturgy at the University of Notre Dame. He is also Editor in Chief of *Orientalia Christiana Analecta*, Liturgical Consultor of the Vatican Congregation for the Oriental Churches, and member of the Vatican Commission for the revision of the Armenian Catholic liturgical books. He is the author of over 250 scholarly publications, including five books.

Louis Weil, a priest of the Episcopal Church, is the Professor of Liturgics at the Church Divinity School of the Pacific in Berkeley, California. He received his doctorate at the Institut Catholique in Paris, and taught at Episcopal seminaries in Puerto Rico and Wisconsin before accepting the post at Berkeley.